MURMURS OF EARTH

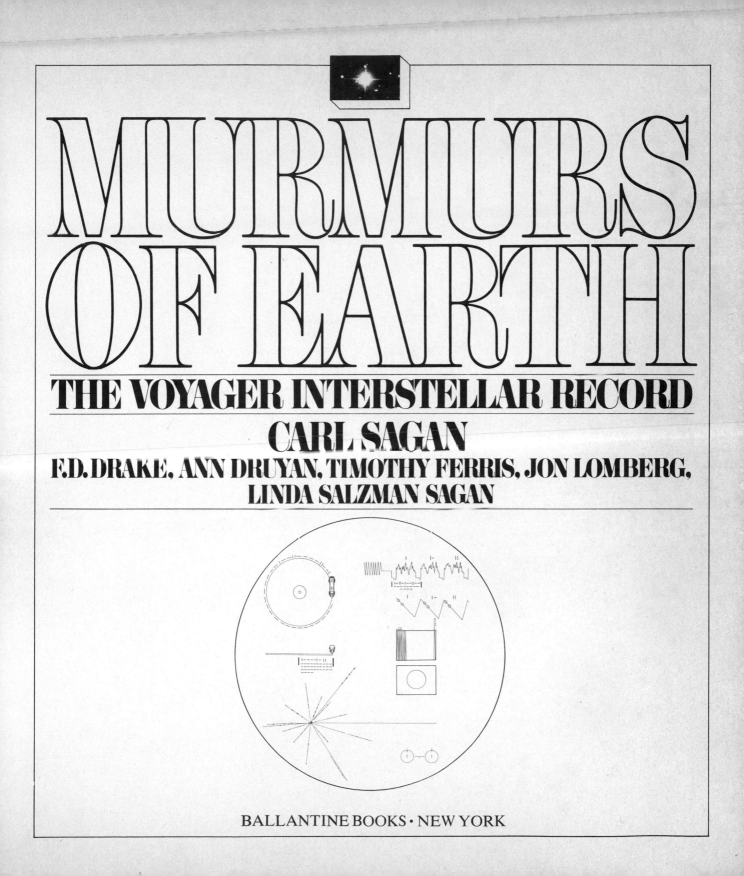

MURMURS OF EARTH

THE VOYAGER INTERSTELLAR RECORD

CARL SAGAN

F.D. DRAKE, ANN DRUYAN, TIMOTHY FERRIS, JON LOMBERG, LINDA SALZMAN SAGAN

BALLANTINE BOOKS · NEW YORK

Library of Congress Cataloging in Publication Data
Main entry under title:

Murmurs of earth.

  Reprint of the ed. published by Random House, New York.
  Includes index.
  CONTENTS: Sagan, C. For future times and beings.—
Drake, F. D. The foundations of the Voyager record.—
Lomberg, J. Pictures of earth.—Sagan, L. S. A Voyager's
greetings.—Druyan, A. The sounds of earth.—Ferris, T.
Voyager's music.—Sagan, C. The Voyager mission to the
outer solar system.—Sagan, C. Epilogue.
  1. Project Voyager—Addresses, essays, lectures.
I. Sagan, Carl, 1934-

[TL789.8.U6V685 1979]   001.55′0999   79-15209
ISBN 0-345-28396-1

This edition published in hardcover by Random House, Inc.

Manufactured in the United States of America

First Ballantine Books Edition: November 1979

1 2 3 4 5 6 7 8 9

To the makers of music — all worlds, all times

The Contents of the Voyager Record

118 pictures

The first two bars of the Beethoven Cavatina

Greetings from the President of the United States

Congressional List

Greetings from the Secretary General of the United Nations

Greetings in fifty-four languages

UN Greetings

Whale Greetings

The Sounds of Earth

Music

Contents

PREFACE

On August 20th and September 5th, 1977, two extraordinary spacecraft called Voyager were launched to the stars. After what promises to be a detailed and thoroughly dramatic exploration of the outer solar system from Jupiter to Uranus between 1979 and 1986, these space vehicles will slowly leave the solar systems—emissaries of Earth to the realm of the stars. Affixed to each Voyager craft is a gold-coated copper phonograph record as a message to possible extraterrestrial civilizations that might encounter the spacecraft in some distant space and time. Each record contains 118 photographs of our planet, ourselves and our civilization; almost 90 minutes of the world's greatest music; an evolutionary audio essay on "The Sounds of Earth"; and greetings in almost sixty human languages (and one whale language), including salutations from the President of the United States and the Secretary General of the United Nations. This book is an account, written by those chiefly responsible for the contents of the Voyager Record, of why we did it, how we selected the repertoire, and precisely what the record contains.

Carl Sagan
F. D. Drake
Ann Druyan
Timothy Ferris
Jon Lomberg
Linda Salzman Sagan

February 1978

1

FOR FUTURE TIMES AND BEINGS,

by Carl Sagan

"I had monuments made of bronze, lapis lazuli, alabaster . . . and white limestone . . . and inscriptions of baked clay . . . I deposited them in the foundations and left them for future times."
—Esarhaddon, king of Assyria,
seventh century B.C.

Courtesy Richard Wurts

The Trylon (right) and Perisphere (center) of the 1939 New York World's Fair. The statuary at left represents Four Victories of Peace, by John Gregory.

In 1939, before my fifth birthday, my parents took me to the New York World's Fair. It exhibited wonders. Lightning was made to crackle, blue and fearsome, between two metal spheres. A sign read "Hear light! See sound!" and it turned out that, sure enough, such things were possible. There were buildings devoted to strange cultures and faraway lands of whose very existence I had been totally ignorant. The centerpiece of that World's Fair was the Trylon and Perisphere, a stately, tapering tower and a building-sized sphere in which was something called "The World of Tomorrow." You walked on a high-railed ramp and below you, in miniature, was an exquisitely detailed model of the future—graceful aerial skyways filled with streamlined automobiles and happy citizens purposefully intent on some futuristic business, the nature of which was difficult to divine from the perspective of my limited experience and abbreviated stature. But one message was clearly communicated: there were other cultures and there would be future times.

The confidence in the future evinced by that World's Fair was dramatically illustrated by the Time Capsule, a chamber "hermetically sealed," filled with newspapers, books and artifacts of 1939, buried in Flushing Meadows to be opened and revealed automatically in some distant epoch. Why? Because the future would be different from the present. Because those in the future would want to know about our time, as we are curious about our antecedents'. Because there was something graceful and very human in the gesture, hands across the centuries, an embrace of our descendants and our posterity.

There have been many time capsules both before and since. Esarhaddon, son of Sennacherib, was a mighty general and an able administrator, but he also had a conscious interest in presenting not just his military glory but his entire civilization to the future, burying cuneiform inscriptions in the foundation stones of monuments and other buildings. Esarhaddon was king of Assyria, Babylonia and Egypt. His military campaigns extended from the mountains of Armenia to the deserts of Arabia. For all that, his name is hardly a household word today, but his works have made a significant contribution to our knowledge of the Middle East in the seventh century B.C. His son and successor, Assurbanipal, perhaps influenced by the time-capsule tradition of his father, accumulated a massive library on stone tablets comprising the

knowledge of all that was known in that remote epoch. The remains of Assurbanipal's library are a remarkable resource for scholars of today. Esarhaddon and Assurbanipal have spoken clearly down through the centuries and millennia. For those who have done something they consider worthwhile, communication to the future is an almost irresistible temptation, and it has been attempted in virtually every human culture. In the best of cases, it is an optimistic and far-seeing act; it expresses great hope about the future; it time-binds the human community; it gives us a perspective on the significance of our own actions at this moment in the long historical journey of our species.

The coming of the space age has brought with it an interest in communication over time intervals far longer than any Esarhaddon could have imagined, as well as the means to send messages to the distant future. We have gradually realized that we humans are only a few million years old on a planet a thousand times older. Our modern technical civilization is one ten-thousandth as old as mankind. What we know well has lasted no longer than the blink of an eyelash in the enterprise of cosmic time. Our epoch is not the first or the best. Events are occurring at a breathless pace and no one knows what tomorrow will bring—whether our present civilization will survive the perils that face us and be transformed, or whether in the next century or two we will destroy our technological society. But in either case it will not be the end of the human species.

There will be other people and other civilizations, and they will be different from us. Our civilization is the product of a particular path our ancestors have followed among the vagaries of historical alternatives. Had events of the distant past taken a slightly different turn, our surroundings and thought processes, what we find natural and hold dear, might be very different. Despite our everyday sense that things should of course be the way they are, the details of our particular civilization are extraordinarily unlikely, and it is easy to imagine a set of historical events which would have led to a rather different civilization—for example, one in which Constantine was converted to Mithraism after the Battle of the Milvian Bridge, in which a subsequent intellectual revolt against institutionalized Mithraism led to a Persian-based Renaissance, in which bulls and scorpions were still dominant cultural motifs. Citizens of such a civilization would consider it to be perfectly ordinary and reasonable and a civilization like ours the merest historical romancing. This lack of historical determinism in the details of a civilization means that those details are of extraordinary value, not just to professional historians but to all who wish to understand the nature of culture. I think it is this respect for the integuments of a civilization that, above all other reasons, makes us sympathetic to the enterprise of time capsuling.

But Earth is only one small planet among nine or so that endlessly circle our star, the Sun; and the Sun is but one of some 250 billion stars that make up a great whirling pinwheel of gas and dust and stars called the Milky Way galaxy. In turn, the Milky Way is one of perhaps hundreds of billions of other galaxies. While we are still profoundly ignorant about many of the details, there is evidence that planets are a common accompaniment of stars and that the chemical steps that led to the origin of life on Earth some four billion years ago require only the most common cosmic conditions.

Many scientists therefore now think it likely—although it is by no means guaranteed—that innumerable other planets have seen the origin of simple forms of life, their slow evolution into more complex forms, the development of beings with some degree of intelligence and ability to manipulate the environment, and eventually the emergence of a technological civilization. The creatures on such other planets would be astonishingly different from human beings or any other creatures that inhabit our little planetary home, the Earth. Like history, evolution proceeds in a multitude of small and unpredictable steps, the variation in any one of which producing profound differences later on. Beings elsewhere might think as well as we do or better; they might be better poets or engineers or philosophers: they might have superior moral or aesthetic standards; but they will not be human beings or anything even close. Likewise, the details and integuments of their civilizations, constructed by beings profoundly different to begin with, on an alien planet with a different environment and different life styles required for survival, should be far stranger than any proposition posed in space fantasy or science fiction.

And yet there is an argument—perhaps it is only a hope—that we might be able to communicate with representatives of such exotic civilizations, because they, like we, must come to grips with the same laws of physics and chemistry and astronomy. The composition of a star and its spectral properties are not fundamentally impositions that scientists have made on nature, but rather the other way around. There is an external reality that we ignore at our peril, and indeed much of the evolution of the human species can be described as an increasing concordance between the images within our brains and the reality in the external world. Thus, whatever the differences in starting points, there must come to be a gradual convergence in intellectual content and discipline between diverse planetary species.

So if it is possible to communicate, we think we know what the first communications will be about: They will be about the one thing the two civilizations are guaranteed to share in common, and that is science. The greatest interest might be in communicating information on music, say, or social conventions; but the first successful communications will in fact be scientific.

And how might such communication be effected? Space vehicles travel very slowly. A typical mission to the Moon lasts a few days, to the nearby planets a few months, to the outer solar system a few years. We do not expect other civilizations among the planets in the Sun's family. Even quite optimistic estimates place the nearest civilization at a few hundred light-years, where a light-year is almost six trillion miles. It would take our present spacecraft some tens of thousands of years to go the distance of the nearest star, and several tens of millions of years to travel this estimated distance to the nearest other civilization.

A much quicker and more reliable means of interstellar communication is to send or receive radio messages that travel at the speed of light. Our present radio technology is fully adequate for this purpose and several attempts have been made to listen to a few hundred nearby stars and galaxies for possible intelligent signals, but so far without positive results. There are so many stars and we have so little information about which are the likely candidates that it would be astonishing if the very first efforts were rewarded with success. A long-term effort of a few dedicated radio telescopes for at least some decades is required. Only one attempt has been made by radio astronomers to send a message into space. This occurred in November 1974 at the dedication of the resurfacing of the great Arecibo radio telescope in Puerto Rico, and was not so much a serious effort at interstellar communication as a demonstration of the great powers that radio technology has put at our command. It is described further in Frank Drake's chapter, "The Foundations of the Voyager Record," below.

There is a major difference between sending and receiving. We have only recently achieved the capability of doing either, and any civilization even a little bit behind us technologically could do neither. Therefore, a baby civilization like ours is not a civilization that might be expected to transmit; the technology of any other communicative civilization should be far in advance of our own. In addition, the immense distances between the stars means that it would be a very long time— probably many hundreds of years—before any signal we transmit could be answered by a civilization on a planet of some other star. As a practical means of instituting interstellar dialogue, neither radio signals nor interstellar spacecraft is appropriate, and we must instead concentrate on the receipt of monologues from elsewhere. The primary approach quite properly is the search for radio messages transmitted in our direction by more advanced civilizations.

But it is hard to resist sending out something ourselves. Most interplanetary spacecraft will pass by the target planet and remain in a long, looping trajectory around the Sun, to become artificial planets of the solar system. Others will orbit or land on the target planet. But occasionally a kind of game of interplanetary billiards occurs, in which the gravity of one planet is used to assist the spacecraft in a short-time fast trajectory to another, more distant, world. The first such missions, by the Pioneer 10 and 11 spacecraft, were launched in 1971 and in 1972 to examine Jupiter. The Jupiter swing-by accelerated Pioneer 11 so that it flies by Saturn in 1979. But the close passage by Jupiter for both Pioneers 10 and 11 results in an extraordinary flight path: they are now irretrievably set on trajectories that will take them out of the solar system. Pioneers 10 and 11 are mankind's first interstellar probes. The characteristic speeds of such spacecraft are about ten kilometers per second with respect to the Earth. They therefore travel about one astronomical unit, the distance between Earth and the Sun, every six months. They take two and a half years to go to Jupiter, five to Saturn, fifteen to Neptune, twenty to Pluto, and more than ten thousand years to the belt of dead cometary husks that slowly orbit the Sun in the dark of the outer solar system. It is only then that they enter the realm of the stars.

The radio transmitters of Pioneers 10 and 11 will be dead long before they reach even the orbit of Pluto, much less the distance to the nearest star. They are condemned to wander passively and forever in the depths of interstellar space. Or at least *probably* forever. The chance of Pioneers 10 and 11 entering another planetary system in, say, the next 10 billion years, is tiny, even if every star in the Milky Way galaxy has planets. The reason is that the distances between the stars are very great, and space is very empty. It is a little like randomly throwing a dart in the dark in Madison Square Garden, to whose walls are affixed twenty balloons. There is *some* chance of puncturing a balloon, but the likelihood of success is stupefyingly small.

Nevertheless, Pioneers 10 and 11 are our first interstellar space vehicles, and they contain a message. Affixed to one of the antenna support struts of each spacecraft is a six- by nine-inch gold-anodized aluminum plaque on which is etched a drawing that describes something of the epoch and locale of our civilization, portrayed in a scientific language we hope is comprehensible to a scientifically literate society with no prior knowledge of our planet or its inhabitants. The plaque also contains a sketch of two representatives of the human species greeting the cosmos with hope. Three of the authors of this book were responsible for the design of the Pioneer 10 and 11 plaques, and more details about it can be found in the next chapter.

In 1974 a small satellite with a heart of solid brass was launched into a very high, very circular orbit around the Earth. It has external facets which make it look something like a giant golf ball. This satellite is called LAGEOS, an acronym for Laser Geodynamic Satellite. One of its jobs is to measure continental drift on Earth, which typically occurs at the very slow rate of an inch per century. To make such precision measurements, LAGEOS must be placed in an extremely stable orbit, which is the reason for the heart of brass and the high trajectory. Compared to other satellites it is impervious to the pressure of sunlight, the drag of the atmosphere and other factors that tend to cause a rapid decay of satellite orbits. Laser transmitters on the continents of Earth will measure with extremely high accuracy their separation each year by bouncing laser signals off LAGEOS. As time goes on, their separation will change.

The estimated lifetime of LAGEOS before it burns up in the

Earth's atmosphere is eight million years. This is sufficiently far in our future that a great deal of information may be lost between now and then—including information on the epoch and purpose of LAGEOS itself. For this reason the National Aeronautics and Space Administration asked me to design a small metal plaque to be affixed to LAGEOS as a kind of a greeting card to our remote descendants. Briefly, the card says, in effect: "A few hundred million years ago the continents were all together, as in the top drawing. At the time LAGEOS was launched the map of the Earth looks as in the middle drawing. Eight million years from now, when LAGEOS should return to Earth, we figure the continents will appear as in the bottom drawing. Yours truly." A picture of the LAGEOS plaque appears on page 10, and more information on it in Appendix A.

The LAGEOS plaque is a time capsule containing extremely limited information intended for the year 8,000,000. It is, like all such spacecraft messages, hitchhiking: the spacecraft is designed for one purpose and the plaque attached (almost always at the last minute) for another purpose. But it is pinpointed for a time in the future far more remote than any attempted before the advent of space flight.

The first detailed and close-up study of Jupiter, Saturn, their twenty or so moons, and the exquisite rings of Saturn is to be made by the Voyager mission. These two spacecraft, formerly called Mariner Jupiter/Saturn, were launched in the summer of 1977, arrive in the Jupiter system in 1979 and in the Saturn system in 1980/1981. One of the Voyagers may, depending on what happens near Saturn in 1981, continue on to explore the system of the planet Uranus. Like Pioneers 10 and 11, the Voyager spacecraft are so accelerated by their close passage by Jupiter, the most massive planet in the solar system, that they will be ejected out of the solar system, and will, like the Sun and the nearby stars, orbit the massive center of the Milky Way galaxy once every quarter billion years, essentially forever. Just as with Pioneers 10 and 11, it seemed a pleasant and hopeful prospect to place some message for a possible extraterrestrial civilization aboard the Voyager spacecraft, and in December 1976, while I was in Pasadena, California, for the mission operations of the Viking spacecraft on Mars, the Voyager project manager, John Casani, asked me to organize the effort to place an appropriate message aboard the two Voyager vehicles.

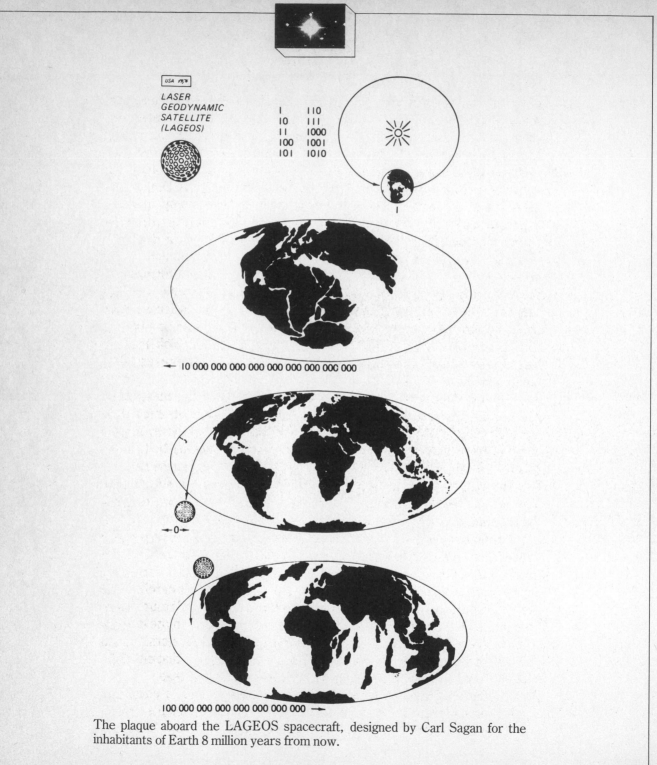

The plaque aboard the LAGEOS spacecraft, designed by Carl Sagan for the inhabitants of Earth 8 million years from now.

My first thought was to make a modest extension of the Pioneer 10 and 11 plaque, perhaps adding some information from molecular biology—for example, on the structure of our proteins and nucleic acids. I organized a small group of scientific consultants to provide advice on the message contents, including Philip Morrison, professor of physics at Massachusetts Institute of Technology; Frank Drake, professor of astronomy and director of the National Astronomy and Ionosphere Center at Cornell; A. G. W. Cameron, professor of astronomy at Harvard; Leslie Orgel of the Salk Institute for Biological Research; B. M. Oliver, vice-president for research and development at the Hewlett-Packard Corporation; and Steven Toulmin, professor of philosophy and social thought at the University of Chicago. Because some science-fiction writers with backgrounds in the sciences have been thinking about such problems longer than most of the rest of us, I also queried my friends Isaac Asimov, Arthur Clarke and Robert Heinlein. A few other scientists were asked to help but were prevented by their schedules.

Many of the consultants emphasized that receipt of the message by an extraterrestrial civilization was chancy at best, while its receipt by the inhabitants of Earth was guaranteed: the public would eventually have access to the message contents, as is in fact accomplished by this book. As Oliver put it, "There is only an infinitesimal chance that the plaque will ever be seen by a single extraterrestrial, but it will certainly be seen by billions of terrestrials. Its real function, therefore, is to appeal to and expand the human spirit, and to make contact with extraterrestrial intelligence a welcome expectation of mankind." Heinlein proposed that Voyager be equipped with a radar corner reflector so that it could be easily found by some future generation of fast terrestrial spacecraft, which could overtake and heave to this ancient derelict. In a telephone message from Sri Lanka on January 3, 1977, Arthur Clarke recommended that the plaque contain a message to our remote descendants saying, "Please leave me alone; let me go on to the stars," which he supported as, among other things, a statement of hope that our civilization would continue long enough for that message to be read.

Cameron proposed that the plaque be painted with a coating of natural uranium whose decay products would give the recipients a rough estimate of the length of time that had elapsed since it was launched.

Toulmin warned against the tendency in all such time-capsule messages to represent human beings as individuals without stressing the importance of community for the human species. He urged that we include some representation of human beings in communities, cooperating together. Several of the scientists suggested that since the spacecraft itself contains so much information on our technology and physical sciences, at least implicitly, the explicit message ought to be oriented in some other direction.

Orgel thought there should be some schematic indication—perhaps wavy lines—that Earth is a water-covered planet, and some indication of the molecular basis of terrestrial biology. The laws of physics are, we already know, the same everywhere in the Galaxy, but the molecules making up living beings may be very different elsewhere than on Earth. Some information on our nucleic acids and proteins might be considered very valuable by a recipient civilization. Several consultants urged that we send information other than scientific. Philip Morrison proposed sending the famous Leonardo da Vinci drawing of a man with arms outstretched and some comparable piece of Oriental art. Oliver proposed that behind a Voyager plaque, in a can, we send a magnetic tape, compatible with the tape recorder on the spacecraft, containing the Beethoven Ninth Symphony, or, if the lifetime of the magnetic pattern on the tape would be too short, a comparable wire recording.

In late January 1977, the American Astronomical Society and its Division for Planetary Sciences were both meeting in Honolulu. As retiring chairman of the DPS I was required to be at this meeting, and as a new member of the council of the parent society, my Cornell colleague Frank Drake was there as well. At the Kawabata Cottage of the Kahala Hilton, Drake made the critical suggestion that determined the subsequent course of the project—namely, that we send a long-playing phonograph record. Because sound information in such a record is physically etched in the record grooves, the information could last for very long times, comparable to or greater than the time for the spacecraft to venture to the stars. This avoided the problem about the lifetime of magnetic tape recordings. In addition, pictures could be encoded in the audio spectrum on such a record, so we could send in the same physical space aboard Voyager many more pictures than we could on a plaque of the Pioneer 10 or LAGEOS sort. I later discovered that 1977 was the hundredth anniversary of the invention of the phonograph record by Thomas Edison (although the original version was a tinfoil disc), so a record would provide a fitting commemoration. (It also transpired, to our great regret, that the inventor of the long-playing record, Peter Goldmark, died in an automobile accident in 1977; the Voyager record can also be considered a memorial to his engineering genius.) Thus, each Voyager spacecraft has a golden phonograph record in a silvery aluminum cover affixed to the outside of its central instrument bay. Instructions for playing the record, written in scientific language, are etched on the cover. A cartridge and stylus, illustrated on the cover, are tucked into the spacecraft nearby. The record is ready to play.

I was delighted with the suggestion of sending a record for a different reason: we could send music. Our previous messages had contained information about what we perceive and how we think. But there is much more to human beings than perceiving and thinking. We are feeling creatures. However, our emotional life is more difficult to communicate, particularly to beings of very different biological make-up. Music, it seemed to me, was at least a creditable attempt to convey human emotions. Perhaps a sufficiently advanced civilization would have made an inventory of the music of species on many planets and, by comparing our music with such a library, might be able to deduce a great deal about us. I was impressed by a paper by Sebastian von Hoerner of the National Radio Astronomy Observatory in Greenbank, West Virginia, which proposed that the physics of sound permitted only a very limited number of musical forms. Perhaps there is a "universal" music. In addition, I was cheered by an earlier remark of the biologist Lewis Thomas, president of the Sloan-Kettering Institute in New York City. When asked what message he would send to other civilizations in space, Thomas replied with words to this effect: "I would send the complete works of Johann Sebastian Bach." "But that," he added as an aside, "would be boasting."

The connection between mathematics and music has been marked at least since the time of Pythagoras. Harmony has a distinct mathematical character, and it is a commonplace that mathematicians and theoretical physicists are often also talented in musical composition and performance. Einstein's passion for the violin is no isolated example.

But so far as we can tell, mathematical relationships should be valid for all planets, biologies, cultures and philosophies. We can imagine a planet with uranium hexafluoride in the atmosphere or a life form that lives mostly off interstellar dust, even if these are extremely unlikely contingencies. But we cannot imagine a civilization for which one and one does not equal two or for which there is an integer interposed between eight and nine. For this reason, simple mathematical relationships may be even better means of communication between diverse species than references to physics and astronomy. The early part of the pictorial information on the Voyager record is rich in arithmetic, which also provides a kind of dictionary for simple mathematical information contained in later pictures, such as the size of a human being. Because of the relation between music and mathematics, and the anticipated universality of mathematics, it may be that much more than our emotions are conveyed by the musical offerings on the Voyager record.

Some months after the Voyager records were launched into space, a science-fiction movie called *Close Encounters of the Third Kind* was released, portraying physical rather than radio contact between an advanced extraterrestrial civilization and us. Unlike the Voyager case, the extraterrestrials are imagined to visit the Earth, rather than a representative of Earth traversing interstellar space. Despite a credulous acceptance of several stories about unidentified flying objects, the movie had at least one virtue: the initial messages were naive, but at least mathematical (showing the geographical coordinates of a future meeting) and musical. Indeed, the climactic scene in the motion picture portrays a kind of fugue between terrestrial and extraterrestrial electronic organs.

I made contact with Tom Shepard, vice-president, Red Seal Division, RCA Records, and established Red Seal's willingness to help us with the early stages of the technical end of the record design. The pressing of an ordinary vinyl twelve-inch long-playing record is made from a mold, which in turn is made from a copper or nickel positive master called a "mother." Since the technology for such an engraving was in hand, it seemed ideal to send a mother to the stars. Its resistance to erosion in space would be considerably greater than an ordinary vinyl record's. Because nickel is ferromagnetic, a nickel mother might interfere with the delicate magnetic field detection experiments of Voyager, so a copper mother was settled upon. By this time, in February and March 1977, because we were thinking of a record to be played at the conventional 33⅓ revolutions per minute, we contemplated something like twenty-seven minutes of playing time on a side, or fifty-four minutes altogether. One side would contain music, and the other the non-musical information—for example, pictures.

But what music? Twenty-seven minutes is barely enough for two movements of a single symphony. How could we send something representative of the music of the planet Earth with its full range of emotion tone and cultural diversity in twenty-seven minutes? I asked for help from many sources. Jonathan Cott, an editor of *Rolling Stone,* and Ann Druyan, a writer, suggested I contact Robert E. Brown, the executive director for the Center for World Music in Berkeley, and Alan Lomax, director of the Cantometrics Project of Columbia University in New York City. Brown's recommendations are reprinted in Appendix C, and his comments represent the first coherent statement we received on possible organizing principles for the diversity of human music to be included. Another early set of recommendations—this by Jon Lomberg of the Canadian Broadcasting Corporation—appears in table form in Appendix D. Murry Sidlin, then the resident conductor of the National Symphony Orchestra in Washington and now the musical director of the New Haven Symphony Orchestra and Tulsa Philharmonic, made a number of proposals both for Western classical music and for music of other cultures, including the happy notion of following the last 4½ minutes of Stravinsky's *Rite of Spring* with the Prelude and Fugue in C, No. 1, from Book 2 of Bach's *Well-Tempered Clavier.* He noted that the emotional contrast would be striking.

Brown's recommendation was for thirty-eight minutes of music, and he clearly would have preferred more. Sidlin stressed the importance of including complete musical selections rather than fragments; and this, especially for Western classical music, would greatly increase the musical time required. Lomberg, independently of Lewis Thomas, felt that a number of pieces by the same composer or a number of pieces in the same form, such as the fugue, would illuminate our music and our intent.

Alan Lomax has devoted his life to recording the ethnic music of the world and to saving it from obscurity and neglect. His Cantometrics

Project has developed a computerized classification of virtually all recorded musical styles. We finally made contact with him after his return from an extensive trip abroad. Most of the music on the Voyager record that is not in the Eastern or Western classical traditions was recommended to us by Lomax. He was a persistent and vigorous advocate for including ethnic music at the expense of Western classical music, and the pieces he brought to our attention were so compelling and beautiful that we acceded to his suggestions more often than I would have thought possible. There was, for example, no room for Debussy among our selections, because Azerbaijanis play bagpipes and Peruvians play panpipes and such exquisite pieces were recorded by ethnomusicologists known to Lomax.

Like Robert Brown, Alan Lomax had a proposed master list of music to include, which we only partially accommodated. After many decades of work, Lomax believes that different stages in the social, economic and technological development of civilization are characteristically reflected by certain styles of music—for example, hunter music, gatherer music, agricultural music, and so on. When Lomax first played Valya Balkanska's soaring Bulgarian shepherdess' aria for Ann, she was moved to spontaneous dance. "Do you hear that, honey?" he drawled, grinning and leaning forward. "That's Europe. That's the first people who had enough to eat." If Lomax's ideas are correct, it might have been possible to communicate something of the evolution of human civilizations through musical motifs alone. But time and other pressures prevented us from giving a full critical hearing to his proposals. (Just as there are today many workers in wildlife conservation dedicated to noting and preserving endangered species, so Lomax has dedicated his life to preserving endangered folk and ethnic music. His Cantometrics Project is clearly operating on a shoestring budget and deserves much wider attention and support. We are particularly grateful to him for his help in broadening our transcultural musical perspectives, as well as in substantially enhancing the beauty of the Voyager record's musical offerings.)

By this time I had asked my friends Timothy Ferris and Ann Druyan to help with the record project. Both had strong musical backgrounds and were enthusiastic about the idea of sending music to the stars. Ferris took charge of many of the production aspects of the project, particularly on the musical end, and Druyan provided vital contributions to all nonpictorial aspects of the record contents. Fortunately, John Casani of the Jet Propulsion Laboratory, NASA, had provided me with some money which permitted the project to partly reimburse these talented people for their time. With these funds I was also able to bring Jon Lomberg into the project. These individuals contributed a great deal of time for which they did not charge the project; and, with a few minor exceptions, all others contributed their time and talent gratis. I detailed Lomberg to work closely with Frank Drake in the selection and design of the pictorial portion of the message. Druyan organized an audio essay, "The Sounds of Earth," an evolutionary sequence on the development of our planet, life, human beings, and the technical civilization responsible for the Voyager mission.

Ferris and I considered a number of schemes for increasing the amount of audio time available. Sending the equivalent of four sides, as two bonded pairs, of the record violated the time scale of the project: the thermal implications only of a single record mounted on the exterior of the spacecraft had been allowed for. The temperature of the delicate electronics on board interplanetary spacecraft must be controlled with great precision if the scientific objectives of such missions are to be realized. Increasing the number of minutes per side much beyond twenty-seven or twenty-eight minutes by using a finer groove interval would result in a substantial loss in fidelity. Eventually we settled on having the record designed for $16^2/3$ revolutions per minute, which would mean some decline in fidelity but not, we believe, an extremely severe loss, especially if the recipients were as clever as they would have to be to acquire the record in the first place. With almost ninety minutes for music we felt we could at least approach doing some justice to the range, depth and magic of the world's music. But this decision came uncomfortably late in the implacable development schedule of a major space mission. Not much time was left to make the selections.

To give some feeling of the nature of the decision-making, let me describe a critical meeting held on May 14, 1977, in Washington, D.C., which lasted until three the following morning. I had been attending a meeting of the Council of the Smithsonian Institution and Druyan, Ferris, Linda Sagan, and Wendy Gradison of my staff had spent part of that time reviewing the nonmusical sound collection of the Library of Congress. Along with Murry Sidlin and his wife Debby, we met in an office at the Smithsonian, which had a small hi-fi musical system and a wall-sized portrait of Louis Armstrong to urge us on. The world's music is very rich, and much of it is unfamiliar even to professional musicians. There is obviously no best answer about what music to send to the stars; there are as many answers as there are people who attempt to make such a decision. In this case it was up to me to make the decision. Many issues were discussed. I had just asked Fred Eggens of the University of Chicago, a specialist in Native American cultures, about some alternative choices in American Indian music. A major decision in the classical repertoire was whether to send several pieces by Beethoven and Bach at the expense of Haydn, say, or Wagner or Debussy, a position Murry Sidlin vigorously opposed. But I was very sensitive to the feeling that Bach and Beethoven represent the best of the musical tradition of the West, the culture that launched the spacecraft. Once I had made this decision, Sidlin was extremely supportive and helped enormously in the individual selections.

One point of debate was whether to send the Miles Davis version of Gershwin's "Summertime." On the one hand, it was argued that this was a pleasing transcultural mixture of African and American musical motifs; but the position that carried the day was that the black tradition in America has been a major, if not the principal, source of important indigenous American music and should be presented without encumberment. To seek advice, Sidlin called Martin Williams, the curator of jazz at the Smithsonian. He introduced himself and explained what we were about, when Williams interrupted: "Now, let's see if I got this straight. You're calling me up at home at eleven o'clock on a Sunday night to ask which jazz to send to the stars?" Sidlin confessed that that was the gist of it and Williams—like all the experts whose advice we sought—was very helpful.

As it turned out, the four pieces of American music included were a Navajo night chant and three pieces from the American black musical tradition. One of them, Louis Armstrong's "Melancholy Blues," which Alan Lomax procured for us later, will always remind me of Armstrong's visage gazing down at us from the wall during our jam session.

At other times there were long debates on Gregorian chants, Charles Ives and Bob Dylan (would the music stand if the words were incomprehensible?); whether we should include more than one Bulgarian or Peruvian composition; an Apache lullaby (and the role of Apaches among Native Americans); the definition of Near Eastern music; whether to include music performed by alleged Nazi sympathizers; whether to include music performed by Pablo Casals, whose spirit we very much admired but whose records were of poor quality; which version of the Second Brandenburg Concerto; the Jefferson Starship, who kindly volunteered their music for the record; Haydn, Vivaldi, Wagner, Tchaikovsky, Purcell, Copland, Rimsky-Korsakov, Debussy, Puccini, Handel, Schoenberg and Shostakovitch; Elvis Presley; and Country and Western music, argued to be the music most enjoyed by those who actually put together the nuts and bolts of the spacecraft. We wanted to send "Here Comes the Sun" by the Beatles, and all four Beatles gave their approval. But the Beatles did not own the copyright, and the legal status of the piece seemed too murky to risk. Many times we expressed our regret at not being able—primarily for reasons of time and space—to include a number of these composers and musicians, and we imagined a cartoon of them, all gathered at Cape Canaveral, gazing wistfully at Voyager being launched to the stars without them. Jon Lomberg was directly responsible for the inclusion of the Queen of the Night aria from Mozart's *Magic Flute,* and of the Bach Partita No. 3 for Unaccompanied Violin. Ann Druyan made a host of essential contributions, on both the creative and production sides of the project, and I can't resist quoting one of her reminiscences:

"Robert Brown had placed Surshri Kesar Bai Kerkar's 'Jaat Kahan Ho' at the top of his list of world music for outer space," she writes. "It was an old recording that had recently gone out of print. After hunting through a score of record stores without any success, I phoned Brown and asked him to suggest an alternative raga.

"He refused.

" 'Well, what happens if we can't find a copy of this one in time to get it on the record?' I pleaded. We had three more days in which to complete the repertoire. I was terribly worried that Indian music, one of the world's most intricate and fascinating traditions, might not be represented.

" 'Keep looking,' he told me.

"When I phoned him the following day after a series of very unrewarding conversations with librarians and cultural attachés, I was desperate.

" 'I promise I'll keep looking for "Jaat Kahan Ho," but you've simply got to give me the name of a piece that we can fall back on. What's the next best thing?'

" 'There's nothing close,' he insisted. 'Keep looking.' The other ethnomusicologists we had been consulting told me to trust him. I started phoning Indian restaurants.

"There's an appliance store on Lexington Avenue in the Twenties in New York City that is owned by an Indian family. Under a card table with a madras cloth thrown over it sits a dusty brown carton with three unopened copies of 'Jaat Kahan Ho.' Why I want to buy all three occasions a great deal of animated speculation on the part of the owners. I fly out of the shop and race uptown to listen to it.

"It's a thrilling piece of music. I phone Brown and find myself saying thank you over and over."

Ten years earlier Ann had heard for the first time the Cavatina from Beethoven's String Quartet No. 13 in B flat, Opus 130, and found herself so moved that then and many times subsequently she wondered how it would ever be possible to repay Beethoven for the experience which he had provided. That debt is at least partly repaid in the Voyager record.

The particular sequencing of compositions which we chose was based on several different criteria. We wished to avoid a Western European musical ghetto on the record, and purposely juxtaposed music from many cultures. In some cases, pieces are coupled because of the emotional and tone contrast, because of a common solo virtuosity on quite different instruments, or because of a similarity of instruments or rhythmic and melodic styles between seemingly disparate cultures. At one point we considered collecting together the five or six pieces that seemed to us most haunting and expressive of a kind of cosmic loneliness. And indeed, the last two compositions, "Dark Was the Night" and the Beethoven Cavatina, are distinctly in that category; for us they express a longing for contact with other beings in the depths of space, a musical expression of the principal message of the Voyager record itself.

Great care was taken with all the musical selections, in an attempt to be as fair and representative as possible in terms of geographical, ethnic and cultural distribution, style of music, and the connection with other selected pieces. After some deliberation we had tentatively selected for "Russian" music a basso, balalaika and chorus selection called "The Young Peddler," with Nicolai Gedda as the soloist. It was rousing and more or less typical of Russian folk music, and had been suggested by Murry Sidlin. But we had lingering doubts. Gedda was a Scandinavian, born of White Russian parents. Was he a true exponent of Russian folk music? How does the authenticity of a folk culture survive a major revolution like that of 1917 in Russia? Was the composition a little too ordinary? Might the entertaining theme of the piece—a capitalist entrepreneur engaged in seducing young women—be considered offensive or at least atypical by contemporary citizens of the U.S.S.R.? To approach these concerns I cabled a scientist colleague in Moscow, briefly outlining our requirements, and indicating that we had, at least for the time being, hit upon this particular version of "The Young Peddler" as exemplar of Russian folk music. Could he suggest one better? The short but not impossible deadline for response came and went without any answer from the U.S.S.R. Many weeks later—too late to affect the outcome—came the reply: an alternative piece was proposed, called "Moscow Nights." This turned out to be a kind of Soviet Mantovani, the blandest, least controversial and also least interesting music imaginable. I later discovered that my request had been given very serious attention, floating toward the top of the scientific hierarchy of the U.S.S.R. Academy of Sciences, and possibly even higher than that. There were debates in which Lenin was quoted to the effect that even capitalist aspects of prerevolutionary Russian culture were important and worth preserving. But it is clear that this position did not carry the day.

Fortunately, we had already selected something which I believe to be much better; Alan Lomax had called our attention to the splendid piece "Tchakrulo" from Georgia in the U.S.S.R. The subject was a revolt against a tyrannical landlord. In the ideal case we would have had extensive consultations with individual musical experts from many nations; while this was possible in some instances—as in our selection of

Chinese music—our time, budgetary and bureaucratic constraints were such that this was not our practice nearly so much as I would have preferred. A detailed discussion of the final musical selections, which Ann described in *The New York Times* as "Earth's Greatest Hits," is presented in Timothy Ferris's article, "Voyager's Music," below, at the end of which is a convenient summary of the pieces chosen.

By late May 1977 the general configuration of the musical selections was becoming clear. Each selection to be included would have to have a copyright release, because the International Copyright Convention restricts the reproduction of a piece of music "for any purposes whatever," presumably including extraterrestrial purposes. In fact, for the flight models, royalties of a few cents per selection were actually paid. The securing of copyright release is sometimes logistically arduous, and NASA, as an agency of the U.S. government, wanted to be completely sure that it was abiding by the copyright convention in every conceivable detail.

We had hoped that RCA Victor's Red Seal Division would be able to secure these copyright releases for us, as well as to help in the actual production of the flight mothers. They had already been of very major assistance in the decision to go to 16⅔ revolutions per minute and in the choice of mother material. But when Tom Shepard discovered that our tentative musical selections included at most one piece recorded by RCA Victor, he gently suggested that RCA might find it difficult to be of much further help. The musical repertoire had been selected entirely without reference to the manufacturer of the recording; but we discovered that a respectable number of our selections had been recorded by Columbia Records. It is not as easy as you might think to attract the attention of the president of a major competitive commercial record company on short notice for any enterprise, much less for volunteering corporate resources to send a record to the stars where, even if there are many potential listeners, no impact on corporate profits is likely to be made, at least in the near future. But, eventually, CBS Records, entirely as a public service, secured all the releases, mixed the music, greetings and sounds, and cut the wax masters from which the metal mothers are made. Worldwide releases were obtained in an unprecedentedly brief time. Since there was no way for CBS Records to increase corporate earnings from this project, their cooperation, although in some quarters reluctant, was on the whole truly remarkable.

Meanwhile, interesting events were occurring on another front. The Pioneer 10 and 11 plaques had, in their most fundamental senses, been visual greeting cards. The Voyager records were messages in the audio as well as the optical domain, and it was natural to consider whether they also should contain explicit greetings. It is barely possible that extraterrestrial civilizations might—by the time the Voyager records are retrieved—know something of human languages, perhaps through the occasional interception of television broadcasts from the planet Earth. This is, to be sure, at best an extremely long shot. By far the most likely situation is that no human language will be remotely intelligible to an extraterrestrial auditor if no primer has previously been encountered. But human spoken language might, nevertheless, be of some interest; and if the record was to be a greeting, it clearly had to include a "Hello." But a "Hello" in English, or in any other single language, seemed particularly chauvinistic. The message in its fundamental sense was to be from all of mankind; therefore it should include greetings in the languages of at least a large proportion of mankind.

Perhaps naively I thought that the most appropriate organization to say "Hello" to the cosmos in a few dozen languages would be the United Nations. In the fall of 1976 I had been invited to give an address on space exploration to the UN General Assembly, and as a result I had met some members of the American Mission to the United Nations as well as members of the UN "Outer Space Committee." But on so weighty a matter as saying "Hello," the United States Mission informed me that it could not act on its own. I then tried the Outer Space Committee, but was told that the committee cannot itself initiate any "action"; this can be accomplished only by national delegations. So back to the U.S. mission. It would act only if so instructed by the State Department. But the State Department, I soon learned, would act only if so requested by NASA, with a firm guarantee by NASA that there was definitely to be a Voyager record and that any UN greetings would be included.

This posed a further dilemma. While my jerry-built committee of professionals and gifted amateurs was working under NASA auspices,

NASA still reserved the right to veto our activities, or, in the ultimate remove, to decide not to include such a record at all. And indeed, when news of some of our activities leaked to the press at a later time, the official posture of NASA's Office of Public Information was that no final decision had been made about having a record on the Voyager spacecraft at all. This bureaucratic Catch-22 soon became still more convoluted. I was informed that I had blundered in making any request directly to the UN Outer Space Committee, because the Voyager record project was now viewed in some sectors of the United Nations organization as an enterprise possibly redounding to the credit of the United States, and therefore to be opposed on those grounds alone.

My suggestion had been that a day or two be reserved at UN headquarters in New York City, and a delegate from each member nation drop by the UN sound studio sometime during that period to say "Hello" in his or her native language. I had hoped that something like half of the voices could be male and half female, in order to reflect the distribution of sexes on the planet Earth. I was told that this was quite difficult on entirely other grounds. Virtually all the chiefs of delegations were male, and it was unlikely that they would delegate the privilege of saying "Hello" to the stars to anyone else. Moreover, what if the chief of delegation was not at the United Nations on the designated day? No, my proposal was entirely impractical even if the U.S. Delegation were to propose it; indeed, even if the Secretary General were to suggest it.

As an alternative, it was suggested to me that each member of the United Nations' Outer Space Committee say "Hello" and we send these voices to the cosmos. The trouble with this was that the languages accidentally represented on this committee do not closely correspond to the languages most commonly spoken on the Earth. China, for example, does not belong to the Outer Space Committee. What is more, the Outer Space Committee would have to *vote* on whether to say "Hello," and its next meeting was to be in Europe in late June. I explained that even if greetings from the Outer Space Committee were desirable, the launch schedule of Voyager would not permit such a dilatory pace. Could we not, I was then seriously queried, postpone the Voyager launch?

I approached Arnold Frutkin, NASA's associate administrator for international affairs, for help. Frutkin eventually succeeded in having the State Department instruct the U.S. Mission to the United Nations to help with this project and also contacted the Secretary General of the United Nations, Kurt Waldheim, directly. But again time was running out. Then late in the afternoon of June 1, 1977, NASA informed me that a UN recording session would take place the following day. There had been no prior notice, and I was not told anything about the format of the greetings that would be given. I asked Timothy Ferris, who lived in New York, to attend the meeting and try to organize it along the lines we needed. In particular, I wanted to be sure that the greetings were very short; the amount of time available on the Voyager record for greetings was strictly limited.

Ferris arrived to find a subset of members of the UN Outer Space Committee assembled and not even a close approximation of the languages spoken on Earth represented. Despite the fact that the Soviet Union is a member of the Outer Space Committee, there was no Russian-speaking delegate at the meeting. Ferris was permitted to given an introductory statement asking for "short greetings," but this phrase means something quite different at the United Nations than in usual spoken language. Each delegate clearly wished to make a speech. Some of the greetings were in fact quite lovely. The French delegate read poetry by Baudelaire and the Swedish delegate by the contemporary Swedish poet Harry Martinson. The Australian delegate made some of his remarks in Esperanto, perhaps on the grounds that Esperanto has been advertised as a "universal" language. The Nigerian delegate included the sentence "As you probably know, my country is situated on the west coast of the continent of Africa, a land mass more or less in the shape of a question mark in the center of our planet." As interesting as these notices were, they were clearly too long to be included in their entirety, and we were forced to make a representative selection of them, being sure to include at least some words from each speech by each member of the Outer Space Committee. A transcript of the messages included appears in Appendix B.

Roger Payne of Rockefeller University is a zoologist who has performed important studies of great whales in the free ocean. From a small boat he has trailed hydrophones beneath the surface of the ocean and recorded the tantalizing, enigmatic, haunting "songs" of the humpback and other whales, some of which last for half an hour or

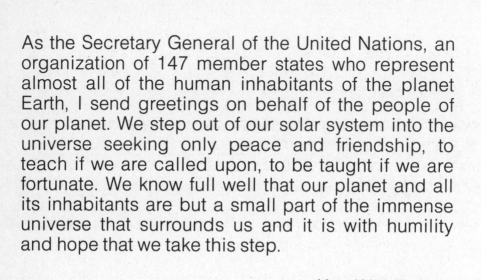

As the Secretary General of the United Nations, an organization of 147 member states who represent almost all of the human inhabitants of the planet Earth, I send greetings on behalf of the people of our planet. We step out of our solar system into the universe seeking only peace and friendship, to teach if we are called upon, to be taught if we are fortunate. We know full well that our planet and all its inhabitants are but a small part of the immense universe that surrounds us and it is with humility and hope that we take this step.

—Kurt Waldheim
Secretary General,
United Nations

more and are later repeated essentially identically. Payne believes that these songs are true communications among the whales when they are so far apart that they cannot see or smell each other, and that one particular kind of song is used as a greeting among the humpback whales. So as to leave no hint of provincialism in the greetings from the UN delegations, we mixed these characteristically human greetings with the characteristic "Hellos" of the humpback whale—another intelligent species from the planet Earth sending greetings to the stars.

Unknown to us, the United Nations had announced the recording session to the press and identified Timothy Ferris as a NASA official. As a result, our wish to keep the enterprise from the attention of the news media until we actually completed it was thwarted. In addition, there were a number of NASA officials who felt miffed at Ferris's misidentification. Our committee could not represent NASA, it was sternly explained to me.

The next day I made still another discovery: Kurt Waldheim had made a speech of cosmic greeting for the Voyager record. While we had never requested it, the speech was so sensitively and gracefully composed, and so appropriate in its sentiments, that I felt it must be included. Waldheim's remarks appear on the opposite page. But now a further question came to mind. Would it be appropriate to have some remarks by the UN Secretary General on board the Voyager spacecraft—an American space vehicle—if there were no comparable remarks from the President of the United States? It seemed to me that the President should at least be given an opportunity to greet the cosmos.

I called the President's science advisor, Dr. Frank Press, who promised he would put the question to the President and give me a rapid response. The reply came back in a few days that the President would like to consider such a message. The President elected to have his message sent to the stars in written form, as one of the 118 pictures, rather than in spoken form like Secretary General Waldheim's remarks. (It is reproduced on page 28.) After the President's statement was released by the White House, commentary in newspapers and the electronic media seemed to me to be almost entirely positive, with the exception of one newspaper which felt it had discovered that the President was a "closet one-worlder."

This Voyager spacecraft was constructed by the United States of America. We are a community of 240 million human beings among the more than 4 billion who inhabit the planet Earth. We human beings are still divided into nation states, but these states are rapidly becoming a single global civilization.

We cast this message into the cosmos. It is likely to survive a billion years into our future, when our civilization is profoundly altered and the surface of the Earth may be vastly changed. Of the 200 million stars in the Milky Way galaxy, some—perhaps many—may have inhabited planets and spacefaring civilizations. If one such civilization intercepts Voyager and can understand these recorded contents, here is our message:

This is a present from a small distant world, a token of our sounds, our science, our images, our music, our thoughts and our feelings. We are attempting to survive our time so we may live into yours. We hope someday, having solved the problems we face, to join a community of galactic civilizations. This record represents our hope and our determination, and our good will in a vast and awesome universe.

Jimmy Carter
President of the United States of America

THE WHITE HOUSE
June 16, 1977

The causal chain continued. NASA officials were concerned that the separation of powers in the U.S. Constitution might imply that if the President could greet the stars, so must the representatives of the legislative branch of the government. After weighing the matter for about a day, NASA decided that it was essential to include on the Voyager record at least the names of a large number of senators and representatives, especially those whose committees had cognizance of NASA activities. As a result, four additional pictures were added at the very last moment to the Voyager record with the information that is contained in the boxes on pages 30 and 31. So in case the reader wonders how it is, say, that Senator John Stennis of Mississippi has his name aboard the Voyager record, I suppose it goes back to Kurt Waldheim and the nature of bureaucracies. I was at least pleased that NASA did not insist on including the names of the members of the U.S. Supreme Court, as the logical conclusion of the separation-of-powers argument. This part of the Voyager message is without doubt a signal to down here rather than to up there.

The late arrival of the presidential and particularly the congressional material caused a range of organizational problems. The 118 pictures had already been transcribed into the appropriate format for the record at Colorado Video in Boulder, Colorado. A special Honeywell 5600-C recorder had been lent to us for this purpose by the manufacturer. The entire technical end of the picture transcription had been supervised as a public service by personnel of the National Astronomy and Ionosphere Center at Cornell. The addition of the new material required reborrowing the Honeywell recorder, flying it out to Boulder again and imposing once more on the good will of Colorado Video, all on an exceptionally tight time scale.

Valentin Boriakoff of NAIC met me at NASA headquarters in Washington, where I gave him the presidential message and NASA's list of members of Congress to be reproduced as 35mm slides in a commercial photography laboratory in suburban Washington. Because the White House understandably wished to release the contents of the President's message itself, Boriakoff was to be present at every stage in the photographic process to make sure that no unauthorized copies were made. This done, he flew on to Denver. Meanwhile, Dan Mittler of NAIC flew

THE UNITED STATES SENATE

WALTER F. MONDALE
PRESIDENT OF THE SENATE

JAMES O. EASTLAND, PRESIDENT PRO TEMPORE
HUBERT H. HUMPHREY, DEPUTY PRESIDENT PRO TEMPORE
ROBERT C. BYRD   HOWARD H. BAKER, JR.
ALAN CRANSTON   TED STEVENS

COMMITTEE ON COMMERCE, SCIENCE, AND TRANSPORTATION

WARREN G. MAGNUSON, CHAIRMAN   JAMES B. PEARSON
HOWARD W. CANNON   ROBERT P. GRIFFIN
RUSSELL B. LONG   TED STEVENS
ERNEST F. HOLLINGS   BARRY GOLDWATER
DANIEL K. INOUYE   BOB PACKWOOD
ADLAI E. STEVENSON   HARRISON H. SCHMITT
WENDELL H. FORD   JOHN C. DANFORTH
JOHN A. DURKIN
EDWARD ZORINSKY
DONALD W. RIEGLE, JR.
JOHN MELCHER

COMMITTEE ON APPROPRIATIONS

JOHN L. McCLELLAN, CHAIRMAN   MILTON R. YOUNG

SUBCOMMITTEE ON HUD-INDEPENDENT AGENCIES

WILLIAM PROXMIRE, CHAIRMAN   CHARLES McC. MATHIAS, JR.
JOHN C. STENNIS   CLIFFORD P. CASE
BIRCH BAYH   EDWARD W. BROOKE
WALTER D. HUDDLESTON   HENRY L. BELLMON
PATRICK J. LEAHY
JAMES R. SASSER

List of some members of the United States Senate responsible, directly or indirectly, for NASA activities. The list was included at the direction of NASA. The illustration was prepared by actually playing the Voyager Record through an audio converter system, and indicates the characteristic departures from perfect reproduction that affect all encoded images on the Voyager Record. The apparent fidelity of reproduction of pictures is much greater than that of printed words.

THE UNITED STATES HOUSE OF REPRESENTATIVES

THOMAS P. O'NEILL, JR., SPEAKER
JAMES C. WRIGHT, JR.   JOHN J. RHODES
JOHN BRADEMAS   ROBERT H. MICHEL

COMMITTEE ON SCIENCE AND TECHNOLOGY

OLIN E. TEAGUE, CHAIRMAN   JOHN W. WYDLER
DON FUQUA   LARRY WINN, JR.
WALTER FLOWERS   LOU FREY, JR.
ROBERT A. ROE   BARRY M. GOLDWATER, JR.
MIKE McCORMACK   GARY A. MYERS
GEORGE E. BROWN, JR.   HAMILTON FISH, JR.
DALE MILFORD   MANUEL LUJAN, JR.
R. H. THORNTON, JR.   CARL D. PURSELL
JAMES H. SCHEUER   HAROLD C. HOLLENBECK
RICHARD L. OTTINGER   ELDON RUDD
THOMAS R. HARKIN   ROBERT K. DORNAN
JAMES F. LLOYD   ROBERT S. WALKER
JEROME A. AMBRO   EDWIN B. FORSYTHE
ROBERT C. KRUEGER
MARILYN L. LLOYD
JAMES J. BLANCHARD
TIMOTHY E. WIRTH
STEPHEN L. NEAL
THOMAS J. DOWNEY
DOUG WALGREN
RONNIE G. FLIPPO
DANIEL R. GLICKMAN
ROBERT A. GAMMAGE
ANTHONY C. BEILENSON
ALBERT GORE, JR.
WESLEY W. WATKINS

COMMITTEE ON APPROPRIATIONS

GEORGE H. MAHON, CHAIRMAN   ELFORD A. CEDERBERG

SUBCOMMITTEE ON HUD-INDEPENDENT AGENCIES

EDWARD P. BOLAND, CHAIRMAN   LAWRENCE COUGHLIN
BOB TRAXLER   JOSEPH M. McDADE
MAX BAUCUS   C. W. BILL YOUNG
LOUIS STOKES
TOM BEVILL
CORINNE C. BOGGS
BILL D. BURLISON
WILLIAM V. ALEXANDER

A comparable list for the United States House of Representatives.

from Ithaca, New York, to Newark, New Jersey, and collected the Honeywell recorder preparatory to flying with it to Denver. The recorder was so rare and the time scale so short that we could not take the risk of having it sent in the baggage section of the airplane. We therefore wanted to reserve a seat for it. It turns out that airlines have difficulty coping with the concept of a seat for a piece of equipment. The solution, we found, was to reserve a seat for an individual named Mr. Equipment. Since Mr. Equipment was under the age of ten, he was able to fly at half fare. *Ad astra per bureaucracia.*

The Outer Space Committee's greetings proved such a poor representation of the languages spoken on the planet Earth that emergency measures had to be instituted. Frutkin thoughtfully proposed giving a cocktail party in Washington for members of various ambassadorial delegations, but I was leery of another diplomatic round with the ponderous bureaucratic machinery. Instead, I recalled that Cornell University, where I teach, has a very wide range of foreign-language departments, and with the aid of Shirley Arden of my staff, Linda Sagan, and many others, a representative set of short greetings from the human community was assembled, beginning with Sumerian, one of the oldest known languages, and ending with this greeting from an American five-year-old: "Hello from the children of planet Earth." They are described further in "A Voyager's Greetings," below.

In early June, immediately after the mixing of the greetings, music, and "Sounds of Earth" portions of the Voyager record, a delegation of NASA officials arrived at the CBS Records recording studio in New York City to be sure that no untoward sound or musical selection, no ditty that might embarrass NASA, had been included. Their responses ranged from recognition (of "Johnny B. Goode") to bland approval, and it was clear that no great passions or dangerous noises had been stirred up. But the next day I received an agitated phone call from a NASA associate administrator concerned that no Irish music had been included in the record. The Speaker of the House of Representatives, it had suddenly been recalled, was of Irish descent, and NASA was concerned not to give unwonted offense. I had to explain that there were many ethnic groups unfortunately unrepresented. There was, for example, no Italian opera, or Jewish folk music. No, it was too late to include "Danny Boy."

There is not the slightest evidence that any member of Congress or of the Executive Office of the President attempted in any way to influence our choice of music. The only such attempt was made by an official of the United Nations who urged us to include a piece by a composer from his homeland. We found ourselves unable to comply.

There were a number of principles behind our selection of pictures for the Voyager record, but the chief one was this: send to any possible extraterrestrial auditors information about the Earth and its inhabitants that they are unlikely otherwise to find themselves in possession of. Extensive information on mathematics or physics or astronomy was therefore excluded. Some scientific and mathematical information was included to begin the picture sequence in a comprehensible way and to provide background for information in subsequent pictures. But the principal focus of the pictorial segment was information that might in some sense be unique to Earth: information on geochemistry, geophysics, molecular biology, human anatomy and physiology, and our civilization. The more specific the information is to Earth, the more anecdotal or idiosyncratic, the more difficult it may be for extraterrestrials to understand—but also the more valuable the information will be, once understood. Here, as with much else on the Voyager record, we recalled that the likely recipients would be much more advanced than we. Since neither Voyager spacecraft would even in ten billion years enter on their present trajectories another planetary system—even if every star in the Milky Way galaxy has planets—the record could be received only by a civilization able easily to traverse the spaces between the stars. Such a civilization must have intellectual and technological gifts far beyond our ken, as well as, perhaps, an acquired inventory of characteristics of diverse planetary biologies and cultures. If such beings had not yet heard *much* about Earth, the record might prove not only readily understandable but also useful. And if they had by this remote time in the future learned much about Earth, the record would at least provide some psychological insights on what a few of us thought important to tell about ourselves. The Voyager pictures are described and reproduced in Jon Lomberg's "Pictures of Earth," below.

Among the pictures we felt important to include was a sequence on human reproduction. There is much that is biologically informative—

including the astonishing fact that there is a one-celled stage in the human life cycle, the stage of sperm and ovum. It did not seem likely to us that any depiction of human reproduction, no matter how graphic, might be perceived as pornographic by the recipients—any more than we might find a scanning electron micrograph of the conjugation of two bacteria uncomfortably stimulating. But NASA had made clear to us that sexual information of a particularly explicit character might have unpleasant repercussions back here on Earth. The depiction of a naked man and woman greeting the cosmos on the Pioneer 10 and 11 plaques was criticized both on the grounds of being insufficiently explicit and on the grounds of "sending smut to the stars."* But the complaints were, on the whole, muted and few, and it hardly seemed possible to describe human reproduction while ignoring the existence of genitalia. Accordingly, we selected a photograph we considered to be extremely tasteful of a young man and woman in whom might be discerned a mutual fond regard, with the woman clearly many months pregnant. They were facing the camera, as required by the logic of the picture sequence, but the amount of prurient interest seemed to us minimal. The picture also satisfied the criteria that it had not appeared in any publication that might reasonably be considered pornographic and that it had not been taken for the purpose of the Voyager message. The picture is reproduced in this book on page 74—but it will not be viewed by any extraterrestrial interpreter of the Voyager message.

After our final selection of the (originally) 120 photographs, I took a 35mm slide of each to Washington to show to NASA officials. Again NASA was concerned about copyright release. On this we satisfied their requirements admirably. But there were questions raised about content. The time was now so late that no new materials could be added. It was a question of either yes or no with each of the 120 pictures. Why no great works of art? Good question—because we did not have time to put together a committee of art historians and critics to make a reasonably professional choice. Why not include the houses of worship and artifacts of the three or four major religions? Because there are at least a dozen

---

*A further discussion of reaction to this aspect of the Pioneer plaques is contained in my earlier book *The Cosmic Connection*.

and probably hundreds of major religions on the Earth, and adherents of the omitted religions would very likely produce an outcry much more serious than any feared because of nonrepresentation of some tradition of ethnic music. Many of the questions were good ones, and all of the answers were accepted—except one. There was no way that NASA was going to launch full frontal nudity to the stars.

We had wanted to keep information about the Voyager record out of the press until all was completed—in part to thwart any temptations to tamper with the repertoire, but also because if information on the various parts of the record came out in bits and pieces, an incomplete impression of our intentions would gain currency. But too many people were involved in too many phases of our work, and leaks occurred. The UN release gave the impression that spoken greetings and nonmusical sounds were the main focus, and thus prompted Charles Osgood of CBS News to offer these verses to his listening audience on May 12, 1977:

> I don't see it mentioned, but please, NASA, please,
> Include on your intergalactic L.P.'s
> The sound of our music. Please give them a song.
> To not put in music would surely be wrong.
> Without Bach or Mozart, the picture's not whole.
> You'd give them our minds; would you leave out our soul?

It was a pleasure to have already anticipated Mr. Osgood's plea. However, in late July, just a few weeks before the Voyager launch and less than two weeks before the planned NASA press release on the record, I was called by Jonathan Spivak of the *Wall Street Journal*. He had clearly ferreted out many of the record selections from various sources and wanted to know the rest. I was as cooperative as I could be within the constraints of not giving him any new information, and on July 26 the first public announcement of the music on the Voyager record appeared. The headline was "Are Jovians Ready for Sweetest Music That Side of Heaven?" But unfortunately, the first paragraph revealed that somehow Spivak had been led to believe that some Duke Ellington music was to be included. The Spivak release forced NASA to issue its own press release far ahead of schedule, resulting in a far less com-

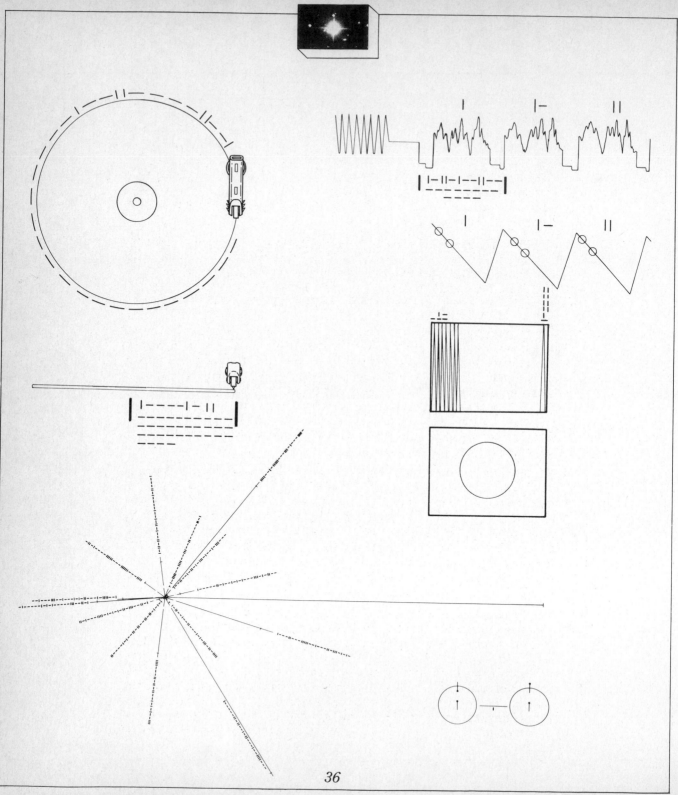

The etched message on the aluminum cover of the Voyager Record. In the upper left-hand corner is an easily recognized drawing of the phonograph record and the stylus carried with it. The stylus is in the correct position to play the record from the beginning. Written around it in binary arithmetic is the correct time of one rotation of the record, 3.6 seconds, expressed in time units of 0.70 billionths of a second, the time period associated with a fundamental transition of the hydrogen atom. The drawing indicates that the record should be played from the outside in. Below this drawing is a side view of the record and stylus, with a binary number giving the time to play one side of the record—about an hour.

The information in the upper right-hand portion of the cover is designed to show how pictures are to be constructed from the recorded signals. The top drawing shows the typical signal that occurs at the start of a picture. The picture is made from this signal, which traces the picture as a series of vertical lines, similar to ordinary television (in which the picture is a series of horizontal lines). Picture lines 1, 2, and 3 are noted in binary numbers, and the duration of one of the "picture lines," about 8 milliseconds, is noted. The drawing immediately below shows how these lines are to be drawn vertically, with a staggered "interlace" to give the correct picture rendition. Immediately below this is a drawing of an entire picture raster, showing that there are 512 vertical lines in a complete picture. Immediately below that is a replica of the first picture on the record to permit the recipients to verify that they are decoding the signals correctly. A circle was used in this picture to insure that the recipients use the correct ratio of horizontal to vertical height in picture reconstruction.

The drawing in the lower left-hand corner of the cover is the pulsar map previously sent as part of the plaques on Pioneers 10 and 11. It shows the location of the solar system with respect to 14 pulsars, whose precise periods are given. The drawing containing two circles in the lower right-hand corner is a drawing of the hydrogen atom in its two lowest states, with a connecting line and digit 1 to indicate that the time interval associated with the transition from one state to the other is to be used as the fundamental time scale, both for the time given on the cover and in the decoded pictures.

Electroplated onto the record's cover is an ultra-pure source of uranium-238 with a radioactivity of about 0.00026 microcuries. The steady decay of the uranium source into its daughter isotopes makes it a kind of radioactive clock. Half of the uranium-238 will decay in 4.51 billion years. Thus, by examining this two-centimeter diameter area on the record plate and measuring the amount of daughter elements to remaining uranium-238, an extraterrestrial recipient of the Voyager spacecraft could calculate the time elapsed since a spot of uranium was placed aboard the spacecraft. This should be a check on the epoch of launch, which is also described by the pulsar map on the record cover.

prehensive announcement and list of acknowledgments than we had anticipated.

Despite these and other impediments, the Voyager record project has attracted and continues to attract substantial interest, most of it favorable. An article in *Science News* by Jonathan Eberhart began:

> Describe the world. Not just that multi-colored ball in the spacecraft photos, but the *world* — its place in space, its diverse biota, its wide-ranging cultures with their lifestyles, arts and technologies — everything, or at least enough to get the idea across. And do it on one long-playing record.
>
> Oh, there's one stipulation: Assume not only that your audience doesn't speak your language, but that it has never even heard of the Earth or the rest of the solar system. An audience that lives, say, on a planet orbiting another star, light-years away from anything you would recognize as home.

After a detailed and entirely accurate account of the record contents Eberhart concluded: "Try it. Make your own list. Or imagine: If you, as an alien, got this message, what would you think?"

Very large numbers of people wrote to ask if a commercially available version of the record might be in the offing. We are still hopeful that such a nonprofit two-record album may be made, even though CBS Records is understandably unsure of how to estimate the sales of such an album.

Most of the comments in the Voyager record project — in the press and in hundreds of letters — were positive and supportive, and encouraged us to think that we had succeeded in communicating something of our vision of the project's purpose. As with Pioneer 10 and 11, a few individuals were worried that the record would "give away" our position in the Galaxy, as a preliminary to some dire interstellar invasion. But at least for the next million years or so the trajectory of the spacecraft itself will quite clearly indicate that it is from the Sun, to say nothing of the sobering fact that our military radar and commercial television indicate the Earth to be an abode of some form of possibly intelligent life — and these signals travel at the speed of light.

Colman S. von Keviczky, the director of something he calls "The International UFO Galactic Spacecraft-Research and Analytic Network," is convinced that we already have clear evidence of extrater-

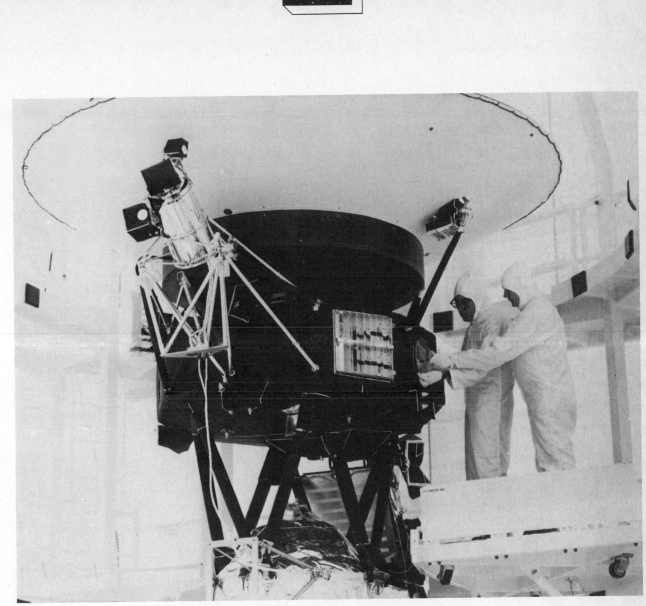

Technicians mounting the interstellar record on the instrument bay of the Voyager spacecraft.

restrial visitation and is concerned that our visitors may be confused by our sending greetings into interstellar space. In a letter to the UN Secretary General, a copy of which von Keviczky was kind enough to send to me, he writes: "The world's military powers have been classified [*sic*] the UFOs strategic survey as espionage, endangering the national security! In light of these accurate military attitudes, the NASA's attempt to seek communication with 'possible' extraterrestrial intelligence is not only brazen inconsistency but seems to be sheer hypocrisy."

A few writers also criticized us for presenting only the favorable circumstances of mankind and chided us for not including scenes of famine, devastation, ravaged cities, and nuclear weapons explosions. This is an issue we debated long and hard during our deliberations on repertoire. There is no question that destruction is a characteristic aspect of what we are pleased to call human civilization. But such a message content might be misinterpreted. Might a photo of a thermonuclear explosion be considered by an extraterrestrial civilization as a pathetically feeble but still palpably nasty attempt at threat? Bernard Oliver had the nice idea of showing a human being with arms outstretched to a galaxy, symbolizing our wish to embrace our fellow creatures among the stars. But a comparable ambiguity seemed to me possible here as well; the gesture could be interpreted by an uncharitable recipient as an intent of galactic aggrandizement. Besides, is it a mistake to put our best face to the cosmos? We tried to send our best music. Why not a hopeful rather than a despairing view of humanity and its possible future?

By the middle of June the deadline John Casani had given us had expired—as well as about ten days he had hidden in his hip pocket, knowing there would be last-minute emergencies. The music had been mixed and a master magnetic tape prepared, which contained all the nonpictorial contents of the record. This was combined at CBS with the pictorial information on two wax masters, which Timothy Ferris then hand-carried to Los Angeles where the copper mothers were prepared. So there would be something done directly by the human hand, Ferris had an inscription etched directly on the record, circumscribing the interior ungrooved portion where the record label ordinarily would be. It reads: "To the makers of music, all worlds, all times." And in place of the label we have photoengraved a photograph of Earth taken from space, to which is added the words "United States of America, Planet Earth."

The bonded pairs of records on each space vehicle are not heavy, but they have a substantial heft. They glisten, golden, in the sunlight. Encased in aluminum cocoons, they were affixed to the flight spacecraft with, in each case, the stylus and cartridge nearby. Each record in fact consists of two one-sided copper mothers, each 0.02 inches thick, bonded back to back with a 0.01-inch bonding thickness, so that the total thickness of the record is 0.05 inches. It weighs about 1.25 pounds. The record, cover, spider support and mounting bracket weigh about 2.4 pounds. The stylus and cartridge are bracketed to the underside of the spider support. The rendezvous of record and spacecraft occurred at the John F. Kennedy Spaceflight Center at Cape Canaveral, Florida, and is shown in the photograph on page 39.

Once the spacecraft were mounted on the top of their Titan III-E Centaur launch boosters they were put through a series of electronic tests to be sure that all was still in working order. All tests were passed, and the day came, August 20, 1977, when the first Voyager was ready to be launched to the planets and the stars. First to leave Earth was Voyager 2. Because of the intricacies of the interplanetary trajectories Voyager 1, although launched later, would arrive at Jupiter earlier. All the authors of this book and many others connected with the Voyager record were at Cape Canaveral on that day for the launch. It had been an arduous and sometimes thankless task, but a supremely satisfying one as well. We had pushed at immobile bureaucracies and let our many other responsibilities slide. Perhaps the Voyagers would never be recovered by some extraterrestrial society. But making the record had provided us with a unique opportunity to view our planet, our species and our civilization as a whole, and to imagine the moment of contact with some other planet, species and civilization. The Voyager 2 launch was flawless, and it was with a sense of exhilaration mixed with many other emotions that we saw it gracefully penetrate the cloud cover and vanish into the blue sky and the black of space beyond. We kissed and embraced, and many of us cried.

Our concern with time and our sense of the Voyager message as a time capsule is expressed in many places on the record—greetings in Sumerian, Hittite and !Kung, photographs of Kalahari Bushmen, music from New Guinea and from Australian aborigines, and the inclusion of the composition "Flowing Streams," whose original structure antedates Pythagoras and perhaps goes back to the time of Homer. The Chinese musicologist Chou Wen Chung had hesitated not one moment in selecting from the 5,000-year-old tradition of Chinese music "Flowing Streams" as the single most important piece for inclusion on Voyager. The record itself is an act of preservation of its musical, pictorial and spoken contents.

In researching "Kinds of Flowers" we came upon a charming and powerful tradition about Javanese gamelan music: there is, it is said, a kind of spirit music in the world, continuously but silently playing. When a gamelan orchestra performs, it is merely making audible the present movement of the music of eternity. Perhaps all of the Voyager record can be viewed similarly—as a local and momentary expression of cosmic discourse, an exchange of greetings and music and information among diverse galactic species that has been in progress for billions of years.

Billions of years from now our sun, then a distended red giant star, will have reduced Earth to a charred cinder. But the Voyager record will still be largely intact, in some other remote region of the Milky Way galaxy, preserving a murmur of an ancient civilization that once flourished–perhaps before moving on to greater deeds and other worlds—on the distant planet Earth.

References

von Hoerner, Sebastian, "Universal Music?" *Psychology of Music*, Vol. 2 (1974), pp. 18–23.

Morrison, Philip, ed., *The Search for Extraterrestrial Intelligence: SETI*. Washington, D.C.: National Aeronautics and Space Administration, 1977.

Sagan, Carl, ed., *Communication with Extraterrestrial Intelligence (CETI)*. Cambridge, Mass.: M.I.T. Press, 1973.

———, *The Cosmic Connection: An Extraterrestrial Perspective*. New York: Doubleday, 1973.

———, and Frank Drake, "The Search for Extraterrestrial Intelligence," *Scientific American*, Vol. 232 (1975), 80–89.

Shklovskii, I. S., and Carl Sagan, *Intelligent Life in the Universe*. San Francisco: Holden-Day, 1966.

2

THE FOUNDATIONS OF THE VOYAGER RECORD,

by F. D. Drake

So deep is the conviction that there must be life out there beyond the dark, one thinks that if they are more advanced than ourselves they may come across space at any moment, perhaps in our generation. Later, contemplating the infinity of time, one wonders if perchance their messages came long ago, hurtling into the swamp muck of the steaming coal forests, the bright projectile clambered over by hissing reptiles, and the delicate instruments running mindlessly down with no report.

—Loren Eiseley

The Voyager record, like its celestial chariot, is one more step toward a very great intellectual and technical goal: contact with an extraterrestrial civilization. How we would communicate with extraterrestrial intelligent life and what we might expect from "Them" are topics that have long obsessed the thinkers of exobiology. Ideas about other worlds have filled the air like confetti. Already the earliest thoughts from the primitive era of, yes, the early 1960's now seem naive. As time has passed, we have seen the power of proposed communication techniques grow explosively. The Voyager record is the ultimate of our "messages"—so far. Even though it has yet to "round the horn" at Jupiter, it too has shown us how to do much better still.

The development of interstellar message techniques began soon after the start of the modern age of the search for extraterrestrial intelligence (SETI). That era began in 1959 with two independent events. At Cornell University, two physicists, Philip Morrison (later to advise on the Voyager record) and Giuseppe Coconni, wondered if perhaps cosmic rays could be used as effective interstellar messengers. While studying the problem, they realized that cosmic rays held little promise after all, but that radio waves could be very effective for interstellar contact. Not only that, they were tremendously excited by their calculation that the developing radio transmission systems and radio telescopes of earth, circa 1959, could communicate over interstellar distances to similar equipment. Recognizing the remarkable threshold in human evolution on which we stood, they published a classic paper in *Nature,* "Searching for Interstellar Communications," calling attention to mankind's abilities. It ended with a statement which still can bring goose pimples: "If signals [interstellar] are present, the means of detecting them is now at hand. Few will deny the profound importance, practical and philosophical, which the detection of interstellar communications would have. We therefore feel that a discriminating search for signals deserves a considerable effort. The probability of success is difficult to estimate; but if we never search, the chance of success is zero."

Meanwhile, at the National Radio Astronomy Observatory, I had independently made those same calculations, showing that the radio telescopes we were then constructing could detect reasonable signals from the nearest stars. I had already started to assemble the special equipment needed to provide high sensitivity to interstellar signals. This equipment was used in 1960, at Green Bank, West Virginia, in a search for signals from two stars, Tau Ceti and Epsilon Eridani. Both this search, called Project OZMA, and the Morrison/Coconni paper received a great deal of publicity and started considerable ferment in the scientific community. Most people supported the search programs, while a few thought that SETI was premature.

Enough interest was generated that in November 1961 a now-famous conference on SETI was held at Green Bank under the auspices, surprisingly, of the prestigious National Academy of Sciences. Attending was virtually every scientist with a serious interest in SETI—all eleven of them! Not many, perhaps, but they were all very good scientists. So good, in fact, that in the middle of the conference the Nobel Prize was awarded to one attendee, Melvin Calvin. The etiquette for celebrating when a visitor gets the Nobel Prize is not well established, but we took a fling at it. Having been tipped off that this might happen, we had stashed away a supply of champagne in the dormitory basement—no mean task in West Virginia, then a semi-dry state. Emily Post would have been pleased, because it turned out that the celebration, which reverberated through the mountains, was just the right thing. Other attendees at that special occasion included Carl Sagan, Philip Morrison, and Barney Oliver, all of whom much later came to play various roles in the making of the Voyager record.

This was the conference where the equations that remain basic to the SETI problem were first written down. It was calculated that the nearest civilizations might be as far as a thousand light-years away and that almost any we could contact would be far more advanced than we. Interest in the intelligence of dolphins was then at a high pitch thanks to the work of John Lilly, one of the attendees. Lilly astonished and stimulated the assembled scientists with his anecdotes concerning the behavior and wit of dolphins. We were impressed with how diverse intelligent life must be. In fact, so fascinating were the dolphin experiments that when the conference was over, the attendees formed an informal group called the Order of the Dolphin and planned to keep in contact and exchange ideas on SETI. Eighteen years later, the Order of the Dolphin is still in existence.

There was some discussion about possible means for constructing a message intended to permit easy communication between civilizations that had had no prior contact. Some ideas, seemingly profound at the time, were to transmit such esoterica as the value of π carried to some very large number of decimal points, or perhaps a sequence of prime numbers (numbers that can be divided only by themselves and by the number one). We thought that such messages would be recognized as evidence of intelligent origin and moreover would give a measure of our intelligence by showing how smart we were to be able to calculate such enormous numbers. In retrospect, I must say that these were bad ideas, because the existence of the transmission itself is already sufficient evidence of the existence of an intelligent civilization.

About this time *Lingua Cosmica,* a book on interstellar codes, was published by Hans Freudenthal, a Yale mathematician. It contained an ingenious method to construct a language by utilizing simple mathematics to establish simple rules and concepts. For example, an equation such as $2 + 3 = 5$ and another equation such as $4 + 5 = 9$ can be used to establish the meaning of the plus sign and the equal sign. The numbers themselves, of course, can be established by representing them as simply as a series of dots equal to their value. Some of these concepts were used in the early part of the picture sequence of the Voyager record. Freudenthal showed that by using such mathematical equations one could develop quite a sophisticated language—in fact, even an ability in the end to express emotions. As ingenious as it was, *Lingua Cosmica* was a rather risky method for interstellar communication, because it assumed that the recipients have brains and logic very similar to ours. More than that, if anywhere along the way a lesson in logic was not understood, all subsequent lessons would be gibberish and the correct coding systems would never be established or understood. A simpler unambiguous method was called for.

About six months after the Green Bank meeting, it occurred to me that a powerful way to send unambiguous interstellar messages was to transmit pictures resembling ordinary television pictures, a procedure very similar to the procedure by which human infants learn to speak. Infants are shown objects and told what the names of these objects are. Would it not make sense in the interstellar context to send images of things and attach to them some linguistic representation, which could then be used to construct sophisticated texts? With a little experimenting, I found that quite a good picture could be made by simply drawing the picture with black and white spots. It is of course useful to have intermediate shades of gray, but in fact the prime characteristics of an image can be expressed quite adequately in nothing more than black and white. The picture could be drawn by taking a rectangular grid of points and making the points black or white, thus constructing the desired pictorial representation. The sequence of black and white spots that make up the picture could then be sent as a sequence of two characters (one for black and one for white), two tones, or perhaps dots and dashes. It should be quite trivial for any intelligent civilization to decode.

As an example of how this might work, I constructed a picture made up of 551 characters. Why 551? Well, it is the product of 19 and 29—prime numbers—and I thought this would help extraterrestrials understand how to lay out the message. It was made in a rectangular grid 29 units high and 19 units across. When extraterrestrials recognize that the number 551 can be divided by 19 and 29 and by nothing else except 1 and 551, it should suggest that the sequence of characters received in the message should be laid out in a format of either 19 rows of 29 characters each, or 29 rows of 19 characters. Which is right must be discovered by trial and error, but it takes only a few minutes to do that.

The message constructed to demonstrate this procedure is shown in Figure 1. At the time, I did it almost as a joke, just to show that if one doesn't try to be too highfalutin, one can come up with a pretty good interstellar language. As a game, I sent out the message, no hints given, to all the members of the Order of the Dolphin and challenged them to decipher its contents. It has surprised me ever since that this exercise in interstellar linguistics, which started out primarily as a source of entertainment, has over the years taken on the aura of a great breakthrough in human intellectual achievements.

In fact, the 551-character message contained a great deal of information—indeed, more than would be allowed by the conventional wisdom of information theory. According to that theory, 551 characters should contain the same information content as about 25 English words. Yet there is much more than 25 words' worth in the message. This is because the message as constructed uses shared concepts of physics and astronomy to impart information, as it were, in a shorthand way.

The decryption is shown in Figure 2, in which the message has been laid out in 29 groups of 19 and the 1's have been made black and

An Example of a Message That Might be Received
from Another Civilization in Space

```
1 1 1 1 0 0 0 0 0 1 0 1 0 0 1 0 0 0 0 1 1 0 0 1 0 0 0 0 0 0 0 1 0 0 0 0 0 1 0 1 0 0
1 0 0 0 0 0 1 1 0 0 1 0 1 1 0 0 1 1 1 1 0 0 0 0 0 1 1 0 0 0 0 1 1 0 1 0 0 0 0 0 0
0 0 1 0 0 0 0 0 1 0 0 0 0 1 0 0 0 0 1 0 0 0 1 0 1 0 1 0 0 0 0 1 0 0 0 0 0 0 0 0 0
0 0 0 0 0 0 0 0 0 1 0 0 0 1 0 0 0 0 0 0 0 0 0 0 1 0 1 1 0 0 0 0 0 0 0 0 0 0 0 0 0
0 0 0 0 0 0 0 1 0 0 0 1 1 1 0 1 1 0 1 0 1 1 0 1 0 1 0 0 0 0 0 0 0 0 0 0 0 0 0 0 0
0 0 0 0 1 0 0 1 0 0 0 0 1 1 1 0 1 0 1 0 1 0 1 0 0 0 0 0 0 0 0 0 1 0 1 0 1 0 1 0 1
0 0 0 0 0 0 0 0 0 1 1 1 0 1 0 1 0 1 0 1 1 1 0 1 0 1 1 0 0 0 0 0 0 0 1 0 0 0 0 0 0
0 0 0 0 0 0 0 0 0 1 0 0 0 0 0 0 0 0 0 0 0 0 0 1 0 0 0 1 0 0 1 1 1 1 1 1 0 0 0
0 0 1 1 1 0 1 0 0 0 0 0 1 0 1 1 0 0 0 0 0 1 1 1 0 0 0 0 0 0 0 1 0 0 0 0 0 0 0 0 0
1 0 0 0 0 0 0 0 0 1 0 0 0 0 0 0 0 1 1 1 1 1 0 0 0 0 0 0 0 1 0 1 1 0 0 0 1 0 1 1 1 0
1 0 0 0 0 0 0 0 1 1 0 0 1 0 1 0 1 1 1 1 1 0 1 0 1 1 1 1 1 0 0 0 1 0 0 1 1 1 1 1 0 0 1
0 0 0 0 0 0 0 0 0 0 0 1 1 1 1 1 0 0 0 0 0 0 0 1 0 1 1 0 0 0 1 1 1 1 1 1 0 0 0 0 0 0
1 0 0 0 0 0 1 1 0 0 0 0 0 1 1 0 0 0 0 1 0 0 0 0 1 1 0 0 0 0 0 0 0 1 1 0 0 0 1 0 1
0 0 1 0 0 0 0 1 1 1 1 0 0 1 0 1 0 1 1 1 1
```

A total of 551 0's and 1's. What does it tell us?

Figure 1
The 551-character "message" constructed to show how a television picture
might be sent simply, and to test the skills of the members of the Order of
the Dolphin. The 0 and 1 characters are used merely to indicate that only
two characters are used. In practice, the message might consist of dots and
dashes or pulses and spaces or two different tones, as in the Arecibo message of 1974.

Figure 2
The decryption of the 551-character message, in which the characters of Figure 1 have been laid out in 29 rows of 19 characters, the 1's have been made into black squares and the 0's have been made white.

the 0's white. What is the message content? I tried to depict what was then thought to be of most interest to another civilization. We see an image of the intelligent creature who composed the message; we see along the left-hand margin of the message a diagram of the creature's solar system, starting with the star at the top, four minor planets, one intermediate planet, two major planets, an intermediate planet, and a final minor planet. In the upper right-hand corner, we see drawings of the atoms of carbon and oxygen, an indication that the creature's life system is like ours, based on carbon, and that the creature's chemistry depends on oxygen in an important way just as ours does. This would indicate to us, of course, that the creature is chemically similar to us.

The characters just below and to the right of the sun are the most difficult to decipher. In fact they are the numerals 1, 2, 3, 4, and 5 written in a binary code. Indeed, this is the simplest numbering system: numbers are based on two rather than the bizarre number ten derived from our fingers. An extra character is added as necessary such that the number of black characters is always odd. In this way, a numbering system is established, and the means by which one can identify what is a number from what is not are clearly identified. If there is an odd number of characters or "bits," then that is a numeral. This method allows us to interpret the three large groups below the atomic symbols. These are groups having an odd number of black characters; therefore we know they are numerals. They are, from the top, 5, 2,000, and 4 billion, approximately. The lowest group is connected by a diagonal line to the figure of the intelligent creature. We can't be sure what these numbers mean, but we notice that they are written alongside planets 2, 3, and 4, suggesting perhaps that there are 4 billion of the creatures on planet 4, evidently its home planet; 2,000 on planet 3, indicating the existence of a large colony on that planet; and finally a group of 5 on planet 2, implying that an exploration on the planet is proceeding. Below the creature is a character sequence; it has an even number of bits, and therefore it can't be a numeral. What else can it be? A word? We can't be sure, but we can guess that the creature is giving us a name, four bits, so that in future messages when the creature wishes to refer to itself it doesn't have to draw a picture but can simply give us the name Four Bits.

Lastly, on the lower right-hand margin, there is a diagram that evidently tells us the size of the creature. The creature is thirty-one somethings high. What can these somethings be? The only length we have in common is the wavelength in the radio spectrum on which this message was transmitted. It is believed that the optimum wavelengths for interstellar communication are about ten centimeters, which would make the creature about ten feet high, and this would, of course, make us feel ten feet high for understanding the contents of this message.

And now, a depressing shock: almost none of the elite members of the Order of the Dolphin were able to interpret this message. Never having seen this kind of message before, it just didn't occur to them to try the picture format. Nowadays thousands of people are aware of this possible format and readily decode it. In any case, in those ancient times, my letters to the members of the Order of the Dolphin enclosing this message elicited only one reply. Back from Barney Oliver came a new message consisting of a sequence of 0's and 1's. But at least I knew what to look for, and indeed it was another very simple and inspiring message, containing just one image: that of a martini glass with an olive in it!

The 551-character message was perhaps quite difficult to interpret even after one did discover the picture format. This was because the message was very tightly structured with all of the symbols and sketches very close together. To one not familiar with such messages it was very difficult to tell what part of the picture was connected to another part of the picture, or what was in fact unrelated to something in the picture. Taking this into account, Barney soon constructed a new message utilizing 1,271 bits, as shown in Figure 3. Its decryption is shown in Figure 4. As is obvious, it gives a much clearer picture. Of course, the information content is not so high, since a lot of the message is devoted to depicting nothing but blank space. But then the amount of ambiguity is much less. As can be seen by looking at this picture, even a small increase in the number of characters has allowed the transmission of much more information and in fact more sophisticated information. In the images of the intelligent creatures here, we see two sexes and a child. It becomes clear that the creatures are not born full-size but develop from smaller versions of the mature ones.

The construction of these two simple binary-code-picture mes-

Таблица 17

Космограмма Дрейка

Неправильная интерпретация (длина строки равна 64). Значение качества (142) значительно меньше, чем для правильной интерпретации, качество которой равно 172

		$u_{i, i+1}$	$u_{i, i+1}$	$u_{i, i+1} + u_{i, i+1}$
0100000100000110000000011000001101100101101100000110011100000000000		0	11	11
100000000000000000000000000000000001000011100000000000000100	1	0	2	2
000000001000010000010001000000000000000000000000000000000010	0	0	0	0
001000010000010000010000001000000000100010000010001001001000	0	0	2	2
010001000100000011110000000000000000100000000010000000000000	0	0	2	2
000000100001000000000000000000000000000000000001000000000010	0	0	2	2
00100001100010000000000000000000000000000000000000001000	0	3	1	4
010100011000011000011000000010010010010010010010010010010110	1	5	9
010100100100001100001100001100001100001000000000000000000001	0	3	6	9
111101000000000000000000000100000010000000000001011011	1	1	7	8
100100000000000001111101000000000000000000000001000000000000	1	0	7	7
000000100010011100000000000010100000000000000101001000011001010	0	2	5	7
111110101000000000000101001000010000000001001000000000000000	1	1	5	6
010010000010000000000011111000000000000011110000011110100000100	0	4	8	12
101000000000000101010000010000000000010100000000010100010	1	8	4	12
000000000000000100010010010001001101100111011010100001000010	0	4	0	4
001010101000100100000000000000010001000100100100010001000000	0	4	11	15
100000000000011100000111100000111000000111110100001010010000 1	1	4	12	16
010000010001000001000000001000001000011100001000001000011000	0	5	1	6
000001000100100010001000000100000100011000010000010001000100	0	4	4	8
010001001000001100000001100001101100011011000001100111000000000	0	—	—	—
		$U_{\text{стр}}$ 47 $U_{\text{столб}}$ 95		$U = 142$

Figure 3

Barney Oliver's 1,271-character message, written in the same way as the message of Figure 1.

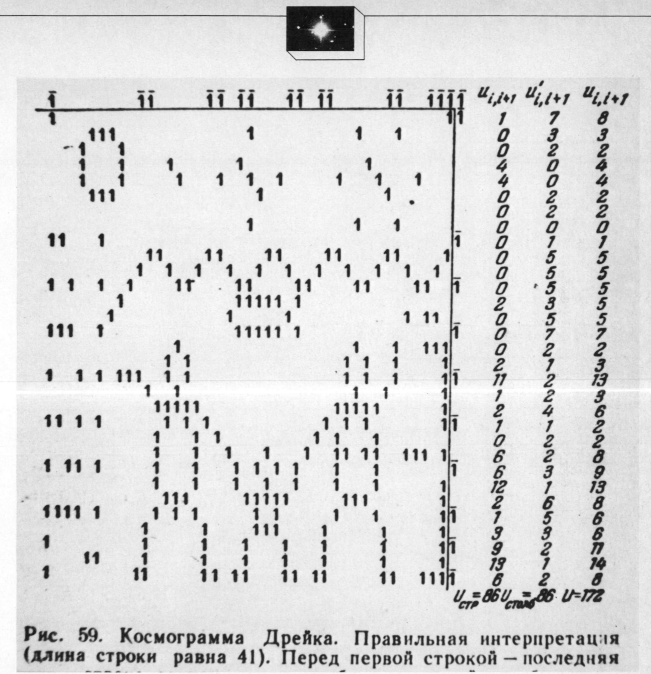

Рис. 59. Космограмма Дрейка. Правильная интерпретация (длина строки равна 41). Перед первой строкой — последняя

Figure 4
The decryption of the 1,271-character message.

sages demonstrated that there is a good means for reliable interstellar communication without prior contact. We need not fear a linguistic problem when we encounter other civilizations even if the means of contact are limited to very simple radio transmissions.

In December 1969 our Arecibo Observatory sponsored a meeting of the American Astronomical Society in a big resort hotel in San Juan, Puerto Rico. During a coffee break, I was chatting with Carl Sagan when he related a fact realized by almost no one: the Pioneer 10 spacecraft soon to be launched on a mission to Jupiter would in fact swing by Jupiter and in the process gain enough velocity to escape the solar system. It would travel indefinitely among the stars to the farthest reaches of the galaxy. This point had first been recognized by a writer for the *Christian Science Monitor,* Eric Burgess, and a planetarium expert, Richard Hoagland, who had suggested that since this would be the first object to leave the solar system, it might well carry on it some message to any intelligent civilization that might someday happen to intercept the spacecraft. Carl had enthusiastically volunteered to construct such a message for NASA. The plan was to engrave something on a metal plate, the idea being that such a metal engraving in a space environment would remain recognizable for a period of perhaps billions of years.

Now in this case, as many as 100,000 characters might possibly be inscribed on the plate if they were crowded in, and so it appeared that a much more sophisticated message than those of the early binary-code pictures could be sent. This time we desired to send some information about the nature of life on Earth and in particular to give the time and place of the Pioneer 10 launching.

Carl asked me how we might express these facts well. In those few minutes before the meeting resumed, we talked about several methods, including the possibility of showing a map of the galaxy with a large number of binary stars indicated, thus perhaps establishing the location of Earth in the galaxy. Carl suggested the possibility of presenting a map showing the Big Dipper and a few other constellations. This would establish the time of launching to within about 10,000 years and the place of launch to within twenty or thirty light-years. At that time, I was very active in research on pulsars, the rapidly pulsating radio sources each of which has a distinct pulsing frequency, and it occurred to me that it would be a much more powerful approach to give the location of the earth with respect to a number of prominent pulsars. The characteristic pulsing frequency of each pulsar would very clearly identify which pulsar was which on the map. More than that, although the pulsing frequencies are well defined, they are gradually changing by a very small amount, which can be accurately measured, small as it is. Some change their pulsing periods by much less than a billionth of a second a day. The amount of change in the pulsar frequency between that shown in the engraving and that determined by those capturing the Pioneer spacecraft would give the time that had elapsed since the picture was drawn. Thus using a pulsar map would allow us to locate the place of origin of the spacecraft in the Milky Way galaxy and would also indicate with very high accuracy how long the spacecraft had been in flight before interception. We adopted this means of achieving the main goals of the Pioneer 10 plaque. This same map is shown on the cover of the Voyager record, and in the picture sequence, to mark the birthplace and cosmic birthday of the Voyager.

Carl asked me if I could construct the pulsar map quickly because time was very short. I said yes and proceeded to do so. As I was doing this, Carl added a diagram of the solar system with relative distances of the planets and the Pioneer trajectory, and his wife Linda drew perhaps the most important information on the plaque, the figures of a man and a woman standing in front of a drawing of the spacecraft itself to give scale. The figures contained characteristics of all human races. The plaque is shown in Figure 5. One of these plaques was launched on each of the Pioneer 10 and 11 spacecraft. Both of these spacecraft have now flown past Jupiter and are on their way into the interstellar space as planned.

The Pioneer 10 and 11 plaque, simple as it was, elicited a public reaction both amusing and amazing. The news and television media were confronted with the problem of showing this plaque in all its details despite the fact that naked humans were depicted on it. For some of the media this was a challenging first. In the *Chicago Sun-Times,* the editors made a frantic effort to airbrush out the sexual parts of the nude figures. For one edition to the next, all on the same day, one titillating bit of anatomy after another disappeared. In the *Los Angeles Times,* there were angry letters to the editor denouncing NASA for using taxpayers' money to send "smut" into space. There were letters from out-

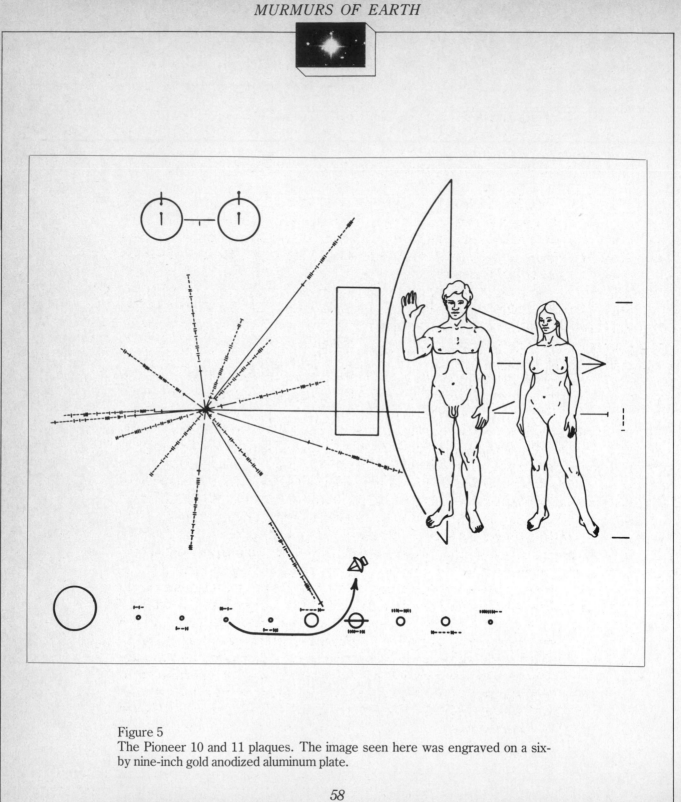

Figure 5
The Pioneer 10 and 11 plaques. The image seen here was engraved on a six-
by nine-inch gold anodized aluminum plate.

raged feminists protesting that the woman on the plaque appeared to be subservient to the man. Was she not in fact standing behind him, and why for heaven's sake was the man's hand raised and not hers? This all came as a shock to the artist, Linda Sagan, who felt herself to be a liberated woman.

Surprise and alarm was expressed by some who felt that the human figures resembled too closely their *own* race, whatever it might be. Surprisingly, this objection was voiced by members of all races; there must be some deep psychological truth here. Perhaps most important were complaints that this message was constructed by a very limited group of humans—in fact, three humans—and thus was neither representative of the human race as a whole nor perhaps as informative as it could be. There were editorials published in the British press demanding that any future similar enterprise be engineered by a large international ecumenical group of scientists and lay people.

After this barrage of criticism, we decided that most of these criticisms had no merit, and we felt that no great mistake had been made. Still, they caused us to look toward the art of constructing interstellar messages with much more humility. We had discovered that there was widespread serious human concern about the content of interstellar messages, even though the chance of reception was very small.

These thoughts were on my mind when the next opportunity to transmit an interstellar message appeared. It was in 1974, and we, at the National Astronomy and Ionosphere Center, had just finished installing a new reflector surface on the Arecibo 1,000-foot radio telescope, and a new transmitter with a power of about half a million watts. The power from this transmitter, when focused by the giant reflector, was to become the strongest signal leaving Earth. In fact, the signal was to be so strong that it was perhaps a million times brighter than the sun at a comparable wavelength, a signal easily detectable by radio telescopes no more sensitive than ours across interstellar distances of many thousands of light-years. A dedication ceremony was to be held at the Arecibo Observatory in November, and it seemed that a striking way to dedicate the "new" telescope would be to transmit an interstellar message from it. This time I sought advice from many more people—most of them scientists, to be sure, but still a much broader cross section than before.

THE ARECIBO MESSAGE, 1974

```
0 0 0 0 0 0 1 0 1 0 1 0 1 0 1 0 0 0 0 0 0 0 0 0 0 0 0 1 0 1 0 0 0 0 0 1 0 1 0
0 0 0 0 0 0 1 0 0 1 0 0 0 1 0 0 0 1 0 0 0 1 0 0 1 0 1 1 0 0 1 0 1 0 1 0 1
0 1 0 1 0 1 0 1 0 1 0 0 1 0 0 1 0 0 0 0 0 0 0 0 0 0 0 0 0 0 0 0 0 0 0 0 0
0 0 0 0 0 0 0 0 0 0 0 0 0 0 1 1 0 0 0 0 0 0 0 0 0 0 0 0 0 0 0 0 0 0 0 0 0
1 1 0 1 0 0 0 0 0 0 0 0 0 0 0 0 0 0 0 0 0 1 1 0 1 0 0 0 0 0 0 0 0 0 0 0
0 0 0 0 0 0 0 0 1 0 1 0 1 0 0 0 0 0 0 0 0 0 0 0 0 0 0 0 0 0 0 1 1 1 1 1 0
0 0 0 0 0 0 0 0 0 0 0 0 0 0 0 0 0 0 0 0 0 0 0 0 0 0 0 0 0 0 1 1 0 0 0 0
1 1 1 0 0 0 1 1 0 0 0 0 1 1 0 0 0 1 0 0 0 0 0 0 0 0 0 0 0 0 0 1 1 0 0 1 0
0 0 0 1 1 0 1 0 0 0 1 1 0 0 0 1 1 0 0 0 1 1 0 1 0 1 1 1 1 1 0 1 1 1 1 1
0 1 1 1 1 1 0 1 1 1 1 0 0 0 0 0 0 0 0 0 0 0 0 0 0 0 0 0 0 0 0 0 0 0 0 0
0 1 0 0 0 0 0 0 0 0 0 0 0 0 0 0 0 1 0 0 0 0 0 0 0 0 0 0 0 0 0 0 0 0 0 0
0 0 0 0 0 0 0 0 0 0 1 0 0 0 0 0 0 0 0 0 0 0 0 0 0 0 0 0 1 1 1 1 1 1 0 0
0 0 0 0 0 0 0 0 0 1 1 1 1 1 0 0 0 0 0 0 0 0 0 0 0 0 0 0 0 0 0 0 0 0 0 0
0 0 1 1 0 0 0 0 1 1 0 0 0 0 1 1 1 0 0 0 1 1 0 0 0 1 0 0 0 0 0 0 0 0 1 0 0 0
0 0 0 0 0 0 1 0 0 0 0 1 1 0 1 0 0 0 0 1 1 0 0 0 1 1 1 0 0 1 1 0 1 0 1 1 1
1 1 0 1 1 1 1 1 0 1 1 1 1 1 0 1 1 1 1 0 0 0 0 0 0 0 0 0 0 0 0 0 0 0 0 0
0 0 0 0 0 0 0 0 1 0 0 0 0 0 0 1 1 0 0 0 0 0 0 0 0 1 0 0 0 0 0 0 0 0 0
0 0 1 1 0 0 0 0 0 0 0 0 0 0 0 0 1 0 0 0 0 1 1 0 0 0 0 0 0 0 0 0 0 0
1 1 1 1 1 1 0 0 0 0 1 1 0 0 0 0 0 0 1 1 1 1 0 0 0 0 0 0 0 0 0 0 0 1 1 0
0 0 0 0 0 0 0 0 0 1 0 0 0 0 0 0 0 0 0 0 0 0 0 0 1 0 0 0 0 0 1
0 0 0 0 0 0 1 1 0 0 0 0 0 0 1 0 0 0 0 0 0 0 1 1 0 0 0 0 1 1 0 0 0 0 0 0
1 0 0 0 0 0 0 0 0 0 0 0 1 1 0 0 0 1 0 0 0 0 1 1 0 0 0 0 0 0 0 0 0 0 0 0
0 1 1 0 0 1 1 0 0 0 0 0 0 0 0 0 0 0 0 1 1 0 0 0 1 0 0 0 0 1 1 0 0 0 0 0
0 0 0 0 1 1 0 0 0 0 1 1 0 0 0 0 0 0 1 0 0 0 0 0 0 0 1 0 0 0 0 0 1 0 0 0
0 0 0 0 0 1 0 0 0 0 1 0 0 0 0 0 0 0 1 1 0 0 0 0 0 0 0 0 1 0 0 0 1 0 0 0
0 0 0 0 0 1 1 0 0 0 0 0 0 0 0 1 0 0 0 1 0 0 0 0 0 0 0 1 0 0 0 1 0 0 0
1 0 0 0 0 0 1 0 0 0 0 0 0 0 1 0 0 0 0 0 0 0 1 0 0 0 0 0 0 0 1 0 0 0 0 0 0
0 0 0 0 0 0 1 1 0 0 0 0 0 0 0 0 0 1 1 0 0 0 0 0 0 0 0 1 1 0 0 0 0 0 0 0
0 1 0 0 0 0 1 1 1 0 1 0 1 1 0 0 0 0 0 0 0 1 0 0 0 0 0 0 0 1 0 0 0 0 0
0 0 0 0 0 0 0 0 1 0 0 0 0 0 1 1 1 1 0 0 0 0 0 0 0 0 0 0 0 1 0 0 0
0 1 0 1 1 1 0 1 0 0 1 0 1 1 0 1 1 0 0 0 0 0 0 1 0 0 1 1 1 0 0 1 0 0 1 1 1
1 1 1 1 0 1 1 1 0 0 0 0 1 1 1 0 0 0 0 1 1 0 1 1 1 0 0 0 0 0 0 0 0 1 0
1 0 0 0 0 0 1 1 1 0 1 1 0 0 1 0 0 0 0 0 0 0 1 0 0 0 0 0 1 1 1 1 1 1 0 0
1 0 0 0 0 0 1 0 1 0 0 0 0 0 1 1 0 0 0 0 0 0 1 0 0 0 0 0 1 1 0 1 1 0 0 0
0 0 0 0 0 0 0 0 0 0 0 0 0 0 0 0 0 0 0 0 0 0 0 0 0 0 0 0 0 0 1 1 1 0 0
0 0 0 1 0 0 0 0 0 0 0 0 0 0 0 1 1 1 0 1 0 1 0 0 0 1 0 1 0 1 0 1 0 1
0 1 0 0 1 1 1 0 0 0 0 0 0 0 0 0 1 0 1 0 1 0 1 0 0 0 0 0 0 0 0 0 0 0 0
0 0 1 0 1 0 0 0 0 0 0 0 0 0 0 1 1 1 1 0 0 0 0 0 0 0 0 0 0 0 0
0 0 0 1 1 1 1 1 1 1 1 0 0 0 0 0 0 0 0 1 1 1 0 0 0 0 0 0 0 1 1 1
0 0 0 0 0 0 0 1 1 0 0 0 0 0 0 0 0 0 1 1 0 0 0 0 0 0 1 1 0 0 1 0 0
0 0 0 0 0 0 1 0 1 1 0 0 0 0 0 1 1 0 0 1 1 0 0 0 0 0 0 1 1 0 0 1 1 0 0
0 0 1 0 0 0 1 0 1 0 0 0 0 0 1 0 1 0 0 0 1 0 0 0 0 1 0 0 0 1 0 0 1 0 0 0 1
0 0 1 0 0 0 1 0 0 0 0 0 0 0 0 1 0 0 0 1 0 1 0 0 0 1 0 0 0 0 0 0 0 0 0 0
0 1 0 0 0 0 1 0 0 0 0 1 0 0 0 0 0 0 0 0 0 0 0 1 0 0 0 0 0 0 0 0 1 0 0
0 0 0 0 0 0 0 0 0 0 0 1 0 0 1 0 1 0 0 0 0 0 0 0 0 0 0 0 1 1 1 0 0 1 1
1 1 1 0 1 0 0 1 1 1 1 0 0 0
```

Figure 6

The Arecibo message of November 1974. In this case, the two characters were sent by switching the radio transmitter between two radio frequencies about 75 cycles per second apart. The basic radio frequency was 2380 Megahertz. The characters were sent at a rate of 10 per second.

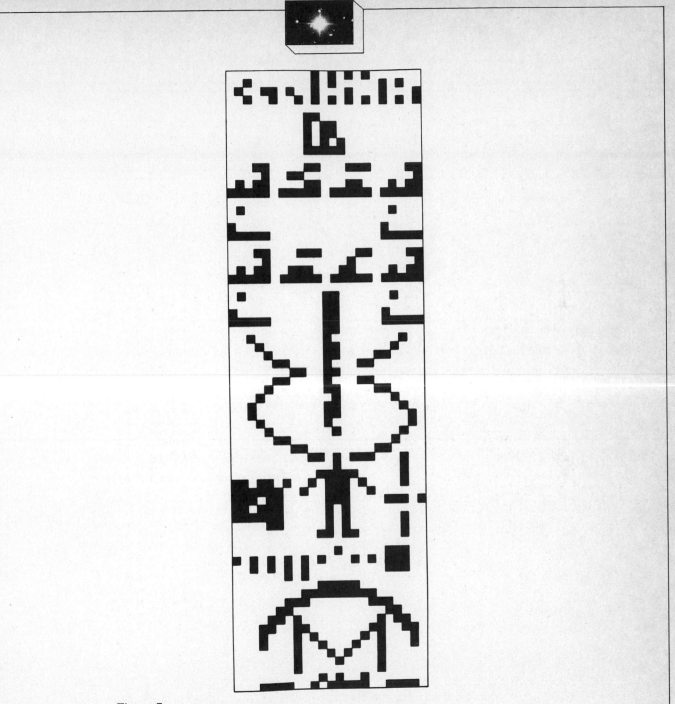

Figure 7
The decryption of the Arecibo message. In this case, the message is written as 73 groups of 23 characters.

In this message, the same format was used as in the early messages—a black-and-white television picture. We wished to send about ten characters a second, both because this would cause the signal to be detectable to very large distances and because such a signal would sound pleasing to the dedication audience. We thought that about three minutes of such a transmission would be enough—more might be boring—and so a message consisting of 1,679 characters was chosen. The number 1,679 is the product of the prime numbers 73 and 23. The characters would be sent as two tones. The movie *Close Encounters of the Third Kind* uses a communication method that mimics this message, but on a trivial level.

I took the ideas, which were suggested by a number of people, and combined them to produce the final message, which is shown in Figures 6 and 7. The first characters appear in the upper right-hand corner of the decryption, and the message reads from right to left and down. This message is considerably more informative than the previous messages, but still is probably among the simplest to decode. We were learning.

The message starts with the numbers 1 through 10, again written in binary code, but intentionally squeezed against the top margin so that we were forced to adopt some convention to indicate how large numbers are to be written where there is not enough space to do so. In this way, the convention would be clearly established. This has to be done carefully and clearly because numbers appear in the message, written not only on several lines but in three orientations. Then follow the numbers 1, 6, 7, 8, and 15, placed in prominent isolation. This is probably the most enigmatic part of the message. The only self-consistent interpretation of these numbers is that they are the atomic numbers of the elements hydrogen, carbon, nitrogen, oxygen, and phosphorus. This makes sense particularly when one explores the next characters in the message, which are sets of numbers in the same locations as the atomic numbers of the various elements. These make up chemical formulas— in fact the formulas of the components of the molecule that determines the nature of terrestrial life, the DNA molecule. Its composition is shown here and even its form, that of a double helix. When one looks at the usual sketches of the complicated DNA molecule, it may not seem possible to depict it clearly and succinctly with the limited imaging capabilities of this type of message, yet when we set out to do it, it turned out to be rather simple after all.

The double helix winds into the head of a human being, indicating a relationship with the intelligent creature. Various attempts were made to make a better unisex version of the human, but the next-best version looked as much like a gorilla as a human, and so I had to settle for this rather masculine-appearing person. That the DNA is important to us is clear. Of equal importance, a large number placed within the DNA molecule tells of the number of nucleotide pairs, or code bits, in the typical human DNA molecule. This expressed something that couldn't be described otherwise in such simple artwork—the level of our evolution, and some measure of the level of our intelligence.

To the creature's right is a measure of its size, given in terms of the wavelength on which the message was transmitted, 12.6 centimeters. To the creature's left is a large number giving the population of humans on earth. Below the human is a sketch of the solar system, including the sun and all nine planets, and showing at least the relative sizes of the planets. Planet 3 is offset from the rest toward the human, showing that there is something special about it, that it is, in fact, the home of the human race. Finally, below the solar system and "up" with respect to the Earth is a sketch of a telescope, a reflector focusing rays to a point. Just below this is a number giving the size of the telescope, about 1,000 feet, again in wavelengths. This is both the size of the telescope that sent the message, the Arecibo radio telescope, and the size of the largest radio telescope on Earth. Thus, we described the state of advancement of our technology. Note that if the message is sent over and over, it will seem to flow out of the telescope, making the point that this is the one that is sending the message.

Carl knew I was constructing this message, and since he was very interested in it, he volunteered to be a proxy extraterrestrial. So one day we went off to the campus faculty club and had a long lunch while I silently laid out the rough drawing of the message in front of him. He cogitated over it, and having grasped the first part of the message, the hardest part, with effort, he proceeded to plow successfully through the whole thing. He had a few suggestions for improvements, but the message worked. I felt full of confidence this time as the computers at Arecibo went to work constructing the commands needed to control the radio transmitters.

The message was successfully sent on November 16, 1974, at 1:00 AST (Atlantic standard time) as approximately two hundred people

PROPOSED MJS RECORD

(12" DISK, ONE SIDE, 33⅓ RPM)

PICTURE	SOUND	ELAPSED TIME
SPACECRAFT AT LAUNCH WITH HUMAN FIGURES		2^m
$H, C, N, O, P \rightarrow$ SYMBOLS (USE OUR ALPHABET)		3
$A, T, C, G, PO_4,$ DEOXYRIBOSE $\rightarrow$ SYMBOLS		5
DNA		7
HUMAN FIGURES (CHILD, ADULT MAN & WOMAN ELDERLY MAN & WOMAN?)		10
A HOUSE (WITH PLANTS, AUTOMOBILE, HUMAN FIGURES)		12
	HUMAN DINNER CONVERSATION	13
TIMES SQUARE (WITH AUTOMOBILE)		15
	SOUNDS OF TIMES SQUARE	16
SYDNEY OPERA HOUSE (WITH BOATS)		18
	SYMPHONY	20
TAJ MAHAL (WITH AIRPLANE, ELEPHANT?)		22
	INDIAN MUSIC	23
MILKY WAY SHOWING SUN, MAGELLANIC CLOUDS M31, SOLAR SPECTRUM		25

PICTURES NOMINALLY 500 × 500 lines = 250000 PIXELS, 4 bits per pixel. HUMAN FIGURES 1.5 TIMES MORE PIXELS.

January 1977 at Kawabata Cottage at Kahala Hilton
Honolulu, Hawaii

Figure 8
The first written plan of the Voyager message, prepared in Hawaii in January 1977. Note how few pictures we then thought were possible, and how the first guess was that it would take several minutes to send each picture.

watched. It was directed toward the great globular cluster of stars in the constellation Hercules known as Messier 13, some 25,000 light-years away. It will take the message 25,000 years to reach the 300,000 stars of Messier 13, passing perhaps 30 other stars along the way. As the audience looked at the huge transmitting structure 500 feet above them, shimmering in the tropical sun, many sensed that there was something very special about the eerie whine, the sound of a message being transmitted to the stars for the first time. It took 169 seconds to send, and as the warbling of the message changed to the steady tone that marked the end of the message, the emotional impact on many of the audience was evident—there were tears in many eyes and sighs to be heard. Brighter than the fires of our own sun, the message was on its way. The first bits of the message were already passing the orbit of Mars. Only seven hours later the message had passed the orbit of Pluto and was plunging at the speed of light into the darkness of the interstellar space. It is now farther from Earth than the distance to the nearest star.

The Arecibo message provoked only two major protests. One was from a few scientists who worried that we hadn't corrected for the speed of the Earth in space in launching the message. Just as a football quarterback must correct the direction he throws a pass to compensate for his own movement, so we must correct for the fact that we are launching the message from a moving platform, Earth. We are moving about 150 miles a second because of our orbital motion around the center of the Milky Way (our motion around the sun gives us just a measly 18.5 miles a second). This speed is enough to divert the course of the message significantly, through an angle about one-tenth the diameter of the moon. We should correct for this. But we don't know our speed through space sufficiently accurately to make a very exact correction. In this case, it doesn't matter because the angular size of Messier 13 is larger than that of the moon, and so the message will arrive at Messier 13 even though we didn't launch it in quite the right direction.

The other protest was a serious one, made by Sir Martin Ryle, a Nobel laureate and the Astronomer Royal of England. He wrote with great anxiety that he felt it was very hazardous to reveal our existence and location to the galaxy. For all we know, any creatures out there were malevolent or hungry, and once they knew of us, they might come to attack or eat us. He strongly recommended that no messages of this sort be sent again and even asked the Executive Committee of the International Astronomical Union to approve a resolution condemning such messages. Many other less knowledgeable people had the same concerns.

The fact is, for better or for worse, we have already announced our presence and location to the universe, and continue to do so every day. There is a sphere of radio transmissions about thirty light-years thick expanding outward at the speed of light, announcing to every star it envelops that the earth is full of people. Our television programs flood space with signals detectable at enormous distances by instruments not much greater than our own. It is a sobering thought that the first news of us may be the outcome of the Super Bowl.

Our radar transmissions similarly spread the signs of human activity to the far corners of the galaxy. Whether or not Sir Martin Ryle is justified in his anxieties about revealing the location of our civilization is of course a debatable subject. Even so, it is too late to worry about it, so we might as well try to be friendly.

Finally, it became Voyager's turn to carry the news of our existence to the cosmos. As we contemplated this message, all the lessons of the past were in our minds. The need for absolute clarity had been learned from the first messages. The fear of sexual content and anxiety about prejudice had surfaced when the Pioneer plaque was unveiled. We heard the calls for ecumenism among the preparers of messages. The pleas that we give special concern to expressing friendship in messages still rang in our ears.

In late January 1977 there was a meeting of the American Astronomical Society, this time in Honolulu, and I had the pleasure of sharing a delightful cottage with Carl and his family at the Kahala Hilton Hotel. In fact, Carl had reserved this cottage many months earlier because the cottage opened out onto a large pool in which two highly trained dolphins were kept. The cottage is known as the Kawabata Cottage because the Japanese Nobel laureate of that name resided there once. There was something inspiring about sleeping in that cottage with the windows open—one could hear our old friends the dolphins slowly swimming by, breathing, playing with one another. Somehow one had the feeling that they weren't just some sea creatures but some very witty and intelligent beings living in the next room.

We were all worrying about the make-up of the Voyager message, because time was short. It had occurred to Carl that perhaps we should just send near duplicates of the Pioneer plaques, thus avoiding any new criticism and the tough problem of selecting a group to construct a brand-new message. We knew that no matter how the group was made up, there would be complaints that someone or some source of wisdom had been neglected. But that seemed a cop-out and an opportunity wasted.

Carl was very interested in sending some music. In fact, Barney Oliver had suggested sending a tape recording that would make this possible. However, we believed a tape recording wouldn't have the required longevity.

Due to our earlier experiences, I was very partial to pictures; they seemed to me the best way to express sophisticated and interesting information clearly. An engraved plaque, as on the Pioneers, is very durable, but it also is very limited. Maybe just one or two pictures—but what could one say about Earth in just two pictures?

Then it occurred to me that we could have our cake and eat it too. A phonograph record is an engraved plaque that can carry sounds. But a television picture is just a collection of signals at various frequencies, just as sound is. If we could translate those picture frequencies to ones that could successfully be recorded on a phonograph record, then we could record pictures too. We could have sound and pictures, and in fact combine them to increase greatly the information content of the "plaque."

The potential information content was enormous. Our first message had contained something like 1,000 characters. The Pioneer plaques could hold as much as 100,000 characters, although we didn't use nearly that many. One side of a long-playing phonograph record can hold 10 million characters!

Thinking this was a good solution, I put together a suggested table of contents for a record. I thought then that we might use one side of a record, and a quick estimate showed that a television picture might take three minutes to send. It seemed a good idea to have a mix of pictures of humans and other aspects of Earth, the sounds that went with the pictures, and some examples of music. This first suggested table of contents, from which the Voyager record grew, is shown in Figure 8.

One of the most remarkable things about the Voyager record is how we found ways to increase greatly its information content. In the end, as described in the previous essay, it was a two-sided record running at half the normal speed, so that we had two hours of playing time. The television pictures took only four seconds each to play (twelve seconds for color photographs). What started out to be about ten pictures ended up being a hundred and eighteen; and there was a whole catalogue of terrestrial voices and sounds and an hour and a half of music. It would have been a lot easier to choose the pictures if we had been limited to ten! It is tantalizing that the 10 million or so characters of the Voyager record are only as many characters as can be sent in a few seconds on a normal television channel. How rich radio interstellar messages could be!

Carl liked the idea of a record and successfully sold it to NASA officials. But we had to wait for weeks while all the necessary people in NASA gave approval to the project. By then it was very late, and the construction of the record became a crash project.

Carl divided up the responsiblities. He carried the ball in arranging the music selections with Tim Ferris; Ann Druyan took over the sounds of earth, and Linda Sagan, the group of greetings in many languages. I quickly assembled as ecumenical and knowledgeable a group as I could, to put together the very challenging picture sequence. Jon Lomberg played a key role in assembling a countless array of candidate pictures from an unbelievable variety of sources including, for example, the Cornell libraries, the libraries of Toronto, the National Geographic Society, and the United Nations, among many others. He helped make selections and did original artwork as necessary. Wendy Gradison helped provide candidate pictures as well as taking care of the onerous task of getting permissions for the use of each individual photograph selected. Amahl Shakhashiri assisted in finding pictures, taking them in some cases, and choosing the ones finally to be used on the record. Herman Eckelmann, our staff photographer, worked as long as needed day after day, both to take special pictures and to make the required prints and slides.

Valentin Boriakoff played a very special and key role in the success of the picture-sequence recording. When we got right down to it, we found to our surprise that the world just didn't make machines that would convert the signals of television pictures to the much lower frequency signals which could be recorded on a phonograph record. Although intellectually the idea was simple, the electronics to carry out the operation didn't seem to exist. Even the vast array of computers we operate at the Arecibo Observatory couldn't cope with the task. The television industry itself had never had a need for such a capability, and so hadn't dealt with the problem.

Valentin is one of our star electronics designers, and we threw the problem to him. Somehow he found a small company in Colorado named Colorado Video, Inc., that had just developed a machine to make the required transformations. They had figured that someday someone would need a machine to send television pictures over telephone lines and the like, and had built the special-purpose computer required. Fortunately their device worked well, and they wanted very much to share in the Voyager record project. They donated the use of their machine and personnel. And so the pictures were successfully recorded at Colorado Video, with Valentin's help, and in only eight seconds each. Without the work of CVI, the information content of the record, the grand pictures of our earth, would have been very much more limited.

The short time available to assemble the record caused a regrettable flaw in the end product. The sounds, music, and pictures are all recorded separately instead of being interrelated. How much better it would be if the human voices were next to the appropriate picture, the sound of a motor next to a picture of a car, or the picture of a violin next to the sound of its music. If ever there are recipients of the Voyager record, they will recognize that we certainly are clever enough to arrange such a helpful combination of sounds and pictures. They may also recognize that the lack of such a mix means one thing: those ancient artists who gave them this record (are any of the artists in the pictures?), now dead a billion years, just didn't have time. Too rushed, no time to organize. Other demands, other commitments. Interstellar messages aren't the most important things in the civilization of this era. Not yet, anyway. This They will know. Perhaps this will be nothing new to Them. Perhaps there will be a motion we wouldn't recognize, to Them a nod, as They realize that a billion years before there had been a civilization little different from Theirs.

References

1. "The Search for Extraterrestrial Intelligence" by Carl Sagan and Frank Drake, *Scientific American,* Vol. 232, No. 5 (May 1975), pp. 80–89.
2. "The Arecibo Message of November 1974" by the staff of the National Astronomy and Ionosphere Center, *Icarus,* Vol. 26 (1975), pp. 462–466.
3. "On Hands and Knees in Search of Elysium" by Frank Drake, *Technology Review,* Vol. 78, No. 7 (June 1976), pp. 22–29.
4. "A Message from Earth" by Carl Sagan, Linda Salzman Sagan, and Frank Drake, *Science,* Vol. 175 (February 25, 1972), pp. 881–884.
5. *Interstellar Communication: Scientific Perspectives,* edited by Cyril Ponnamperuma and A. G. W. Cameron. Boston: Houghton Mifflin, 1974.

3
PICTURES OF EARTH,
by Jon Lomberg

"I think an extraterrestrial message will be much more like a discipline of learned study than like a series of headlines."

Philip Morrison

When Carl Sagan first mentioned the Voyager record to me, I didn't expect to end up constructing a pictorial message for extraterrestrials. I had written a paper a few years earlier entitled "Some Thoughts on Art, Extraterrestrials, and the Nature of Beauty," which was printed and distributed by the National Air and Space Museum of the Smithsonian Institution. Referring to the work of various philosophers and aestheticians (such as Pythagoras and Gustav Fechner), I had suggested that some of the aesthetic principles of human art forms, especially music, were based on physical constants and the mathematical order of nature. Thus different intelligent species, observing the same universe, might produce art forms with some similar characteristics. In particular, I had speculated that certain highly ordered structures like fugues (especially those of Bach) might be accessible to minds all though the inhabited galaxy, if they could hear them.

Sagan, sensing my enthusiasm for a project that actually involved sending music into interstellar space (my excited response to his proposed plan for Voyager took approximately one nanosecond to manifest itself) said, "Consider yourself co-opted," and asked me to submit ideas and proposals.

As it turned out, I had a hand in the design of three areas of the record: the choice of music (mostly in the classical selections, especially the Bach and Mozart pieces), the sound montage (having worked for some years in the production of radio montages on scientific topics for the *Ideas* program of the Canadian Broadcasting Corporation, I submitted a proposed montage that suggested and outlined an evolutionary sound sequence—a sequence that was in part incorporated into the sound essay produced by Ann Druyan) and the picture package, where most of my efforts were directed.

When Frank Drake had decided that a metal phonograph record would be more efficient for information storage than an engraved plaque (such as the Pioneer 10 plaque), he thought that a few pictures might be encoded on the record. The original idea was to have six pictures. It was thought that we might show Earth, the DNA molecule, and a few shots of humans and animals. Since I am a painter with a longstanding professional interest in interstellar communication, Sagan suggested to Frank Drake that my ideas might be useful.

I arrived at Cornell in early May 1977. In previous weeks, Frank and Carl had contacted various members of the CETI* "brain trust," including such scientists as Philip Morrison, Bernard Oliver, Leslie Orgel and A. G. W. Cameron, men who had been thinking about interstellar communication for a long time. The question was, Which pictures of Earth and humanity should be sent? By comparing responses and seeing what common suggestions were made independently, Drake compiled a list of subjects. At this point, no actual photographs had been selected or even submitted—just general subjects. Frank said to me, "Your job is to find the photographs and construct diagrams if necessary."

There was one catch. Though NASA felt that the project was a good idea, time constraints forced them to insist on receiving the finished record in about six weeks. Not only did they require a formal proposal with actual submissions of pictures, voices, sounds and music, they needed an approved and fabricated record, ready to bolt onto the spacecraft. This meant that we had something like a month to find all the photographs, prepare them, secure legal permission for their use, draw all the diagrams, photograph everything to format, convert the pictures into a sound signal suitable for recording on a phonograph record, and devise an instruction sheet for the cover of the record to tell anybody who found it how to play it.

Since NASA was not prepared to sink a lot of money into this endeavor, Drake had to find some cheap system that already existed for converting pictures into sound. He worked with Valentin Boriakoff, a research associate at the National Astronomy and Ionosphere Center, who located a suitable system belonging to Colorado Video, a company that was willing to convert the pictures into sound on their equipment free of charge as a public service. It is a tribute to Frank and Val's combined ingenuity and expertise that within a week they had reduced the record time required to record a picture from close to a minute per picture to eight seconds per picture, had solved the problem of how to record in color, and had worked out a way of recording different pictures

---

*Communication with Extraterrestrial Intelligence—an acronym coined at an international conference attended by these and other scientists.

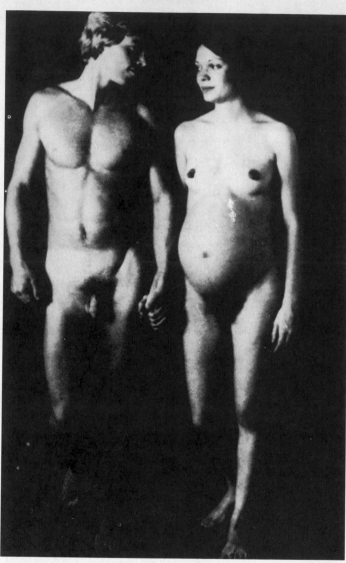

Our original proposal to NASA included this picture of two nude human beings to show recipients how our bodies look. We wanted to be neither sexist, pornographic, nor clinical. After looking through medical textbooks and anatomy books, we chose this photograph as the best and most inoffensive compromise. NASA refused to include it, perhaps because of possible adverse public reaction. We decided to keep the silhouette of this picture in the package because we felt that without it the continuity of the human reproduction sequence would be broken.

on each of the two stereo channels without getting crossover "ghost" images.

It was soon apparent that we could fit over a hundred pictures in the few minutes of the record allotted to the picture package. Even so, we didn't know exactly how many pictures we would send. A message of only black-and-white pictures could have three times as many pictures as a message of only color pictures, since a color picture took three times as long to record as a black-and-white one. We decided to compromise and send a mix, but up until the last minute we didn't know what the proportion of black and white to color would be. Where we felt color was vital (as in the solar spectrum) or desirable to give the best picture of our planet (by showing human skin tones or the color of trees, for example), we recorded in color. Of the one hundred and eighteen pictures in the finished package, twenty are in color.

The team that worked on selecting the pictures consisted of Frank Drake, me, Amahl Shakhashiri of the National Astronomy and Ionosphere Center, and Wendy Gradison, of the Laboratory for Planetary Studies at Cornell, who assisted in finding pictures and securing permissions. Technical support was provided by Dan Mitler, NAIC engineer, and Herman Eckelmann, the NAIC staff photographer, who had the tedious and frustrating job of photographing all pictures to format—and often rephotographing them several times as various problems came up. Eckelmann also took several photographs composed especially for the message. Draftsman Barbara Boettcher assisted me in preparing most of the diagrams in the package.

Wendy and I scoured the Cornell and local public libraries and amassed a stack of coffee-table and picture books that would have done credit to a major bookstore at Christmastime. *The History of Toys, Birds of North America, The Family of Man, Plant-Devouring Insects, The Age of Steam,* and a hundred others teetered in precarious stacks alongside every issue of the *National Geographic* back to 1958.

There were a few topics that we intentionally avoided. We reached a consensus that we shouldn't present war, disease, crime, and poverty. It would be naive to deny the importance of these phenomena in human culture and history—after all, more human beings have killed one another or starved to death than have written string quartets. Yet we felt that we were making something that would survive us and our time—something that might be the only token of Earth the universe would have. We decided that the worst in us needn't be sent across the galaxy. Also, we wanted to avoid any sort of political statement in this message, and a picture of Hiroshima or My Lai—or of a noble and heroic warrior, for that matter—seemed more an ideological statement than an integral part of an image of Earth. Nor did we want any part of the message to seem threatening or hostile to recipients ("Look how tough *we* are"), which is why we didn't send a picture of a nuclear explosion.

Similarly, we decided not to include any picture that was specifically religious. The music of Bach or the ch'in piece on the record certainly convey something of human spirituality and our sense of awe, but there are so many human religions that if we had shown any, we felt we would have to give equal time to all. If we'd included a picture of a cathedral, we felt we would also have to include one of a mosque, a synagogue, a lamasery, and so forth. Since there was no way of explaining each religion, inclusion of all faiths would be merely a political sop to people on Earth viewing our work.

Finally, we decided not to include artwork—mostly because we didn't feel competent to decide what art should be sent. A great deal of human art is shown in the music, which comprises the bulk of the record, but there was enough time to gather a panel of musicological experts to advise on balance and selection. We were so rushed in putting together the picture message that we couldn't assemble experts in all the various visual arts and have them agree. And we thought extraterrestrials would have enough trouble interpreting photographs of reality or simple diagrams without our including a photograph of a painting, which is itself an interpretation of reality. Even though we have some acknowledged "great art" in the pictures (Ansel Adams, for example, is generally considered one of the world's great photographers), the criterion for the picture message was informative, not aesthetic, value.

As we plowed through material, we began contacting individuals and organizations who had access to cross-indexed picture libraries that contained some of the subjects we were looking for. Of the greatest assistance was the National Geographic Society, which provided us with transparencies of published and unpublished material and was in general invaluable. In a way, they do routinely and on a larger scale what we were trying to do—give a full picture of Earth and its inhabitants. The UN picture library was also extremely cooperative. *Sports Illustrated* and NASA's photo services were contacted as well for specific shots.

I found myself increasingly playing the role of extraterrestrial, a mental exercise I had done in fun for many years (while playing Frisbee, for example, I'd ask myself, "What would ETI make of this?"). Only now it was in earnest. I would look at pictures and try to imagine that I'd never seen the subject before. How could the photograph be misinterpreted? What was ambiguous? How could scale be deduced? That bird in the distance flying past the man, a wingtip partly obscured by the man's outflung arm—*I* knew that the bird was a second creature in the distance, but if I didn't, couldn't it be a growth on the man's arm? The late anthropologist and poet Loren Eiseley wrote perceptively that "one does not meet oneself until one catches the reflection from an eye other than human." These words echoed in my mind during this whole process.

I was much influenced, in trying to adopt this mode of thought, by physicist Philip Morrison and by the science-fiction author Robert Heinlein. Each had pointed out in correspondence to us that the concept of "picture" as we understand it is by no means "universal" even on Earth, and that human beings from cultures that don't use pictures have to be educated to the concept before they see photographs as Westerners do. How dangerous to assume that ETI could understand pictures, even if they were tremendously intelligent!

It may be an insoluble problem, especially in the unlikely case that those who find Voyager (whom I will refer to as "recipients") have no senses as we understand them. In choosing pictures, we were faced with two contradictory demands: the pictures should contain as much information as possible, and they should be as easy to understand as possible. It seemed to me that one solution would be to have on board *some* pictures with very little information, primarily to help the recipients understand how to see pictures. So the first two pictures in the sequence are of objects elsewhere on Voyager—two of the engravings on the record's cover. As engravings, they can be perceived by senses other than vision. We hope that beginning with these will give the recipients a way of comparing a photograph with an object they can touch.

It also occurred to me that silhouettes of photographs might be a kind of insurance. A silhouette maximizes the figure/background contrast and might show how we separate the various objects in a photograph by their outlines. It's a way of saying "This is what we want you to see in this picture." So in a number of places I drew silhouettes of photographs and inserted them in sequence.

In two cases, the pressure of events caused us to depart from a regular sequence of silhouette/photograph. Last-minute permission problems led to a change in the photograph of the fetus (originally there was a photograph of a fetus and embryo that matched the silhouette), and NASA decided not to include the photograph of two human nudes (who appear in silhouette in picture 32). We decided to keep this silhouette anyway because it showed that the fetus was inside the mother, and in the time that remained before the pictures were to be recorded (a few hours), we couldn't find another representation. The vetoed photograph is reproduced on page 74.

It also seemed a good idea to use recurrent images, such as the elephant in pictures 66 and 67 and the circles of people in pictures 36, 74, and 81. I've enumerated some of these "links" in the individual descriptions of pictures. It may be an interesting parlor game for people to find some of the others.

Here, in sequence, are the Voyager pictures:

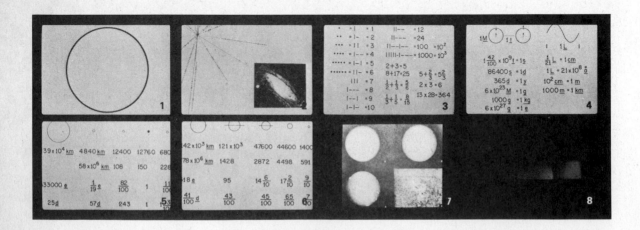

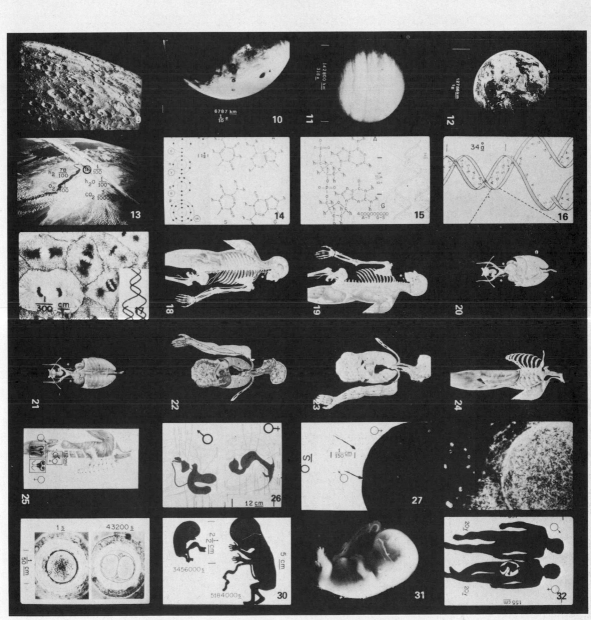

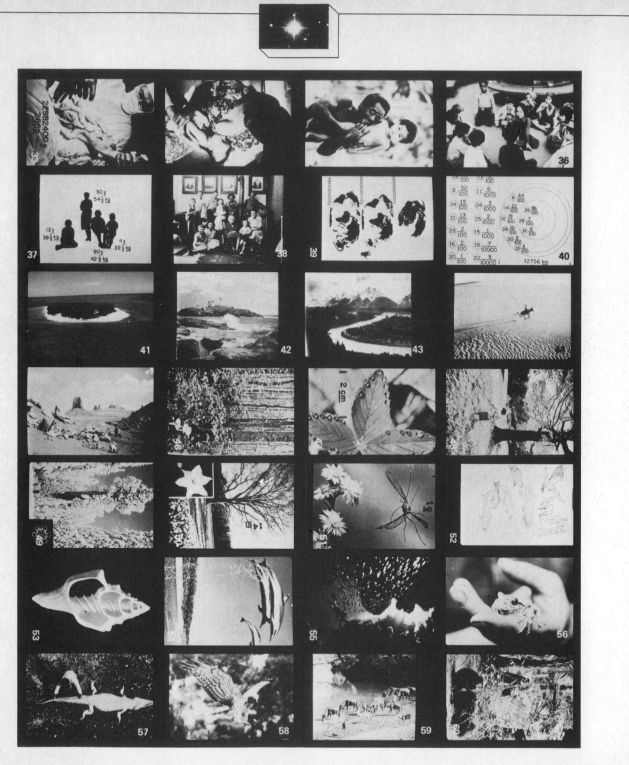

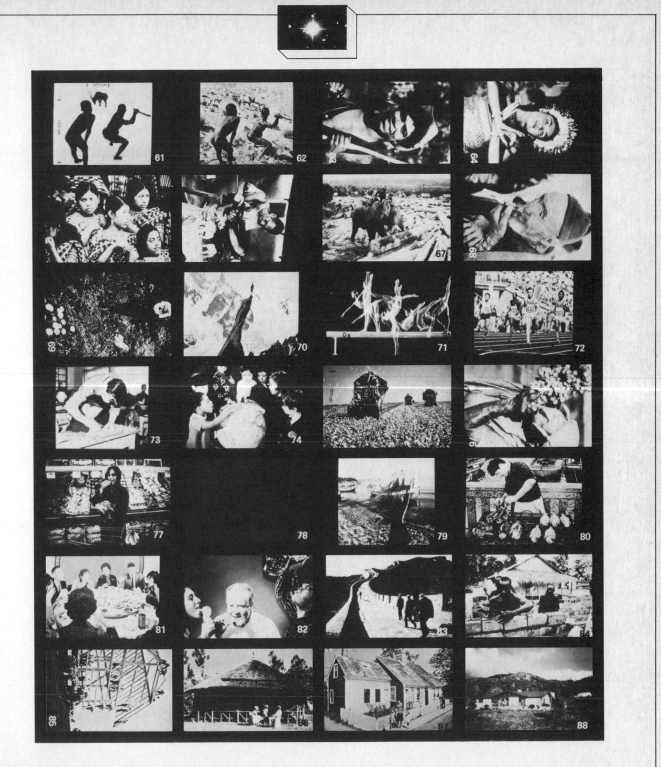

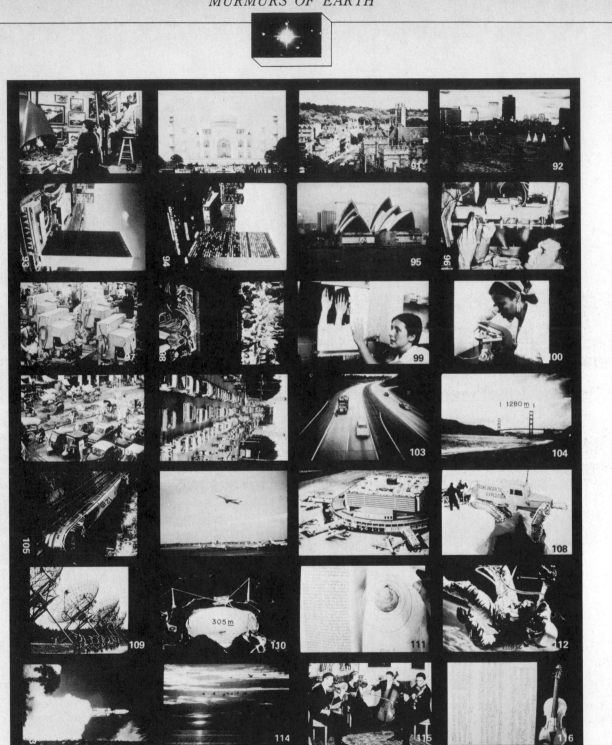

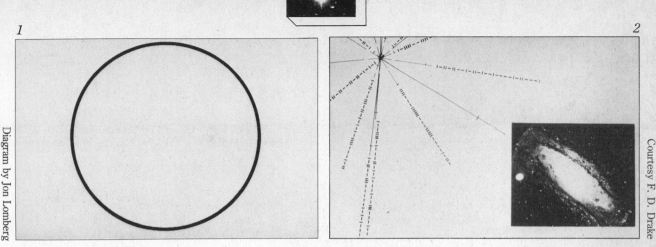

Diagram by Jon Lomberg

Courtesy F. D. Drake

1. Calibration Circle

Physicist Philip Morrison of M.I.T. suggested that the first picture be of some very simple geometrical form. Although we believe that the reconstruction of pictures from the audio signal should be simple for any civilization able to find Voyager in the first place, it seemed wise to begin with something easy. The diagram on the cover of the record, which shows how the audio signal is to be reconverted back into video, ends with a picture of a circle. Thus if recipients follow the instructions correctly, the first picture they reproduce will be the circle shown on the cover. This will tell them they are proceeding correctly. A circle also has the advantage of confirming the correct ratio of height to width in the picture raster.

2. Solar Location Map

In a way, this repeats the idea of the circle, since the solar location map, which shows the position of the sun relative to some astronomical "landmarks" called pulsars, also appears on the cover of the record. The original idea was to reproduce the whole map. But the resolution of the pictures on the record is equivalent only to the resolution of a television picture, and in that resolution the binary code, which gives the characteristic period of each pulsar, falls just below the resolution limit of the television picture. We wanted to make sure that the recipients recognize this picture as equivalent to the map on the cover, so the binary notation had to be clear. We therefore reproduced just a part of the map and added to it, as another reference point, a picture of M31, the Andromeda galaxy in its position relative to our sun at the time of the launch.

The Andromeda galaxy is our galaxy's nearest large neighbor in space, and the close-up view of the core and dust lanes should make it an obvious landmark. In fact, if the recipient race is very old or has good astronomical measurements of the internal motions of Andromeda or of the motion of its companion galaxy M32, or has access to the records of some other very old civilization, this image of Andromeda may help date the age in which Voyager was launched. Andromeda should appear about the same from any viewing position in our own galaxy, and millions of years from now the pattern of stars and dust will have changed slightly in Andromeda. Recipients may be able to look up (or even remember!) when it was that Andromeda looked the way it does in our photograph; in fact, it may be the only object in the whole package of pictures that both we and the recipients have seen firsthand.

This picture also provides a check to the "handedness" of all the pictures—that is, it will tell the recipients which is supposed to be the left-hand side and which the right-hand. Since it must match the map on the cover and the real appearance of Andromeda in the sky, this picture assures recipients that they haven't processed all the pictures backwards.

3. Dictionary—Mathematical Definitions

The cover of the record uses binary notation and units equal to the period of the 21-centimeter emission characteristic of neutral atomic hydrogen to tell recipients how fast to play the record, how to reconstruct the pictures, and which pulsars we are using as reference points. We wanted to superimpose measurement and notation on the pictures to indicate the sizes, weights, and so forth of various objects, but we felt that the "hydrogen binary" was too clumsy to use throughout. (For example, the length unit of the hydrogen emission is 21 centimeters; to express the diameter of the earth in units of 21 centimeters requires a very long binary number!) So our "dictionary" introduces a more convenient notation. The first picture shows groups of dots (one dot, two dots, three dots, and so forth) and their equivalent notation in both binary and Arabic numerals. We then show how our numbers are used in exponents, fractions, arithmetical operations, and so forth. So now if we want to say that something is 1½ units long, recipients will understand what we mean by 1½. In some cases, we give more than one example of a particular usage so there will be something to confirm their hypotheses.

4. Dictionary—Physical Unit Definitions

The second picture in our dictionary is a conversion table that defines common units in terms of the "hydrogen binary" units of length, time, and weight. The two drawings at the top of the picture represent the hydrogen atom (whose mass is 1 $\underline{M}$) undergoing a change of energy states that emits radiation at a frequency which is the reciprocal of 1 $\underline{t}$ with a wavelength of 1 $\underline{L}$. From these three units, we derive metric units of weight and distance (plus the angstrom as a distance unit in notating atomic and molecular diagrams); we invented a unit called $\underline{e}$ to measure one earth mass, and employed units of time (seconds and years). We had now defined a plethora of symbols, with more to come when we introduced symbols for elements, atomic number and nucleotide base pairs. We began to worry that things might be getting confusing, so to help matters a bit we distinguished all the units of measure by underlining them.

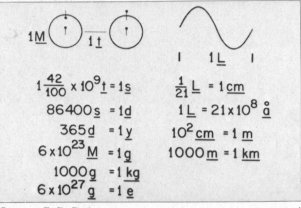

Courtesy F. D. Drake   3

Courtesy F. D. Drake   4

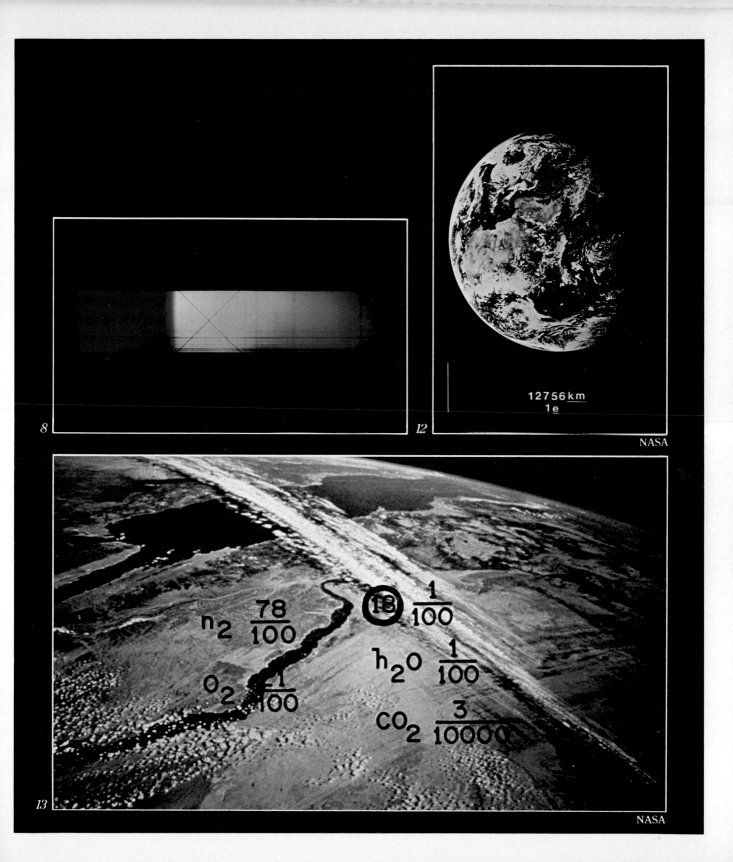

8

12

12756 km
1e

NASA

13

n_2 $\dfrac{78}{100}$

18 $\dfrac{1}{100}$

o_2 $\dfrac{1}{100}$

h_2o $\dfrac{1}{100}$

co_2 $\dfrac{3}{10000}$

NASA

23

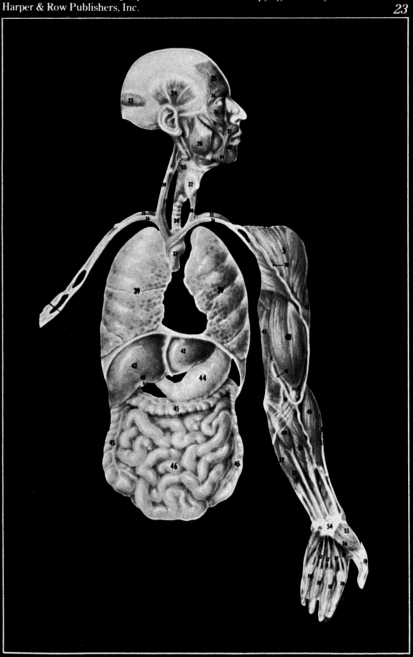

United Nations

34

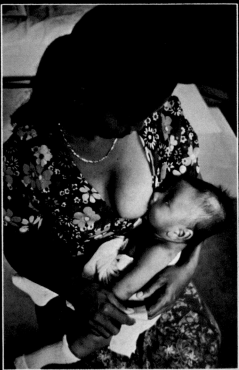

35

David Harvey from Woodfin Camp, Inc.

36

Photo by Ruby Mera, UNICEF

45

46

Jodi Cobb, © National Geographic Society

48

Photo by Josef Muench

Robert F. Sisson, © National Geographic Society

49
49a

Courtesy of The Henry Francis du Pont Winterthur Museum

50
50a

David Doubilet, © National Geographic Society

55

60

Vanne Goodall, © National Geographic Society

89

James L. Amos,© National Geographic Society

94   United Nations

97

Photograph by Fred Ward: *Factory Interior*

112

114

5 and 6. The Solar System

Frank Drake, who devised the dictionary, also did this diagram of the solar system, which shows our sun and planets along with the diameter, distance from the sun, mass, and period of rotation of each. The poor TV quality resolution of the pictures made it necessary to use two pictures for this. Coincidentally, since the first picture ends at Mars and the second begins at Jupiter, we also indicated the partitioning of the sun's family into an inner solar system (composed of small and rocky planets) and an outer solar system (composed of large and gassy planets). Note that the recently discovered rings of Uranus, omitted in the Pioneer 10 and 11 plaques, have been included.

7. The Sun

This Hale Observatory photograph shows four views of the sun taken through different kinds of filters, showing sunspots and the granular texture of the surface. Together with the next picture this should indicate the nature of our star to extraterrestrials.

5

139×10^4 km	4840 km	12400	12760	6800
	58×10^6 km	108	150	228
333000 e	$\frac{1}{19} e$	$\frac{82}{100}$	1	$\frac{11}{100}$
25d	57d	243	1	$1\frac{3}{100}$

Courtesy F. D. Drake

6

142×10^3 km	121×10^3	47600	44600	14000
778×10^6 km	1428	2872	4498	591
318 e	95	$14\frac{6}{10}$	$17\frac{2}{10}$	$\frac{9}{10}$
$\frac{41}{100} d$	$\frac{43}{100}$	$\frac{45}{100}$	$\frac{65}{100}$	$\frac{7}{10}$

Courtesy F. D. Drake

7

Photo: Hale Observatories

8

9

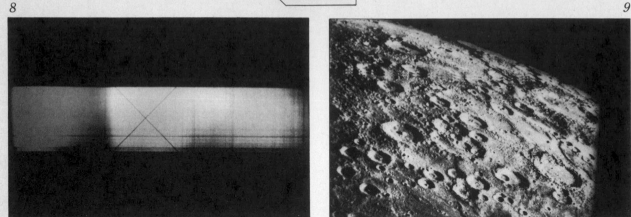

NASA

8. Solar Spectrum

Once extraterrestrials begin to reconstruct the pictures, they will notice a curious thing: most of the pictures are recorded in one burst of information, as shown on the cover. Yet about twenty of the pictures, beginning with this one, are recorded not once, but three times in a row. The only difference between the three is in the relative values of the grays. Recipients will wonder what this means. The answer is that these triple-imaged pictures are the ones we recorded in color; each shot represents a color separation (similar to that used in photo-offset color printing) indicating the amount of red, blue, or green in each picture. But how do we tell them that?

The solution we came up with relies on a fact of stellar astronomy that should be common knowledge to astronomers throughout the galaxy. The atmosphere of a star, any star, contains elements that absorb some of the light the star is emitting. When you look at the spectrum of a star, you see that the rainbow pattern is broken by an array of dark lines called absorption lines. These lines have been studied and mapped with precision by astronomers; they serve as a kind of fingerprint that tells a great deal about the star emitting the light. In particular, they tell the precise temperature of the stellar surface, and thus how much light the star emits at each wavelength. The "color" of the star is given exactly by these lines. Their displacement by the Doppler shift (called the red shift when the star is moving away from the sun) tells about the motion of the stars and galaxies emitting the light and provides much of the observational basis for studies of other galaxies and of the structure of the universe as a whole.

We think that the absorption lines in the picture of the solar spectrum, even when reproduced in black and white, should shout out "G 2 star! G 2 star!" loud and clear. So the recipients will know that our sun is a G 2 star—and they should also know exactly what the spectrum of this kind of star "really" looks like in color. Even if the recipients' eyes don't utilize exactly the same portion of the electromagnetic spectrum we call visible light, the absorption lines will tell them that *we* wish to indicate something about this portion of the spectrum. Their task is to combine the three-color separations of the solar spectrum into one picture that presents the spectrum as it really is—as they know from their own observations of common yellow stars like the sun. They have to work backward from information they already know to understand our concept of color separations. Then they'll be able to reconstruct the other color pictures correctly and see flowers, coral reefs, and skin tones in the colors of the original photographs.

Oddly enough, the Cornell Astronomy Department's books turned up no photograph of the sun's spectrum that was exactly what we wanted. So NAIC staff scientist Valentin Boriakoff and NAIC staff engineer Dan Mitler photographed the sun, using a simple prism and film typical of that used in many of the other color pictures.

10

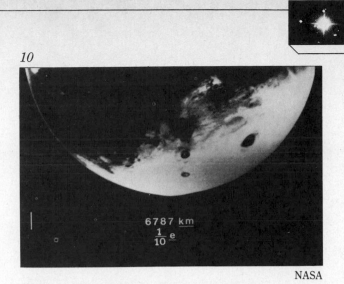

6787 km
$\frac{1}{10}$ e

NASA

11

142800 km
318 e

NASA

9, 10, and 11. *Mercury, Mars and Jupiter*

As we make our first tentative exploration of the solar system, we feel a sense of adventure exploring its distant worlds. Yet from an interstellar point of view, the solar system is a little family huddled around a little star, and if we wish to tell extraterrestrials that "this is home," Jupiter and Mars are as much a part of home as New York or New Delhi. At the suggestion of astronomer A. G. W. Cameron, we included a few pictures of the other planets: Mercury, as seen by Mariner 10; Mars, as Viking saw it when it was approaching and preparing to land; and Jupiter from our first close-up look furnished by Pioneer 11. Thus we restate the implied message of Voyager: we are spacefaring and wish to explore and contact—the universe around us.

The diameter and mass of Jupiter and Mars, shown on the pictures, provide a cross reference to the solar-system chart on pictures 5 and 6.

12. *Earth*

Photographed in color, this is a snapshot of home, the "meadow in the middle of the sky," in Sagan's words, from which these pictures were launched.

The pictures of planets should be objects that spacefaring races will recognize. Of course they won't have seen these planets, but in other solar systems they should have seen gas giants like Jupiter, cratered and airless wastes like Mercury, and perhaps even lovely blue water/oxygen worlds like Earth. Looking at objects that are at least somewhat familiar should help the recipients calibrate their system for reproducing pictures and understand our concept of a picture—how we represent reality on a two-dimensional surface. Certainly it will help them to see something familiar before moving on to those pictures of things that are totally unfamiliar to them.

12

12756 km
1 e

NASA

13. *Egypt, the Red Sea, the Sinai Peninsula and the Nile, with the Composition of Earth's Atmosphere*

Descending to the surface of the blue planet, another color photograph establishes the idea that *this* is the planet we live on. The cloud patterns and the views of land and water may provide clues to our meteorology. The relative abundance of gases in the atmosphere is shown, in symbols defined in the following pictures. The five most important biological atoms have been given letter symbols; all others are indicated by showing their atomic number in a circle. (So, for example, argon becomes ⑱.) Pictures 9 through 13 were selected by Sagan.

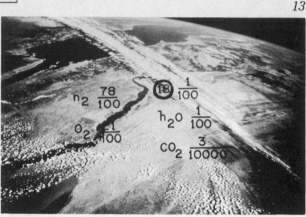

NASA

14, 15, and 16. *DNA Structure and Replication*

One of the crucial and unanswered questions of biology is whether the chemical make-up of life on Earth is the *only* way matter can form the structures we call living, or whether there are other ways. Is carbon chemistry the only viable one? Must replication of life involve helical molecules? What is necessary about our biology, and what merely an accident of our evolution? One of the reasons biologists are so eager to find life elsewhere—say, on Mars—is to try to answer these questions. We felt that some hint of the chemical nature of our biology would be of great interest to the scientists of the race that finds Voyager.

On Earth, all life uses the DNA molecule to store and replicate the information that tells an organism how to grow itself from scratch. So the structure of DNA seemed a good thing to show. However, it is possible that DNA *is* the only way, in which case we will be telling them something they already know. At the same time, we will reveal our ignorance: "The Earthlings don't know yet that *everybody* is made of DNA!"

Diagraming the DNA molecule proved difficult, since it is a complex molecule with many atoms and a twisting, helical structure, difficult to show clearly in a drawing. None of the ordinary diagrams or models—stick and ball or space filling—seemed clear enough, so with the help of Dr. Stuart Edelstein, a biochemist at Cornell, I devised a diagram.

The shaded portion on the left-hand side of picture 14 shows schematically the five atoms that compose DNA. The indicated size of the hydrogen atom (1 angstrom) should make it obvious that we are talking about atoms (nothing else is that small). Atoms are given letter symbols and symbols for their atomic number (the number inside a circle). Note that

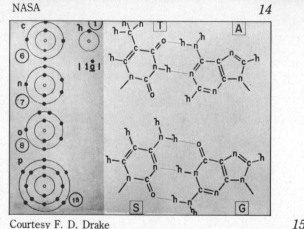

Courtesy F. D. Drake

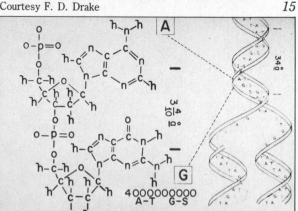

Diagram by Jon Lomberg

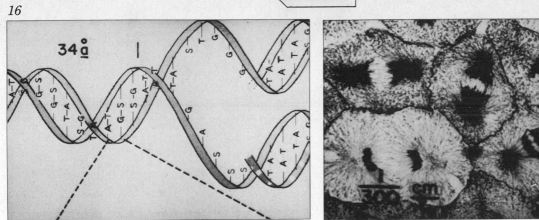

Diagram by Jon Lomberg   Turtox/Cambosco, Macmillan Science Co., Inc.

we had to put a little tail on the *h* of hydrogen, to eliminate the possibility of confusing it with the *n* of nitrogen.

The right-hand part of the picture shows the four bases that connect the two twisting spirals of the DNA backbone. The four bases are always found paired—thymine with adenine, and guanine with cytosine. These base pairs are the two letters of the genetic alphabet. The composition of the two possible pairs are shown. The bases are indicated by a letter in a square. Here we confronted a problem that cropped up all the time. We had to try to eliminate all possible sources of ambiguity, and it seemed ambiguous to use the same symbol for two different things: "cytosine" begins with a C, but we had already used a C to define carbon. I brought the problem up with Frank, and he shrugged and said, "Spell it with an S." "Cytosine with an S?" I said dubiously. "The biochemists will have a fit." "Do it anyway," Frank said. "It'll be a good object lesson in the special problems of communicating with extraterrestrials." "Cytosine with an S?" Edelstein complained. I'm not sure our explanation convinced him.

The left-hand portion of picture 15 shows the composition of the backbone of the DNA molecule with two of the bases attached, and the right-hand portion is a diagram of the whole molecule, showing how the backbone and base pairs form a helical structure capable of self-replication. On the bottom of the picture appears the legend "4000000000 A–T G–S," indicating that a molecule of DNA uses a large number of base pairs to code the information necessary to construct a living being (the number shown is the number of base pairs in a DNA strand from a human being).

In our working room at Cornell we had a small television camera and screen so we could look at the pictures in the resolution at which they would be recorded. The letters indicating the base pairs in the helix of picture 15 were close to the resolution limit, so for insurance we repeated a close-up of this portion of the diagram in picture 16.

17. Cell Division

This superb photograph shows DNA replication in action. The scale "1/300 cm." indicates that we are showing something that is much larger than the molecules of the previous photographs but is still quite small. As a clue we show the same shape that appears in picture 16—the DNA double helix unwinding and replicating. The cells shown, from the blastula of a frog, exhibit several of the phases of cell division.

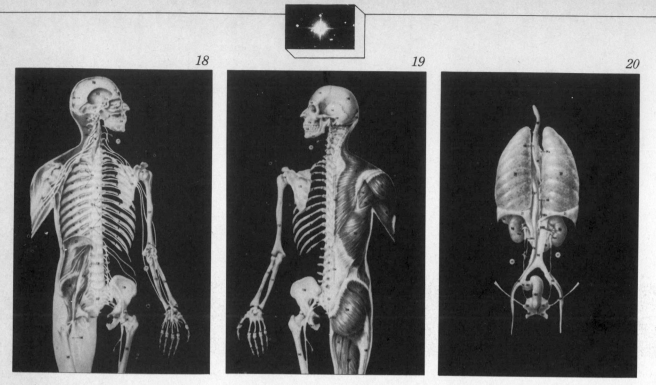

18 through 25. Human Anatomy

Frank Drake thought that the transparent overlays of human anatomy found in encyclopedias would be ideal for showing structural (if not functional) human anatomy, and he obtained a set of the acetate overlays used in *The World Book Encyclopedia*. These eight pictures show superficial and deep human anatomy, including skeletal structure, the nervous system, the circulatory system, and so forth. Picture 23 was recorded in color to emphasize the difference between veins (blue) and arteries (red). Unfortunately, the figure in the overlays is neuter—where its sex organs should be is a gaping void. Both to emphasize our sexuality (a nontrivial aspect of human anatomy) and to link the anatomy diagrams with the pictures to come, we added to picture 25 a rough sketch showing that in the area of the groin there existed either of two sets of organs—and introduced the male and female symbols to distinguish them. We used these symbols again in pictures 26, 28, and 32.

We'd noticed that the overlays were covered with hundreds of tiny black numbers, to relate the parts of the body to a list of names that appeared, in the encyclopedia, alongside the overlays. The *World Book* staff couldn't provide us with a set that didn't include these little numbers, so Linda Sagan, who is a painter, painted out all the numbers on the acetate, skillfully matching the colors. Many tedious hours later, she had finished. But after the paint had dried, it flaked off the acetate. All Linda's work was wasted, and there was no time to redo it. It is anybody's guess what extraterrestrials will make of the myriad of black spots covering our ribs, spleen, and biceps. (Photographs © 1978 World Book–Childcraft International, Inc. Used with permission of the publisher. The artwork was adapted for the exclusive use of *The World Book Encyclopedia* from *The Human,* copyright 1955 by Harper & Row Publishers, Inc.)

26. Diagram of Human Sex Organs

The symbols for male and female should link this picture with pictures 25 and 32. This picture and the seven that follow form a sequence describing human reproduction. Not only did this sequence have to be clear, it also had to be cleared by a NASA approval board. It isn't difficult to understand the reluctance of a government agency, which has to get its funds from Congress every year, to swim in the murky waters of human sexuality. That NASA approved this portion at all was something of a wonder, but they did veto the picture we submitted (shown in this article, but not on the Voyager record), of a man and a pregnant woman quite unerotically holding hands. A silhouette of this photograph, showing the position of the fetus, appears in picture 32. (From *Life: Cells, Organisms, Populations,* by E. O. Wilson et al. Copyright © by Sinauer Associates, Inc. Drawing by Sarah Landry.)

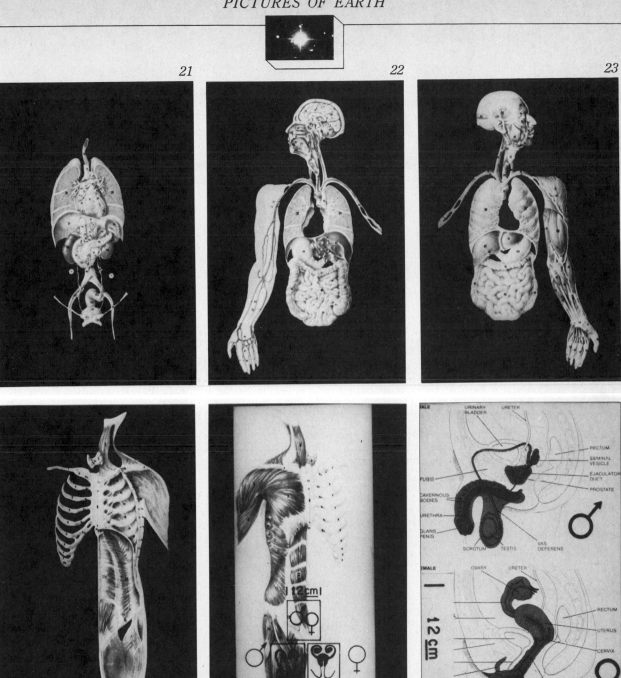

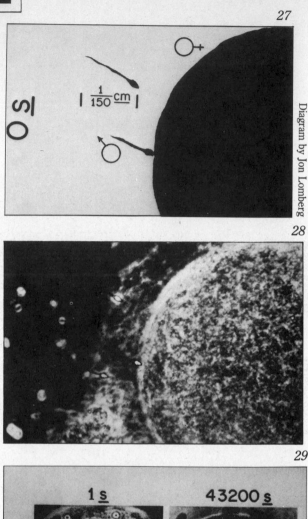

27

28

29

Diagram by Jon Lomberg

27 and 28. *Conception with Silhouette*

The Swedish physician/photographer Lennart Nilsson is renowned for his beautiful photographs of all stages of human prenatal development. We included a photograph of human conception taken by him, but we took a small liberty with it. To show the time it took to grow a human being in the womb, we wanted to start at the beginning, or "0 seconds." Nilsson's photograph, certainly the finest we could find, was of a sperm a fraction of a second before it reached the egg. It seemed vital to make clear that the moment of conception was the moment the sperm actually reached the egg. I decided to draw in a sperm just touching the egg so we could more accurately label this picture "0 seconds."

This is the first time we used a silhouette before the photograph, and on it we indicated, besides "0 seconds," the size of the sperm and the fact that the sperm was male and the egg female. (Photographs of conception and fertilized ovum from original edition of *A Child Is Born* by Lennart Nilsson. Copyright © 1965 by Albert Bonniers Förlag, Stockholm. English translation copyright © 1966 by Dell Publishing Company, Inc. Photographs by Lennart Nilsson for the book *Ett Barn Blir Till* by Albert Bonniers Förlag AB, Stockholm, 1976. Used by permission of Delacorte Press/Seymour Lawrence.)

29. *Fertilized Ovum*

These two photographs, also by Lennart Nilsson, show the fertilized egg at two stages. The left-hand picture, "1 second," shows the thickening of the membrane around the egg immediately after conception. The right-hand picture shows the time until the first cell division, about "43,200 seconds." The cell membranes have been enhanced to make the cell division more obvious. (Photographs of conception and fertilized ovum from original edition of *A Child Is Born* by Lennart Nilsson. Copyright © 1965 by Albert Bonniers Förlag, Stockholm. English translation copyright © 1966 by Dell Publishing Company, Inc. Photographs by Lennart Nilsson for the book *Ett Barn Blir Till* by Albert Bonniers Förlag AB, Stockholm, 1976. Used by permission of Delacorte Press/Seymour Lawrence.)

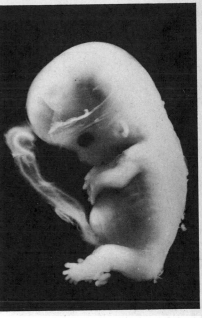

Photo by James Kendrick—George Washington University Collection

30 and 31. *Fetus and Silhouette*

The photograph, by Dr. Frank Allan of George Washington University, shows a fetus after about sixty days of development. The silhouette shows an embryo after about forty days and a silhouette of a fetus the same age as the fetus in the photograph. In the silhouette, the time from conception is given, and also the size of the developing child. Originally we planned to use a photograph of an embryo and a fetus that matched the silhouette exactly, but last-minute permissions problems forced us to substitute a different picture of a fetus.

32. *Silhouette of Male and Female*

This is the fetus of the previous picture shown in its position inside the mother. The male and female symbols distinguish the mother from the father, and the typical sizes of human beings are shown. At this point, the recipients should begin to have a good idea of the body shape of human beings.

30

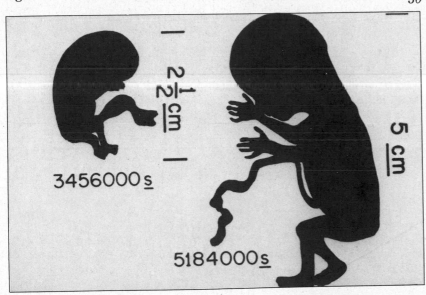

Diagram by Jon Lomberg

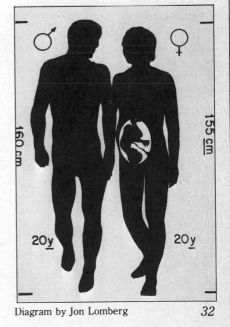

Diagram by Jon Lomberg 32

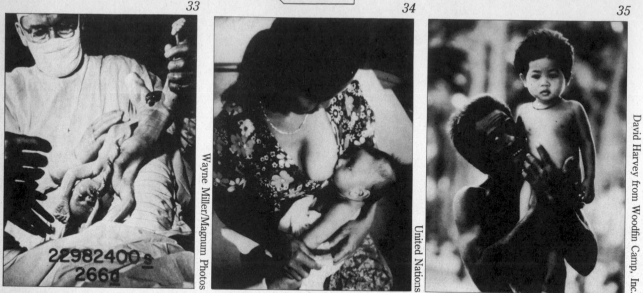

33. *Birth*

This photograph is from the famous collection *The Family of Man*. We had hoped to find a photograph that showed a child actually emerging from its mother, but in all such photographs we looked at, the mother was so hidden by sheets that it wasn't clear that it was a woman (or even a person) that was giving birth. We called Wayne Miller, who took this picture, to get permission for its use. He was out of town, so we spoke to his son, who sounded as if he were in his twenties. When we explained the nature of the project, he gasped and said, "You want to send that picture into space forever? *That* birth picture? That's *me* being born! Of course you can use it! I guarantee my father's permission!" Interestingly enough, it turned out that the physician delivering the younger Miller was the boy's grandfather—and the photographer's father.

Up to now the picture sequence has consisted largely of scientific information, mostly diagrammatic, to introduce ourselves. From this point on, most of the pictures are photographs, and while the major criterion for selection was still the information conveyed, the information is often cultural and many different kinds of information may appear in the same photograph. For example, the two pictures that follow the birth picture each show a parent and a child. We wanted to convey some sense of the parent/child relationship. We also wanted to show close-up views of the human face and hands.

34. *Nursing Mother*

This color photograph shows a woman from the Philippines nursing her child. A secondary kind of information is present in the design of the woman's dress, showing perhaps that we enjoy making printed fabric and adorning ourselves with it. It is even possible that the recipients may make some association between the flowers on the dress and flowers appearing elsewhere in other pictures.

35. *Father and Child*

To humans, this picture, also sent in color, embodies the pride of parenthood. For us selecting it, it was a source of pleasure for additional reasons. You can see *everything*—the man's ears (amazing how many pictures do not show ears) and teeth (ditto teeth); the child's toes. The man's eyes are directed toward the child (a girl, by the way), while the child looks at the camera—a clue that, along with other pictures, might suggest that eyes are organs of vision. Their possible motion is clearly shown here. The muscles in the man's arm are well-defined. The skin tones show perfectly. And it is a beautiful, well-composed picture to boot.

36. Group of Children

Early on, when the picture package was going to consist of a half-dozen photographs, someone suggested showing a group of humans of various races and cultures doing something together. The idea resulted finally in this color photograph and numbers 72 and 74. Ruby Mera, a photographer working for UNICEF, took the picture at the UN International School, a school for the children of delegates in New York City. As well as including a spectrum of racial types and nations, the picture shows human beings sitting in a circle, that almost archetypal arrangement for a group of people. It illustrates various forms of sitting and kneeling, as well as various positionings of the hands and arms. Seeing human bodies rotated through 360 degrees should give the recipients a good sense of the volume of the human form in space.

Photo by Ruby Mera, UNICEF

37 and 38. Family Portrait and Silhouette

This photograph of a Midwestern American family is also from *The Family of Man* collection. Five generations of the family are present, with a sixth generation in the portraits on the walls (in fact, one of the men in the paintings is the father of the old woman). The silhouette gives the estimated weight and age of some members of the group, with the implication that the oldest member of the group is approximately the age of the oldest human being. We hope that recipients will reason that we would want to show how long people live, and if there was a person a thousand years old, we would show that.

While I was in New York to get permission to use this picture from Time/Life, Nina Leen, the photographer, happened to be in the office. I told her we wanted to send her photograph to the stars, perhaps to be viewed by the beings of another world. She was willing and seemed pleased but somehow unimpressed. "You see," she told me, "I've been in contact with Them for years anyway—but I know They're glad you're doing this."

Pictures 32 through 38 introduce human beings. Before presenting any more information about our culture, we give a more detailed picture of our planet—its landscapes, oceans, and biology.

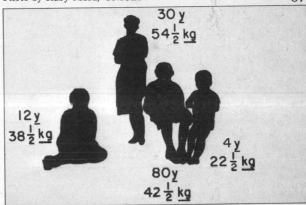

Diagram by Jon Lomberg

Nina Leen, *Life* Magazine, copyright 1947 Time, Inc.

39. *Diagram of Continental Drift*

The upwelling and obliteration of large chunks of Earth's surface by the process called plate tectonics is a relatively recent geological discovery. Its implications for meteorology, geology, and the evolution of life are not well understood, but it seems to have been an important factor in the history of our planet—and perhaps in the histories of other planets in the galaxy as well. It certainly reveals something about the structure of the Earth. This diagram shows Pangaea, the primordial continent, as it existed three billion years ago; the continents now; and the continents as they will appear ten million years from now. The time scale dates from the formation of the Earth, so the present time is four and a half billion years since the Earth was formed, and this gives a strong clue to what the phenomena are that we are talking about; if we are talking about billions of years, we must be talking about something either astronomical or geological, and pictures 12 and 74 also show the continents of Earth. The human hand marks the era of man. It says, "This is the era when the hand that launched the spacecraft existed." The basic diagram comes from Sagan's design of the LAGEOS plaque.

40. *Structure of the Earth*

This diagram was prepared with the help of Dr. Steven Soter of Cornell University. Earth is shown schematically, though it is identifiable by the diameter and earth mass that appear beneath it, and echoes slides 5 and 12. The fourteen most abundant elements are shown, using their atomic numbers to identify them in their proportions in the planet as a whole. Inside the schematic of Earth is shown the composition, by relative atomic abundance, of the interior regions of the planet, called the core and the mantle.

Pictures 41 through 45 show some typical landscapes.

41. *Heron Island*

An island along the Great Barrier Reef in Australia. Coral formations can be seen in the water. We start with scenes of the ocean to suggest that water dominates the surface of Earth.

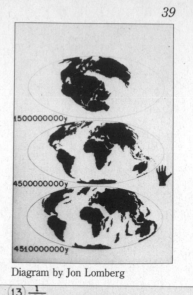

39

Diagram by Jon Lomberg

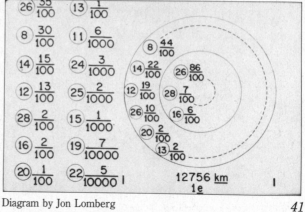

40

Diagram by Jon Lomberg

41

Courtesy Jay M. Pasachoff, Williams College, Williamstown, Mass.

42

43

Dick Smith

44

42. Seashore

Cape Nedick in Maine. Waves crashing on a rocky shore. A sky full of puffy clouds. This shows that there is solid rock and that there are winds.

43. Snake River and the Grand Tetons

Ansel Adams's breathtaking photograph showing mountains, a river, and forests gives evidence of tectonic activity in our continent. (Photograph by Ansel Adams: *The Tetons and the Snake River, Grand Teton National Park, Wyoming, 1942*)

44. Sand Dunes

This contains a lot of information about aeolian processes and dust-transport mechanisms in arid regions. A rider and his dog leave their tracks in the sand. We were afraid that the rider might be mistaken for a centaur. Later pictures make it clear that we have animals like horses and that we ride them.

George F. Mobley, © National Geographic Society

45

45. Monument Valley

Some of the rugged geology of the American Southwest shown in color. The eroded volcanic plugs should be of interest, as should the humans with their flocks of sheep.

Ray Manley, Shostal Associates

46

47

48

Bruce Dale, © National Geographic Society

2 cm

J. Arthur Herrick

Jodi Cobb, © National Geographic Society

Pictures 46 through 50 show vegetation in various seasons.

46. *Forest Scene with Mushrooms*

Tree trunks, a secondary growth of bushes and shrubs, and mushrooms, in color. This gives a sense of the ambience of a forest. It could well be that trees are rare in the universe. If you had never seen a planet and were designing one, you might never imagine something like a tree.

47. *Leaf*

A close-up of a strawberry leaf with the size indicated. The droplets of water beading the edge of the leaf are not dew but water actually oozing out of the leaf by transpiration. Recipients might recognize this object as a biological food factory.

48. *Fallen Leaves*

The growth on the trees has fallen off, and a human being seems to be collecting or raking it. This photograph was sent in color, and the fact that the fallen leaves have changed from the green color seen in the leaves of other trees might indicate to the recipients this tree's deciduous nature, and perhaps even something about the existence of several different photosynthetic pigments.

49

50

Photo by Josef Muench

Robert F. Sisson, © National Geographic Society

Courtesy of The Henry Francis du Pont Winterthur Museum

14 m

49a   50a

49 and 49a. Sequoia and Snowflake

Sometimes it was possible to make a photocomposite—essentially getting two pictures in one frame—where the connection between the different pictures seemed obvious. Here is an example in color. The huge sequoia trees are covered with snow, and we have inserted a picture of a snowflake at the bottom right. Like the appearance of planets from space, the hexagonal crystalline structure of water should be familiar to extraterrestrials. Water is a common substance throughout the galaxy, and its crystal form should be known and recognized. One might even speculate that snowflakes—all the same and yet all different—are regarded as objects of beauty by beings treading the snowy worlds of other stars. The insert not only identifies the white substance covering the tree but also emphasizes again the presence of water on Earth. The small human figures give an indication of the size of the trees. The picture also shows that things live naturally where temperatures fall below freezing on Earth.

50 and 50a. Tree and Daffodils

This picture shows the branchy pattern of a tree in color. The insert is a close-up of the flowers surrounding the tree; we hoped that the similarity in color between the insert and the flowers in the larger picture would help recipients connect the two—and also show them the relative size of trees and flowers. In picture 49, the size of a tree is shown relative to a human being. Here the size is shown in absolute units (14 m). Considering that our ancestors lived in trees, our emphasis on them does not seem inappropriate.

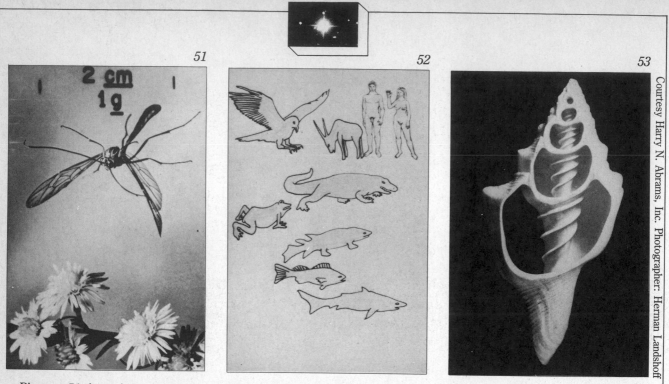

Courtesy Harry N. Abrams, Inc. Photographer: Herman Landshoff

Pictures 51 through 60 show other representatives of the Earth's biosphere, from various phyla.

51. *Flying Insect*

The flowers here are similar to the flowers in picture 69, again providing both an absolute and a relative indication of the size of the objects depicted. Even if the notation is obscure to recipients, it should be evident that humans are much larger than, and insects nearer the same size as, daisies. The wings of the insect are particularly well shown. The insect is a yellow ophion ichneumon wasp, whose life style strikes me as particularly unpleasant. Its larvae inhabit the bodies of other insects, burrowing through and devouring the flesh of their unwilling hosts until they grow big enough to gnaw their way to the surface. Other insects, like bees, have lives more in keeping with our moral and social sense, but this creature is an inhabitant of Earth too, and who were we to pass judgment on its way of life?
(Copyright © 1975 by Stephen Dalton; *Borne on the Wind* published by Reader's Digest Press, New York)

52. *Diagram of Vertebrate Evolution*

This sketch shows a very rough evolutionary sequence, to try to give some idea that animals on Earth have evolved together into the present various species, and that there was a movement from the sea to the land. With the exception of the shark (which is similar to the dolphin of picture 54) and the fish with feet, all the animals shown also appear in other pictures. The bird and the deer are outlined as they appear in pictures 58 and 62. The two humans may look familiar—they are the same pair that appeared on Sagan and Drake's Pioneer 10 and 11 plaques, drawn by Linda Sagan. There was criticism of that plaque from some quarters, because the man was shown raising his hand in greeting while the woman stood in a pose that struck a number of viewers as unduly passive. In the interests of fairness, we show the couple again, and this time it is the woman whose arm is raised in cosmic greeting. *Pace,* feminists.* (Diagram by Jon Lomberg. Adapted from *Life: Cells, Organisms, Populations,* by E. O. Wilson et al. Sinauer Associates, Inc., Fig. 18, p. 367)

---

*A more detailed discussion of the design of the Pioneer plaque and the reaction it aroused can be found in *The Cosmic Connection* by Carl Sagan.

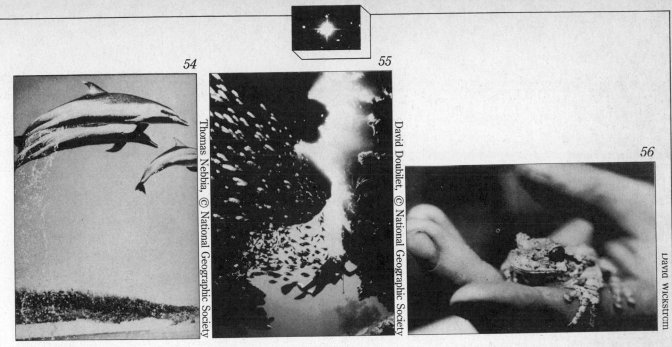

54

55

56

Thomas Nebbia, © National Geographic Society

David Doubilet, © National Geographic Society

David Wickstrom

53. *Seashell*

Seashells have been a favorite subject of mine for painting, and the perfection of their form has reminded me of the forms of much larger objects, such as galaxies. I also have a gut conce as indefensible as any other intuition—that the order of their form gives them a beauty other intelligences may appreciate, if they have an aesthetic sense at all. (This is the same logic that led us to suspect that snowflakes and Bach might appeal to the senses and brains of another race.) This Xancidae, from the collection *The Shell: Five Hundred Million Years of Inspired Design,* has long been a favorite of mine.

Frank Drake and Carl Sagan both felt this might be one of the more confusing pictures in the package, since it isn't clear that the shell is a product of a living creature. It could equally well be a sculpture, a machine tool, a propeller or an architect's model. Its placement among other living things may help resolve the confusion.

54. *Dolphins*

Whales and dolphins are, along with great apes and human beings, the most intelligent animals on the planet. Whale songs are included among the greetings on the record, so it seemed courteous to show dolphins in the pictures. The dripping water and the hydrodynamic streamlining (similar to the shark in picture 52) should be strong clues that this is an aquatic creature—and an energetic and exuberant one.

55. *School of Fish*

Sagan, Drake and I are all enthusiastic scuba divers, and we wanted some good underwater shots. But as we were looking through pictures of reefs and fish, we realized there was no way one could tell for certain that the scene was underwater. The most unambiguous way of showing an underwater scene was to have a diver present, since the air bubbles rising from the regulator should furnish clear evidence of the aqueous medium. In addition, the presence of the diver would show that human beings were interested in exploring and adapting to various environments. It is no accident that many space buffs (including science-fiction writers and astronauts) are scuba divers. The weightlessness, the life-support system, and the complex and gorgeous world of the reef seem a preview of interstellar exploration. It's as close as most of us can ever get. This color photograph was taken in the reefs of the Red Sea off Na'ama Bay in Sinai.

56. *Tree Toad*

This little fellow was found and photographed in a backyard in Enfield, near Ithaca, New York. The picture also provides a close-up of a human hand, including a dirty fingernail.

57. *Crocodile*

In many of the pictures showing animals, a human being is present observing, photographing, or measuring the animal (see picture 60, for example). We hope this will indicate something of our curiosity about the natural world. This picture also shows a ventral view of a vertebrate.

58. *Eagle*

This picture, along with picture 114, should give some sense of the winged creatures of Earth, and how they fly. The eagle here is frozen in flight, with the structure of the wings very clear. (From the book *Donana: Spain's Wildlife Wilderness.* Copyright © 1974 by Juan Antonio Fernandez. Reprinted by permission of Editorial Olivo, Spain, Taplinger Pub. Co., New York)

59. *Waterhole*

One of the earliest ideas Frank Drake had was to show animals around a waterhole, which would include a number of different species in the same photograph. The waterhole is also an in joke for devotees of interstellar communications. The likeliest means by which widely separated races in the galaxy will contact one another is by radio communication, and there has been much discussion as to the best frequency at which to search the skies for messages from the stars. One band of frequencies in the microwave region, a region of relatively low noise on the radio spectrum which is bounded by the emission of hydrogen on one side and the hydroxyl radical (OH) on the other, has been dubbed "the waterhole" because hydrogen and OH are products of the breakdown of water. Since water may be a crucial component of life throughout the galaxy, some poetic astronomers have suggested that this region might be the best place to search for messages. Just as human beings and animals historically meet at the waterhole, so might the water-based life of different planets meet at the radio waterhole.

57

Photographer: Peter Beard

58

59

Courtesy of South African Tourist Corporation

60   Vanne Goodall, © National Geographic Society

60. *Scientists and Chimpanzees*

This color picture shows our near relatives being observed by two scientists, one of them the famous Jane Goodall. From the point of view of an extraterrestrial, chimps and human beings may be nearly identical—it seems likely that pictures of chimps dressed in cowboy suits would pass unnoticed by extraterrestrials. More human beings, they'd probably think. The fact that the human beings in this picture are studying the chimps may be a weak clue that the latter aren't members of the race that made Voyager. On the other hand, it might appear that the chimps are the masters because the human beings are toting the gear. But we couldn't leave out the primates. Also, the background shows a kind of vegetation not seen elsewhere: jungle growth. This photograph was taken by Jane Goodall's mother, Vanne Morris-Goodall. When we wrote her that we wanted to use the picture, she replied: "I am completely overawed by the knowledge that I once pressed the button for a photograph which is now on its way to outer space, and still more so because my daughter, Jane, has merited the unique honor of representing an area of study on the planet Earth."

61 and 62. *Bushmen Hunters and Silhouette*

Another photograph from *The Family of Man* collection, showing a typical human/animal relationship: the human being is about to kill the animal. Hunting is a primal human activity, but this picture illustrates teaching as well: the boy is observing his father. The silhouette restresses the human form and separates the deer from the background. We estimated that the boy and the deer were about the same size. In perspective, the deer looks much smaller. Perspective conventions may be one of the most difficult concepts for an extraterrestrial to grasp (human beings from cultures where perspective isn't used have to learn how to see it). Since the boy and the deer are marked in the silhouette as being the same size, we hope we have provided a clue that will help recipients see this picture as we do—and apply this knowledge to all the other photographs as well.

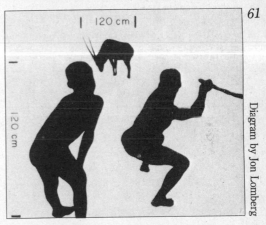

61   120 cm   120 cm

Diagram by Jon Lomberg

62   N. R. Farbman, *Life* Magazine, copyright 1946 Time, Inc.

All the remaining pictures in the package concern human beings and our culture and artifacts.

63. Man from Guatemala

This picture was chosen for its close-up view of hands and face. The opposition of the thumb is shown and also a machete, one form of a basic and important human tool—the knife.

64. Dancer from Bali

This picture provides a clear presentation of human facial features and hands, and some suggestion of the complexities of dress and ornamentation found in most human cultures.

65. Andean Girls

Here are more hands and faces from a different human gene pool and culture, and more examples of human dress. The Peruvian music included on the record was made by such people.

63

United Nations

64

Donna Grosvenor, © National Geographic Society

65

Joseph Scherschel, © National Geographic Society

66

67

68

66 and 67. *Thai Craftsman and Elephant*

The craftsman demonstrates some of the varied uses of the human hand and hand tools. The following picture shows the animal that is being carved (and also demonstrates how we have domesticated animals and put them to work). We hope recipients will recognize the similarity between the carving and the animal and thus get a sense of our concept of symbolic reproduction of real forms.

68. *Old Man from Turkey*

This close-up of hands and face furnishes some additional information, such as the existence of facial hair. The hat is clearly an object on the head, and this may make the less obvious head gear (as in pictures 63 and 64) more understandable. The spectacles are also obviously artificial, and a clever recipient might eventually guess that there were lenses in the frames, especially if evidence from other pictures had suggested that eyes were organs of vision. When I spoke to the photographer, he made some obscure remarks about the substance the old man was smoking.

69. *Old Man in a Field*

This is one of three pictures (the other two are 44 and 61) that show dogs accompanying human beings. We hope the recipients will guess that dogs are our friends.

70. *Mountain Climber*

This picture shows the French climber Gaston Rébuffat atop a spire of rock in the Alps. If the recipients recognize the silhouetted human figure, they may guess that it was both difficult and seemingly pointless to scale this rock needle. The only point would be the accomplishment of doing it. If this message is communicated, it will tell extraterrestrials something very important about us. *(Escalade par Gaston Rébuffat, guide de Chamonix, du Grand Gendarme du Pic de Roc, Massif du mont Blanc [cliche Gaston Rébuffat]).*

71. *Gymnast Cathy Rigby*

Sports Illustrated provided this stroboscopic picture, taken by Phillip Leonian, of Cathy Rigby on the balance beam. If this had been the only picture of a human being we sent, what a strange image of us recipients might have! But it should be clear that this is one person in movement, and it probably gives a better sense of how we move than anything else could have. The picture shows that we stand on one foot, on two feet or (some of us) on our hands, and that we can roll over backwards. On the balance beam, we superimposed the approximate time it would take to execute this part of a routine. This seat-of-the-pants estimate may not be highly accurate (maybe it took her ten or fifteen seconds), but the important point is that we move in seconds as opposed to microseconds or years.

69

Bruce Baumann, © National Geographic Society

70

© 1971 Phillip Leonian
Photographed for *Sports Illustrated*

71

72

72. *Olympic Sprinters*

Like picture 36, this selection grew out of the desire for a picture that showed representatives of various races of human beings, and it occurred to us that the Olympics were a good place to look for such a scene. Here a white man (the Russian champion Valery Borzov), two black men and an Oriental sprint toward the finish line. The musculature of the leg, which did not appear in the anatomy pictures 18–25, is shown, as are various positions in the act of running. Careful study may also reveal the presence of other people standing around, perhaps giving a clue that we are not just runners but also spectators in our sports events, and that there is competition.

Recipients will have learned Arabic numbers from our dictionary. They may be confused by the numbers on the chests of the runners, perhaps thinking they have been put on the picture for their benefit (to measure something, as in the Cathy Rigby picture). Or perhaps the wrinkles in the numbers will indicate that they are really on clothing and that they were put there not for the extraterrestrials but for the human audience.

Picturepoint London

73

73. *Japanese Schoolroom*

This shows the important human activity of learning how to write; it also shows that we still educate children en masse rather than by private tutors or teaching machines—at least so far.

74. *Children with Globe*

Like picture 36, this was taken at the UN International School in New York City. Again, the children are shown in a circle, their eyes directed to the hands on the globe. The portion of the globe shown—Africa and the Mideast—is the same portion shown on picture 12 of Earth from space. If recipients make the connection and realize that the children are looking at a globe of their home planet, they may notice that the land on the globe is broken up by a complex pattern of lines. Perhaps they will deduce that these represent some sort of political or territorial boundaries, boundaries that are concepts, not real markings on the planet.

United Nations

74

United Nations

75. Cotton Harvest

We felt we had to have a picture of mechanized agriculture, and these cotton pickers were chosen because the white cotton shows up the swath of the harvester clearly. In fact the cotton can be seen, tossed into the air above the machine. There is enough similarity in appearance between the field of cotton and the field of daffodils (picture 50) to make it obvious that something growing is being picked. The following pictures show how we obtain and eat our food, and this picture serves as an introduction, even though cotton is not normally thought of as a food (unless you are Milo Minderbinder in *Catch-22*).

76. Man with Grapes

Originally selected as a close-up of hands and a face, this plainly shows a human being stuffing his mouth. Functional anatomists may note that three very different functions of the hand are also shown. The things he is eating look as if they may be of natural origin, suggesting that we don't yet produce food in factories. (Photograph by David Moore: *Grape Picker*)

77. Supermarket

Here is another person eating grapes, but this time in a location that adds more information—namely, that we don't all get grapes from the fields; some of us buy them in markets. There are a variety of other foodstuffs in bins in the background, some marked numerically with prices. A recipient society with an economy that involves money, buying, and selling might even deduce that these are in fact prices. Frank Drake had decided that we had to have a picture of a market or food store, and it was easier to take our own picture than to spend days looking for one. Five of us, including Herman Eckelmann, the NAIC staff photographer, trooped off to the local supermarket. With Frank in the lead, we began loading up carts with foods. Eckelmann ran around taking photographs. The other shoppers soon gave us a wide berth. Predictably, the manager came over and politely asked what the hell we were doing. Frank did the talking, and while the rest of us tried to look appropriately serious, one of the world's great astronomers explained to a suspicious store manager that we wanted to send his supermarket to the stars. We put most of the food back on the shelves (causing more bewilderment), paid for the grapes, and left.

75

Howell Walker, © National Geographic Society

76

77

Photo: Herman Eckelmann, NAIC staff photographer

United Nations

78. Diver and Fish

[Unfortunately we were unable to reach a satisfactory arrangement with the photographer to include this picture in this book. It was chosen to add more information on the undersea environment.]

79. Fishing Boats

It may be deduced that the nets these Greek fishermen are pulling in are for catching the fish, since the next picture shows fish being cooked. The boat is primitive in relation to the technology in some other pictures, showing various stages in our technological development.

80. Cooking Fish

The fish are being broiled on an open grill in Portugal. On one side of the grill the fish are raw and wet (looking very much like the fish in picture 78). They become progressively more cooked (and carbonized) along the grill. The message is that we catch animals and then cook them. (From *The Cooking of Spain and Portugal*, a title in the Foods of the World series. Photograph by Brian Seed. Courtesy Time-Life Books, Inc.)

81. Chinese Dinner Party

We wanted to show a group of people eating together. The fact that this party is sitting in a circle around a table echoes the circles of pictures 36 and 74. Several of the people are holding utensils; some are dipping into their bowls, and some are raising their spoons to their mouths. Plates of food and a bottle of liquid appear on the table. This is also one of the few pictures that show people in typical modern dress. Westerners may find the man's gesture puzzling. He is playing a table game common in the Orient, in which players have to guess how many fingers a person will hold out. The women are evidently amused. (From *Chinese Cooking*, a title in the Foods of the World series. Photograph by Michael Rougier. Courtesy of Time-Life Books, Inc.)

82

82. *Demonstration of Eating, Licking and Drinking*

We wanted to make sure that the eating and drinking functions of the mouth were clear. The mouth performs a variety of functions in eating, and we could not find one picture that made them all plain, so Amahl Shakhashiri suggested that we take one of our own. She envisioned three people—one drinking water from a jug, one eating a sandwich (to show how we bite), and one licking an ice cream cone (to show the tongue, which doesn't appear elsewhere in the photographs). It was an inspired and efficient suggestion, resulting in a highly informative (if somewhat bizarre) picture. Under Amahl's direction, the three principals—Wendy Gradison, Val Boriakoff, and George Helou, a Cornell graduate student—gathered in Eckelmann's studio. Wendy got her ice cream cone, Val was handed a sandwich made with tuna fish (which he loathes), and George got his jug. The first results were disappointing. The white bread of the sandwich made it impossible to see the shape of the bite, and the stream of water spilling out of an opaque earthenware jug could be mistaken for a silvery pipe leading into George's mouth. On the second try Val had a sandwich made with dark rye toast and George had a glass pitcher so that the water could be seen pouring out. George had to be actually pouring water into his mouth while the photographer focused, checked reflections and took a few shots; he swallowed half the pitcher before Eckelmann was finished. Although the picture is somewhat comic to us, it presents a great deal of information about how our mouths work. It also tells the galaxy that we live by bread, water and ice cream.

Photo: Herman Eckelmann, NAIC staff photographer

83

H. Edward Kim, © National Geographic Society

83. *Great Wall of China*

This was another suggestion made by Philip Morrison. The Great Wall is one of the most tremendous engineering achievements of man, and it is also a product of one of the oldest and most important human cultures. It was difficult to find a shot that showed both the scale of the wall and a view of it close up. The National Geographic Society helpfully provided us with a number of photographs to choose from.

84. *Construction Scene (African)*

This picture shows a man building a four-sided walled structure out of brick, the same material used to construct the Great Wall. Another man holds bricks ready. The structure is clearly something human beings can be inside. A completed structure is in the background for comparison.

84

United Nations

85

86

87

85. Construction Scene (Amish)

This picture of a barn raising shows construction as a cooperative activity. On the right-hand side, the first planks of the walls are being nailed to the frame of the building.

86. House (Hut)

We decided to show human dwellings—and immediately found it hard to decide what a typical human dwelling was. This picture and the two that follow show a few of the many kinds of houses we live in.

87. House (New England Frame)

A typical North American house. The picture may seem a bit dated to us, but that shouldn't matter too much millions of years from now.

88

89

Courtesy F. D. Drake

James L. Amos, © National Geographic Society

90

Photo: David Carroll

91

88. House (Modern)

This house, in Cloudcroft, New Mexico, is the residence of John V. Evans, a well-known solar astronomer.

89. House Interior

We selected this picture primarily because it had a fireplace, and we thought fire had to be shown somewhere. It is made possible by our oxygen atmosphere, described in picture 13. The photograph happens to contain a lot of other information as well—how we sit on a stool, for instance. Perhaps the activity of the man might be connected with the paintings already on the wall, showing something of our creative drives (at least in landscape painting). This picture was sent in color to show the fire most clearly.

90. Taj Mahal

Pictures 84 through 88 show some typical buildings. We also wanted to show some more impressive architecture, and the variety of buildings we build. Out of a host of possibilities—the Eiffel Tower, a Gothic cathedral, a Mayan pyramid—we chose the Taj Mahal. The Taj Mahal is a monument not to religion but to love, and thus was an appealing choice. It is also generally regarded as one of the world's most beautiful buildings.

91. English City (Oxford)

The next few pictures show several kinds of human cities. The information from other pictures (101 and 102) should help recipients identify the objects seen in the street. (Douglas R. Gilbert, from *C. S. Lewis: Images of His World*, Wm. B. Eerdmans Pub. Co.)

Ted Spiegel, © National Geographic Society

92. *Boston from the Charles River*

This represents the skyline of a modern city, showing skyscrapers. From the sailboats on the river it may be deduced that we like to live along rivers and coasts and that we use them for transportation (again emphasizing the importance of water on our planet and in our culture).

93 and 94. *UN Building, by Day and by Night*

We wanted to show how we light our cities, so we looked for a shot of a city taken from the same angle by day and by night. This shot of the UN building was the best one we could find. It also seemed an appropriate structure to show, symbolizing to us (though not to the recipients) that we hoped this message would represent global humanity, not just Western humanity. The night scene was sent in color.

United Nations

93

United Nations

94

95

95. Sydney Opera House

Frank Drake urged us to include a shot of this Australian building as an example of modern architecture substantially different from that of any other building shown (i.e., involving shapes other than rectangles and domes). The picture was taken while the opera house was still under construction, as the crane and scaffolding may indicate.

Michael E. Long, © National Geographic Society

96. Artisan with Drill

This picture is the same kind of hands-and-face close-up as can be found in pictures 63, 64, and 68, but here we show the use of hands in an industrial process involving a machine. (Bill St. John of the Whittier [CA] Gem and Mineral Society, operating a drill machine, designed by Sol Stern, a fellow member. Photograph courtesy of Frank Hewlett. From the book *Gem Cutting* by John Sinkankas, Fig. 72)

96

97. Factory Interior

Just as the construction pictures 84 and 85 show first individual construction, then construction by a group, this picture follows naturally from picture 96. A group of men operate machines in a modern factory that makes precision instruments. It was necessary to send this picture in color to show the incandescent glow of the electrical equipment. (Photograph by Fred Ward: *Factory Interior*)

97

98. *Museum*

Here is a group of people looking at the bones of ancient animals in a museum. Behind them is a mural that shows the animals as they were when they were alive. The anatomy overlays (pictures 18–25) and the following picture (99) may help recipients recognize the bones in this picture.

99. *X-ray of Hand*

The versatility of the human hand has played no small part in our cultural evolution, and we showed hands performing a large variety of tasks—we felt we had to stress their importance by repetition. We also wanted a picture that gave some hint of medical technology. It occurred to us that an X-ray photograph of a human body might indicate that we could direct our technology toward our own biology. And we decided, after looking at various X-rays, that a human hand showed up best and would be a part of the human body that recipients should recognize easily. Herman Eckelmann and I went out to the Tompkins County Hospital and took this picture in their radiology department. Teresa Cima, a radiology technician, is holding up her hand for comparison.

100. *Woman with Microscope*

If Voyager is ever recovered by extraterrestrials, they will find actual examples of some of our automatic scientific instruments on board the spacecraft. We wanted to show a scientific instrument being operated by a human being. If the evidence of other pictures suggests to recipients that eyes are our organs of vision, and if the function of the spectacles in picture 68 is guessed, then the function of the microscope may also be inferred. The light source under the microscope may give an additional clue. The photomicrograph of dividing cells (picture 17) will prove that we've discovered microscopy. Carl Sagan deduced that the microscope in this picture couldn't have been the one that took picture 17. Nevertheless, recipients will know that we have microscopes, so they may figure out that this is an example of one. The woman is wearing earrings. We hope that these will be recognized as jewelry and not, say, a miniature radio à la *Star Trek*, or a name tag.

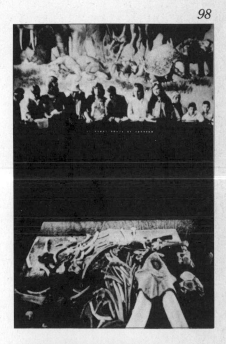

98

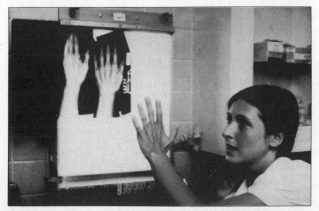

99   Photo: Herman Eckelmann, NAIC staff photographer

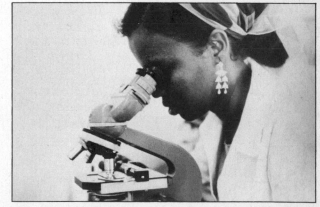

100

United Nations

101

103

United Nations

United Nations

102

Photo: Herman Eckelmann, NAIC staff photographer

Pictures 101 through 108 show various forms of human transportation.

101. Street Scene (Pakistan)

This picture may have the highest information density of any in the whole message. Frozen in a busy rush to somewhere are automobiles (four- and three-wheeled), bicycles, motorbikes, horsecarts, and pedestrians, going in both directions along a two-way street, while sacred cows idle lazily along the median strip. This is a virtual cross section of short-range ground transportation, and an ambiguity that may exist throughout the rest of the sequence is cleared up. Some of the pictures show people in primitive or at least pretechnological situations. Others show sophisticated machinery and technology. Recipients might think that we are showing various stages in our history, and that the world is now completely technological. This picture makes clear that the advanced and the primitive exist at the same time, that human beings at the time Voyager was launched used both powered vehicles and vehicles drawn by draft animals. This could indicate that we are a very young scientific civilization with uneven technological development.

102. Street Scene

Rush hour in India. A subtle point that extraterrestrials from crowded cities may note is that there are four lanes of traffic going in one direction and only one in the opposite direction, suggestion that a majority of people go to or come from some place at the same time.

103. Highway

Eckelmann took this picture on Route 13 in Ithaca. Unlike the other street scenes with vehicles, the setting is rural, not urban. This shows that ground transport is used for long-range movement of people and goods (the logs in the truck) and not just for transport within a city.

104

106

Photograph by Gordon W. Gahan, © National Geographic Society

104. *Golden Gate Bridge from Baker's Beach*

Philip Morrison suggested that we include a picture of a suspension bridge, since its form so directly follows its function and its shape is determined entirely by the laws of physics. Both these facts make it a structure that extraterrestrials ought to recognize and understand. It also shows that our roads span rivers. This photograph was taken by Ansel Adams. (Photograph by Ansel Adams: *The Golden Gate and Bridge from Baker's Beach, San Francisco, California, c. 1953*)

105. *Train*

A turbo train on the Boston–Washington run. The second set of tracks indicates the nature of the vehicle and distinguishes it from the trucks and cars of previous photographs. A face is visible in the front window.

106. *Airplane in Flight*

Frank Drake took this photograph on the runway of Syracuse airport, one jump ahead of the security guards, who undoubtedly wondered what he was doing there. Anything for science! The jet is plainly taking off, and smaller airplanes of different types are visible on the ground.

Courtesy F. D. Drake

105

107. *Airport*

An aerial view of Toronto International Airport showing planes of various sizes and types. Recipients will recognize the airplanes as the same vehicles they saw in the previous picture. This shot informs them that our transport system involves terminals—centralized points of arrival and departure—and therefore we use airplanes extensively, not just for exploration or some limited purpose. Smaller ground vehicles can be seen servicing the aircraft.

108. *Antarctic Sno-Cat*

Well, we're not perfect. This picture, which concludes our transportation sequence, was taken on Sir Vivien Fuchs's trans-Antarctic expedition of 1958. A crevasse has opened in the ice beneath the sno-cat, which totters precariously, unable to move either forward or backward. The explorers stand around in a "What do we do now?" stance. We could justify inclusion of this picture by pointing out that it shows polar terrain and a vehicle with treads. In fact it's a joke—the only deliberate humor in the picture portion of the Voyager record. The more we looked at this picture, the funnier it seemed. The vehicle almost looks embarrassed, dangling helplessly, with the expedition's name in bold lettering on its side (painted for whom to see, we wondered, the penguins?). The crew of the starship that salvages Voyager may have had their own experience with ships, tractors, or sleds stuck in the unimaginable muds of distant planets. Freeing stuck vehicles may be an experience we share with alien explorers, no matter how advanced. These explorers, incidentally, managed to pull their sno-cat back from the lip of disaster with another sno-cat, and continued on to cross Antarctica overland.

Pictures 109 through 113 show some aspects of our emergence as a spacefaring civilization.

109. *Radio Telescope (Westerbork Interferometer)*

An interferometer is an array of radio antennas that can function as a single telescope. Here a group of humans on bicycles (recognizable from picture 101) is sightseeing. Like a suspension bridge, the shape of a dish antenna is determined entirely by the job it must perform, and so it should be recognized by the radio astronomers of another species.

107

Lawson Graphics (Pacific) Ltd.   108

© National Geographic Society   109

James P. Blair, © National Geographic Society

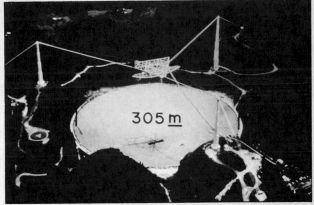

110. *Arecibo Observatory*

The 1,000-foot-diameter radio telescope built into a natural bowl-shaped valley in Puerto Rico is the largest radio/radar telescope in the world. The Observatory is part of the National Astronomy and Ionosphere Center and is funded by the National Science Foundation. Frank Drake is director of NAIC and has used the telescope to conduct searches (so far unsuccessful) for artificial radio signals beamed our way from civilizations elsewhere in space. Advanced civilizations may use radio telescopes to talk to one another. This picture shows that Earth is ready to enter the conversation.

Photo: Herman Eckelmann, NAIC staff photographer

111. *Page from a Book*

Books have been the means by which humans have stored and remembered information not coded into their genes or brains. Without books and writing, our civilization couldn't have developed. Our use of notation throughout the picture package shows our use of symbols. We wanted to show the form these symbols take on our home world; we wanted to show a page from a book. But which page from which book?

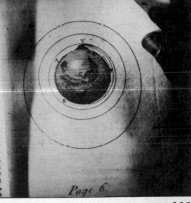

I spent a wonderful hour with Donald Eddy, the curator of rare books at the Cornell University Library, looking at the most beautiful books I had ever seen—a first-folio Shakespeare, a Renaissance edition of Chaucer with exquisite woodcuts, an edition of Euclid's Geometry that is four centuries old. Philip Morrison suggested that the most appropriate page to send would be the one from Sir Isaac Newton's *System of the World* on which, for the first time in human history, the procedure for launching an object into orbit was correctly explained and diagramed. In a way, this page was the first step on the path that led to Voyager. And beyond its historical importance, the diagram of cannonballs being launched in various orbital and suborbital trajectories might just be decipherable by recipients, who would certainly know the ballistics of launching satellites. Moreover, the diagram is marked by letters (AFB representing the surface of Earth, C the center of Earth, and so forth), and these letter groups reappear in the text. It might be possible for recipients to associate the letter groups in the diagram with those in the text. We have shown a hand turning the page, to give the idea that a book consists of more than one sheet of paper. The page numbers 6 and 7 can be seen—and recipients will already have learned what the numbers mean. The edition we photographed was printed in 1728. It was the smallest book we were considering, which meant that in terms of the TV quality resolution of the pictures, the lettering on the page would be larger, sharper and clearer. All the lettering can be read, even when this picture is reproduced as a TV image.

The following two pictures show Newton's principles in practice, giving another clue as to the meaning of the text.

112. *Astronaut in Space*

American astronaut James McDivitt on a walk in space from a Gemini orbital flight. His hand is visible, which should make certain that recipients recognize that this is a human figure. This picture was sent in color to link the planet positively with Earth of pictures 12 and 13.

113. *Titan Centaur Launch*

Voyager was launched atop a Titan Centaur rocket identical to the one shown here blasting off from Cape Canaveral in 1975, launching Viking on its trip to Mars.

114. *Sunset*

We felt that at least one picture ought to be chosen purely for its beauty, to say nothing more than how lovely our planet is. A sunset seemed a good choice. But I might point out that the reddening of light contains information about our atmosphere, and the silhouetted birds show the mechanism of avian flight. This photograph was taken by David Harvey, who also took the father-and-daughter photograph (picture 35).

112

NASA

114

David Harvey from Woodfin Camp, Inc.

113

NASA

115

116

Courtesy Phonogram International

Three-quarters of the Voyager record is music, and the final two pictures try to explain explicitly what the sounds are that constitute the bulk of our record, using as example a string quartet.

115. String Quartet

This photograph of the Quartetto Italiano shows people engaged in making music. An individual musician wouldn't have conveyed the idea that music can be a social activity, and pictures of a symphony orchestra had too many people and instruments for anything to be really clear. In this picture, each person is playing an instrument, and the instruments are identical in shape but different in size. They are stringed instruments, and it should be plain that the people are striking or rubbing the strings. The vibration of a string is one of the things whose characteristics (the production of overtones and harmonics) ought to be the same everywhere, and extraterrestrials should know or be able to figure out that a vibrating string makes a certain kind of sound.

116. Score of Quartet and Violin

The violin seen in the last picture is shown here next to a page of musical score. The score is the Cavatina from Beethoven's String Quartet No. 13, which is the last piece on the record. After this picture, we play a few seconds of the quartet that appears again later on the record. These few seconds are the measures scored on the sheet music. We hope that recipients will realize from analyzing the sound that it has been produced by vibrating string. From there it should be an easy jump to associate the instruments and the people playing them with the vibrating strings of the music. In a real way musical notation reflects the sound of music—a higher note is higher on the staff. Clever extraterrestrials might look at the notation on the score and guess that each note connects in a one-to-one relationship with the marks on that score. If they can figure this out, they will know that music is composed and written down and that we are showing them the notation. We hope this will give them some idea of what the rest of the sounds on the record are all about.

4
A VOYAGER'S GREETINGS,
by Linda Salzman Sagan

It's gayer than a greeting, and it's sadder than a sigh.
— "Aloha Oe," Don Blanding

The Voyager spacecraft hurtling through space as I write these words resembles a glistening cocoon carrying on it a gold record, a gift to all our intelligent counterparts inhabiting the universe. The greetings part of the record is a celebration of the human spirit, emphasizing our gregariousness, our joy in being the social creatures we are, and expressing our desire to be thought of as eloquent in this, our first speaking engagement to the universe. We are saying that language is important here, and that we would welcome—indeed, relish—a dialogue with another interlocutory civilization elsewhere in the cosmos.

We are Robinson Crusoe on island Earth—inventive, resourceful and creative, but alone. We scan the rim of the horizon for any passing ships that might be sailing the star-encrusted ocean. Hoping to make contact, we call across the vastness of space; cupping our hands to our mouth we shout, "Hello out there, is anybody home?"

What if there is no reply? Are we just crying in the wilderness? How sad it would be if our cosmic yoo-hoo echoed through the canyon of space and reached no one on the other side of the chasm. All we'd hear would be our own greetings, warm and heartfelt, sounding as hollow as pennies dropped into a glass jar.

Under a sun-drenched Florida sky, a few hundred people gathered, outfitted with special gear for the occasion—sunglasses, binoculars and cameras—to watch Voyager rise from Earth in a blast of white light, a puff of sunset-colored smoke and a sky-splitting roar. Watching Voyager flash out of our sight, and eventually out of our jurisdiction, on its one-way ticket to who-knows-where, one hopes that, like Marco Polo, it will find itself at the gates of some ancient and great civilization. As our emissary, it will extend greetings and present our calling card (or disc, in this case), as any well-mannered Victorian guest would do when out visiting in the neighborhood.

And what an enticing assortment Voyager is instructed to present to these extraterrestrial hosts, a package of great interest and importance—providing they have ears. Eyes would also be a great help. But since I'm unable to conceive of an organism that is highly developed intellectually and does *not* have sense organs, I must adopt the assumption that such beings will be able to experience Voyager with both their senses and their intellects.

If you had the opportunity to send a greeting to another sentient being living on another world, what would you convey in the brief seconds you would be allowed to speak? Would your message be a general one, expressing good will from everyone here to everyone there, or would it be a message from you as an individual? Would it sound like the regards one sends to a distant relation, or would the tone be warm and effusive? Perhaps you would be most comfortable with a formal greeting, one set in tradition, or would you just send the basics—"Hi there, we don't bite, what's it like where you are? Yours truly, Earth."

Essentially, all the elements mentioned are contained in the fifty-five salutations, each one of which is spoken in a different language. The speakers were chosen because of their fluency in the language, not because of any special scientific knowledge. They were given no instructions on what to say other than that it was to be a greeting to possible extraterrestrials and that it must be brief. A few of the languages, such as Sumerian, Akkadian and Hittite, are no longer heard in our modern world, and although Latin is, it is used primarily for religious or ceremonial occasions; but because these languages have historic importance, they were taken down from the shelf, dusted off and allowed to shine in their own right, as in the almost biblical Latin message, "Greetings to you, whoever you are: we have good will towards you and bring peace across space." The Swedish message was personal: "Greetings from a computer programmer in the little university town of Ithaca, on the planet Earth." I especially like the Mandarin Chinese greeting; its casualness reminds me of a postcard to friends—"Hope everyone's well. We are thinking about you all. Please come here to visit us when you have time."

A few people asked the extraterrestrials to be in touch, such as the Indian speaking in Gujarati: "Greetings from a human being of the Earth. Please contact." A fellow Indian speaking in Rajasthani had other sentiments: "Hello to everyone. We are happy here and you be happy there." The Turkish speaker made a leap of faith when he assumed not only that he would be talking to friends, but that they would be fluent in Turkish: "Dear Turkish-speaking friends, may the honors of the morning be upon your heads."

Those of us who worked on this part of the message realized that the most conscientious alien linguist, smarter than our own brilliant Jean François Champollion, couldn't decipher the vast majority of the languages we sent. But there was not enough physical space on the recording to provide a Rosetta stone, let alone a pocket dictionary to accompany each language. During the entire Voyager project, all decisions were based on the assumption that there were two audiences for whom

The Principal Languages of the World
Source: Sidney S. Culbert, Associate Professor of Psychology,
University of Washington
Total number of speakers of languages spoken by at least one million
persons (Midyear 1978).

Language	*Millions*
Achinese (Indonesia)	2
Afrikaans (S. Africa)	7
Albanian	3
Amharic (Ethiopia)	9
Arabic	138
Armenian	4
Assamese[1] (India)	13
Aymara (Bolivia; Peru)	1
Azerbaijani (USSR; Iran)	8
Bahasa (*see* Malay-Indonesian)	
Balinese	3
Baluchi (Pakistan; Iran)	3
Batak (Indonesia)	2
Bemba (S. Central Africa)	2
Bengali[1] (Bangladesh; India)	136
Berber[2] (N. Africa)	
Bhili (India)	4
Bihari (India)	22
Bikol (Philippines)	2
Bisaya (*see* Cebuano, Panay-Hiligaynon, and Samar-Leyte)	
Bugi (Indonesia)	2
Bulgarian	9
Burmese	24
Byelorussian (mainly USSR)	9
Cambodian (Cambodia, Asia)	7
Canarese (*see* Kannada)	
Cantonese (China)	49
Catalan (Spain; France; Andorra)	6
Cebuano (Philippines)	9
Chinese[3]	
Chuang[7] (China)	

Language	Millions
Chuvash (USSR)	2
Czech	11
Danish	5
Dayak (Borneo)	1
Dutch (*see* Netherlandish)	
Edo (W. Africa)	1
Efik	2
English	374
Esperanto	1
Estonian	1
Ewe (W. Africa)	3
Fang-Bulu (W. Africa)	1
Finnish	5
Flemish (*see* Netherlandish)	
French	98
Fula (W. Africa)	9
Galician (Spain)	3
Galla (*see* Oromo)	
Ganda (or Luganda) (E. Africa)	3
Georgian (USSR)	4
German	120
Gilaki (Iran)	2
Gondi (India)	2
Greek	10
Guarani (mainly Paraguay)	3
Gujarati[1] (India)	32
Hakka (China)	22
Hausa (W. and Central Africa)	20
Hebrew	3
Hindi[14]	224
Hindustani[4]	
Hungarian (or Magyar)	13
Ibibio (*see* Efik)	
Ibo (or Igbo) (W. Africa)	11
Ijaw (W. Africa)	1
Ilocano (Philippines)	4

Language	*Millions*
Iloko (*see* Ilocano)	
Indonesian (*see* Malay-Indonesian)	
Italian	61
Japanese	114
Javanese	46
Kamba (E. Africa)	1
Kanarese (*see* Kannada)	
Kannada[1] (India)	30
Kanuri (W. and Central Africa)	3
Kashmiri[1]	3
Kazakh (USSR)	6
Khalkha (Mongolia)	2
Kikongo (*see* Kongo)	
Kikuyu (or Gekoyo) (Kenya)	3
Kimbundu (*see* Mbundu-Kimbundu)	
Kirghiz (USSR)	2
Kituba (Congo River)	3
Kongo (Congo River)	2
Konkani (India)	2
Korean	56
Kurdish (S.W. of Caspian Sea)	7
Kurukh (or Oraon) (India)	1
Lao[5] (Laos, Asia)	3
Latvian (or Lettish)	2
Lingala (*see* Ngala)	
Lithuanian	3
Luba-Lulua (Zaire)	3
Luganda (*see* Ganda)	
Luhya (or Luhia) (Kenya)	1
Luo (Kenya)	2
Luri (Iran)	2
Macedonian (Yugoslavia)	2
Madurese (Indonesia)	8
Makua (S.E. Africa)	3
Malagasy (Madagascar)	8
Malay-Indonesian	103

Language	Millions
Malayalam[1] (India)	28
Malinke-Bambara-Dyula (Africa)	6
Mandarin (China)	680
Marathi[1] (India)	53
Mazandarani (Iran)	2
Mbundu (Umbundu group) (S. Angola)	3
Mbundu (Kimbundu group) (Angola)	2
Mende (Sierra Leone)	1
Meo (*see* Miao)	
Miao (and Meo) (S.E. Asia)	3
Min (China)	40
Minankabau (Indonesia)	4
Moldavian (inc. with Romanian)	
Mongolian (*see* Khalkha)	
Mordvin (USSR)	1
Moré (*see* Mossi)	
Mossi (or Moré) (W. Africa)	3
Ndongo (*see* Mbundu-Kimbundu)	
Nepali (Nepal; India)	10
Netherlandish (Dutch and Flemish)	20
Ngala (or Lingala) (Africa)	2
Norwegian	5
Nyamwezi-Sukuma (S.E. Africa)	2
Nyanja (S.E. Africa)	3
Oraon (*see* Kurukh)	
Oriya[1] (India)	25
Oromo (Ethiopia)	7
Panay-Hiligaynon (Philippines)	4
Panjabi (*see* Punjabi)	
Pashto (*see* Pushtu)	
Pedi (*see* Sotho, Northern)	
Persian	26
Polish	37
Portuguese	137
Provençal (Southern France)	5
Punjabi[1] (India; Pakistan)	60

Pushtu (mainly Afghanistan) 17
Quechua (S. America) 7
Rajasthani (India) 21
Romanian 22
Ruanda (S. Central Africa) 7
Rundi (S. Central Africa) 4
Russian (Great Russian only) 253
Samar-Leyte (Philippines) 2
Sango (Central Africa) 2
Santali (India) 4
Sepedi (*see* Sotho, Northern)
Serbo-Croatian (Yugoslavia) 19
Shan (Burma) 2
Shona (S.E. Africa) 4
Siamese (*see* Thai)
Sindhi (India; Pakistan) 10
Sinhalese (Sri Lanka) 11
Slovak 5
Slovene (Yugoslavia) 2
Somali (E. Africa) 5
Sotho, Northern (S. Africa) 2
Sotho, Southern (S. Africa) 3
Spanish 231
Sundanese (Indonesia) 16
Swahili (E. Africa) 25
Swedish 10
Tagalog (Philippines) 23
Tajiki (USSR) 3
Tamil[1] (India; Sri Lanka) 55
Tatar (or Kazan-Turkic) (USSR) 7
Telugu[1] (India) 55
Thai[5] 34
Thonga (S.E. Africa) 1
Tibetan 6
Tigrinya (Ethiopia) 4
Tiv (E. Central Nigeria) 1
Tswana (S. Africa) 3

[1]One of the fifteen languages of the Constitution of India.
[2]Here considered a group of dialects.
[3]See Mandarin, Cantonese, Wu, Min and Hakka. The "national language" (Guoyu) or "common speech" (Putonghua) is a standardized form of Mandarin as spoken in the area of Peking.
[4]Hindi and Urdu are essentially the same language, Hindustani. As the official language of India, it is written in the Devanagari script and called Hindi. As the official language of Pakistan, it is written in a modified Arabic script and called Urdu.
[5]Thai includes Central, Southwestern, Northern and Northeastern Thai. The distinction between Northeastern Thai and Lao is political rather than linguistic.
[6]Yiddish is usually considered a variant of German, though it has its own standard grammar, dictionaries, and a highly developed literature, and is written in Hebrew characters. Speakers number about 3 million.
[7]A group of Thai-like dialects with about 9 million speakers.

this message was being prepared—those of us who inhabit Earth, and those who exist on the planets of distant stars.

We were principally concerned with the needs of people on Earth during this section of the recording. We recorded messages from populations all over the globe, each representative speaking in the language of his or her people, instead of sending greetings in one or two languages accompanied by keys for their decipherment. We were aware that the latter alternative might have given the extraterrestrials a better chance of understanding the words precisely, though it would have raised the thorny question of which two languages to send. We felt it was fitting that Voyager greet the universe as a representative of one community, albeit a complex one consisting of many parts. At least the fact that many different languages are represented should be clear from the very existence of a set of short statements separated by pauses and from internal evidence—such as the initial greeting *"Namaste,"* which begins many of the greetings from the Indian subcontinent. The greetings are an aural Gestalt, in which each culture is a contributing voice in the choir. After all, by sending a spaceship out of our solar system, we are making an effort to de-provincialize, to rise above our nationalistic interests and join a commonwealth of space-faring societies, if one exists.

We made a special effort to record those languages spoken by the vast majority of the world's inhabitants. Since all research and technical work on the record had to be accomplished within a period of weeks, we began with a list of the world's most widely spoken languages, which was provided by Dr. Steven Soter of Cornell. Carl suggested that we record the twenty-five most widely spoken languages. If we were able to accomplish that, and still had time, we would then try to include as many other languages as we could.

The organization of recording sessions and the arduous legwork involved in finding, contacting and convincing individual speakers was handled by Shirley Arden, Carl's executive assistant, Wendy Gradison, then Carl's editorial assistant, Dr. Steven Soter, and me. The master table, reproduced on pages 134 through 143, which shows each of the languages, the speaker's name, their comments in the original language, an English translation, and the real and fractional number of human beings who speak that language, was largely Shirley's idea. We contacted various members of the Cornell language departments, who cooperated with us on very short notice and provided numerous speakers, even though school was ending and many people were leaving for summer vacations. Other speakers were more difficult to find. Sometimes it meant sitting for hours, telephoning friends of friends who might know someone who could speak, let's say, the Chinese Wu dialect. After finding such a person, we had to determine whether he or she would be available during the hours when the recording sessions had been scheduled. Even while the recording sessions were going on, we were still trying to find and recruit speakers of languages not yet represented. Often people waiting to record would suggest names of individuals fluent in the very languages we were looking for. Immediately we called these people, explained the project and our plight, and asked them to come at once. Many people did just that.

Bishun Khare, a senior physicist in the Laboratory for Planetary Studies, was responsible almost singlehandedly for the participation of the Indian speakers. He personally called friends and members of the Cornell Indian community, explained the undertaking to them, and asked for and received their cooperation.

There were only a few disappointments, where someone had agreed to come to a recording session, could not and forgot to let us know in time for us to make other arrangements. It wasn't always possible to find replacements at the last minute, so there are some regrettable omissions—Swahili is one.

The greetings were recorded in two sessions in the administration building of Cornell University. The first session was recorded on June 8, 1977, by Joe Leeming of Cornell's Public Relations Department. While one person was being recorded, the others waited in a connecting office just outside the studio. Leeming left the audio speakers in the office on so that the people who were about to record could actually hear the voice of the person being recorded in the studio. This led to a warm feeling of camaraderie and excitement among the participants. The second recording session took place on June 13, and was recorded by Cornell film-maker David Gluck and his assistant Michael Bronfenbrenner.

Voyager has been compared to a bottle with a note inside tossed over the railing of a ship at sea. It is, though the bottle is custom-built and the note scribbled in computer instead of pencil. We are tossing our bottle into the void of the sky. Whether it will ever be found by someone walking on a galactic beach will not be known by our generation. Our distant progeny will have this to look forward to.

GREETINGS ON THE VOYAGER SPACECRAFT
(in the order presented)
(prepared by Shirley Arden)

Language	Greeting
Sumerian	Silima khemen

Greek

οἵτινες, ποτ᾽ ἔστε, χαίρετε. εἰρηνικῶς, πρὸς φίλους ἐληλύθαμεν φίλοι.

Portuguese	Paz e felicidade a todos.

Cantonese

各位好嗎？祝各位平安健康快樂。

Akkadian	Adannish lu shulmu.

Russian

Здравствуйте, приветствую вас!

Thai

สวัสดีค่ะ สหายในธรณีโพ้น พวกเราในธรณีนี้ขอส่งมิตรจิตรมาถึงท่านทุกคน

Arabic

تَحِيّاتُنَا لِلْأَصْدِقَاءِ فِي النُّجُوم

يَالَيْتَ يَجْمَعُنَا الزَّمَان

Romanian	Salutări la toată lumea.

English Translation	Speaker's Name	Countries Where Language Is Spoken	Millions of Speakers	Percent of World's Population
May all be well.	David I. Owen	Ancient Sumer (2000 B.C.) (Modern Iraq)	2×10^{-4} (spoken by about 200 academics)	
Greetings to you, whoever you are. We come in friendship to those who are friends.	Frederick M. Ahl	Greece, Cyprus	10	0.2
Peace and happiness to all.	Janet Sternberg	Portugal, Brazil Angola, Mozambique, Guinea-Bissau	133	3.3
Hi. How are you? Wish you peace, health and happiness.	Stella Fessler	Southern China	48	1.2
May all be very well.	David I. Owen	Mesopotamia (500 B.C.)	5×10^{-4}	
Be healthy—I greet you.	Maria Rubinova	U.S.S.R.	246	6.1
We in this world send you our good will.	Ruchira Mendiones	Thailand	35	0.8
Greetings to our friends in the stars. We wish that we will meet you someday.	Amahl Shakhashiri	Algeria, Bahrain, Egypt, Iraq, Jordan, Lebanon, Libya, Morocco, Oman, Qatar, Saudi Arabia, S. Yemen, Sudan, Syria, Tunisia, Yemen	134	3.3
Greetings to everybody.	Sanda Huffman	Romania, Moldavian S.S.R.	22	0.5

French	Bonjour tout le monde.

Burmese	ကောင်းသော ညခင်းပါ ။ Ma-ye. la: hkamya
Hebrew	Shalóm
Spanish	Hola y saludos a todos.

Indonesian	Selamat malam hadirin sekalian, Selamat berpísah, Sampai bertemu lagi dilain waktu.
Kechua (Quechua)	Kay pachamanta pitapas maytapas rimapayastin, runa simipi.
Punjabi	ਜੀ ਆਇਆ ਨੂੰ . ਤੁਹਾਨੂੰ ਮਿਲਕੇ ਬੜੇ ਖੁਸੀ ਹੋਈ.
Hittite	Ashshuli.

Good day to the entire world.	Alexandra Littauer	France, Belgium, Quebec — Canada, Switzerland, Benin, Cameroon, Chad, Central African Republic, Congo, Dahomey, French Guinea, Gabon, Guadeloupe, Haiti, Ivory Coast, Luxembourg, Martinique, Mali, Niger, New Caledonia, Reunion, (Indian Ocean), Senegal, Togo, Upper Volta	95	2.5
Are you well?	Maung Myo Lwin	Burma	24	0.6
Peace.	David I. Owen	Israel	3	0.07
Hello and greetings to all.	Erik J. Beukenkamp	Argentina, Bolivia, Chile, Colombia, Ecuador, Paraguay, Trinidad and Tobago, Uruguay, Venezuela, Costa Rica, El Salvador, Guatemala, Honduras, Nicaragua, Panama, Mexico, Cuba, Dominican Republic, Haiti, Puerto Rico, Spain, parts of Morocco and Western Africa	225	5.6
Good night ladies and gentlemen. Goodbye and see you next time.	Ilyas Harun	Indonesia	101	2.5
Hello to everybody from this Earth, in Kechua language.	Fredy Amilcar Roncalla Fernandez	Peru, Bolivia, Equador	7	0.17
Welcome home. It is a pleasure to receive you.	Jatinder N. Paul	India, Pakistan	58	1.4
Hail.	David I. Owen	Anatolia (Turkey) until 1200 B.C.	2×10^{-4}	

Bengali	নমস্কার ! বিশ্বে শান্তি হোক
Latin	Salvete quiquumque estis; bonam erga vos voluntatem habemus, et pacem per astra ferimus.
Aramaic	Shalám
Dutch	Hartelghe groeten aen iadereen.
German	Herzliche grüsse an alle.
Urdu	ہم زمین کے باشندوں کی طرف سے آپکو خوش آمدید کہتے ہیں
Vietnamese	Chân thành giu dén cáo ban lò'i chào thân hu'u.
Turkish	Sayın Türkçe bilen arkadaşlarımız: Sabah şereflerinizi hayırlı olsun!
Japanese	こんにちはお元気ですか。
Hindi	हम धरती के निवासी आप का स्वागत करते हैं।
Welsh	Iechyd da i chwi yn awr ac yn oes oesoedd.
Italian	Tanti saluti e auguri.
Sinhalese	ආයුබෝවන්
Nguni (Zulu)	Siya nibingelela maqhawe sinifisela inkonzo ende.

Greeting	Author	Region	Speakers (millions)	%
Hello! Let there be peace everywhere.	Subrata Mukherjee	Bengal, India; Bangladesh	131	3.7
Greetings to you, whoever you are: we have good will towards you and bring peace across space.	Frederick M. Ahl	National and international in Europe until the mid-Renaissance	scholarly and ecclesiastical circles only	
Peace.	David I. Owen	Ancient Near East Present-day: some Syrians in Syria and Iraq	3×10^{-2}	
Heartfelt greetings to everyone.	Joan de Boer	Netherlands, Surinam, Antilles	20	0.4
Heartfelt greetings to all.	Renate Born	Germany, Austria, Switzerland	120	3.0
Peace on you. We the inhabitants of this earth send our greetings to you.	Salma Alzal	Pakistan, central India	60	1.5
Sincerely send you our friendly greetings.	Tran Trong Hai	Vietnam	38	0.9
Dear Turkish-speaking friends, may the honors of the morning be upon your heads.	Peter Ian Kuniholm	Turkey, minorities in Bulgaria, Greece, Cyprus	41	1.0
Hello. How are you?	Mari Noda	Japan	113	2.8
Greetings from the inhabitants of this world.	Omar Alzal	North Central India: Uttar Pradesh, Madhya Pradesh	180	4.4
Good health to you now and forever.	Frederick M. Ahl	Western Wales	0.6	0.01
Many greetings and wishes.	Debby Grossvogel	Italy, southern Switzerland	61	1.5
Greetings.	Kamal de Abrew	Sri Lanka	11	0.3
We greet you, great ones. We wish you longevity.	Fred Dube	Southeast Africa	5	0.1

Sotho (Sesotho)	Reani lumelisa marela.

Wu 祝 你们 大家 好

Armenian

Korean 안녕하세요?

Polish Watajcie, istoty zza światów!

Nepali पृथ्वीवासीहरूबाट शान्तिमय भविष्यको शुभकासना !

Mandarin Chinese 各位都好吧，我們都很想念你們, 有空請到這來玩.

Ila (Lambia) Mypone kabotu noose.

Swedish Hälsmingar från en data programmerare
i den lilla universitats staden Ithaca
på planeten jorden.

Nyanja Mulibwanji imwe boonse bantu bakumwamba.

Gujarati

Ukranian ПЕРЕСИЛАЕМО ПРИВІТ ІЗ НАШОГО СВІТУ, БАЖАЕМО ЩАСТЯ, ЗДОРОВЯ, І МНОГАЯ ЛІТА.

Persian

A VOYAGER'S GREETINGS

Greeting	Name	Region		
We greet you, O great ones.	Fred Dube	Sotho (Pedi), Lesotho, N. Transvaal, Tswana	5	0.6
Best wishes to you all.	Yvonne Meinwald	China: Shanghai, Chekiang	43	1.1
To all those who exist in the universe, greetings.	Araxy Terzian	Armenia, minorities in U.S.S.R., Lebanon, Syria, Iran, Turkey	4	0.1
How are you?	Soon Hee Shin	North Korea, South Korea	55	1.4
Welcome, creatures from beyond the outer world.	Maria Nowakowska-Stykos	Poland	36	0.9
Wishing you a peaceful future from the earthlings!	Durga Prashad Ojha	Nepal	10	0.2
Hope everyone's well. We are thinking about you all. Please come here to visit us when you have time.	Liang Ku	China	670	16.7
We wish all of you well.	Saul Moobola	Zambia	0.75	0.02
Greetings from a computer programmer in the little university town of Ithaca on the planet Earth.	Gunnel Almgren Schaar	Sweden	10	0.2
How are all you people of other planets?	Saul Moobola	Malawi, Zambia	3.0	0.07
Greetings from a human being of the Earth. Please contact.	Radhekant Dave	Western India	31	0.7
We are sending greetings from our world, wishing you happiness, good health and many years.	Andrew Cehelsky	Ukranian S.S.R.	42	1.0
Hello to the residents of far skies.	Eshagh Samehyeh	Iran, Afghanistan	26	0.6

Serbian	ЖЕЛИМО ВАМ СВЕ НАЈБОЉЕ СА НАШЕ ПЛАНЕТЕ
Oriya	ସୂର୍ଯ୍ୟ ତାରକାର ଦୂରସ୍ଥ ଗ୍ରହ ପୃଥିବୀରୁ ବିଶ୍ୱ ବ୍ରହ୍ମାଣ୍ଡର ଅଧିବାସୀମାନଙ୍କୁ ଅଭିନନ୍ଦନ।
Luganda (Ganda)	Musulayo mutya abantu bensi eno mukama abawe emirembe bulijo.
Marathi	नमस्कार. ह्या पृथ्वीतील लोक तुम्हाला त्यांचे शुभविचार पाठवितात. आणि त्यांची आज्ञा भेट कि तुम्ही ह्या जन्मी धन्य रे.
Amoy	太空朋友 你們好！你們吃過飯 嗎？有空來这兒坐坐。
Hungarian (Magyar)	Üdvözletet küldünk magyar nyelven minden békét szeretö lénynek a világegyetemen.
Telugu	నమస్తే. తెలుగు మాట్లాడే జనముల నుండి మా శుభాకోరుట.
Czech	Mily přátelé, přejeme vam vše nejlepši.
Kannada (Kanarese)	ಕನ್ನಡಿಗರ ಪರವಾಗಿ ಶುಭಾಶಯಗಳು
Rajasthani	सब भाइयो ने म्हारो राम राम पहूँचे। हमा अँटे खुशी हाँ तुम्हा वहाँ खुशी रहीमो।
English	Hello from the children of the planet earth.

We wish you everything good from our planet.	Milan M. Smiljanic	Yugoslavia	19	0.4
Greetings to the inhabitants of the universe from the third planet Earth of the star the Sun.	Raghaba Prasada Sahu	Eastern India	24	0.5
Greetings to all peoples of the universe. God give you peace always.	Elijah Mwima-Mudeenya	S. Uganda, Kampala	3	0.07
Greetings. The people of the Earth send their good wishes.	Arati Pandit	Maharashtra (W. India)	53	1.3
Friends of space, how are you all? Have you eaten yet? Come visit us if you have time.	Margaret Sook Ching See Gebauer	Eastern China	30	0.7
We are sending greetings in the Hungarian language to all peace-loving beings in the Universe.	Elizabeth Bilson	Hungary, minority in Rumania	13	0.3
Greetings. Best wishes from Telugu-speaking people.	Prasad Kodukula	Andhra Pradesh, (Southeast India)	53	1.4
Dear Friends, we wish you the best.	V. O. Kostroun	Czechoslovakia	11	0.2
Greetings. On behalf of Kannada-speaking people, "good wishes."	Shrinivasa K. Upadhyaya	Karnataka (Southwest India)	29	0.7
Hello to everyone. We are happy here and you be happy there.	Mool C. Gupta	Rajasthan (Northwest India)	22	0.5
Hello from the children of planet Earth.	Nick Sagan	Australia, Bahamas, Botswana, Canada, Gambia, Ghana, Great Britain, Grenada, Guyana, Ireland, Jamaica, Liberia, Mauritius, New Guinea, New Zealand, Rhodesia, Sierra Leone, Tanzania, Trinidad and Tobago, Uganda, United States of America, Zambia	369	9.2
			TOTAL	87.13

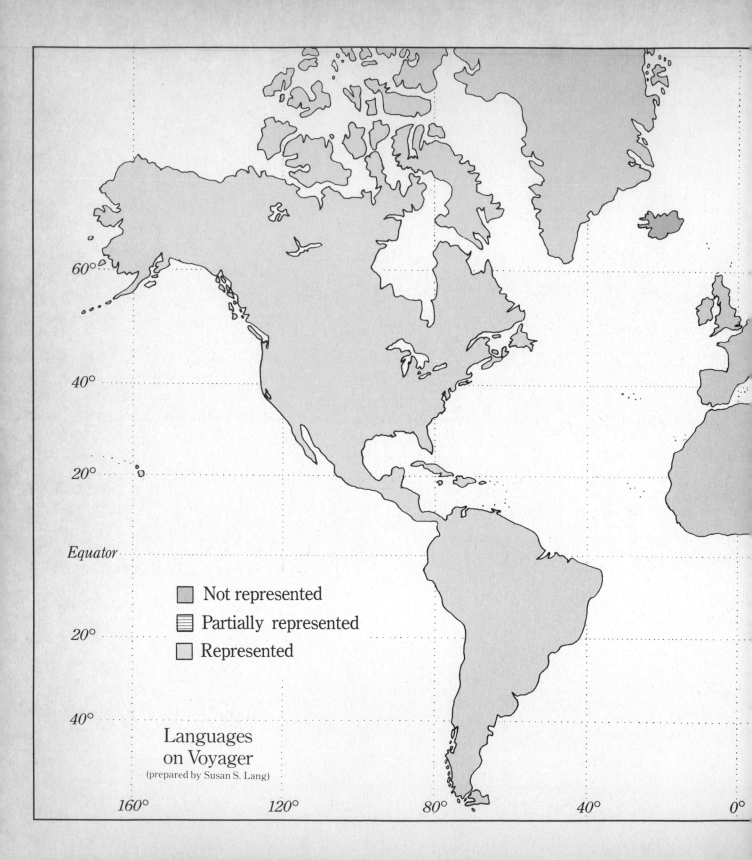

Not represented

Partially represented

Represented

Languages
on Voyager
(prepared by Susan S. Lang)

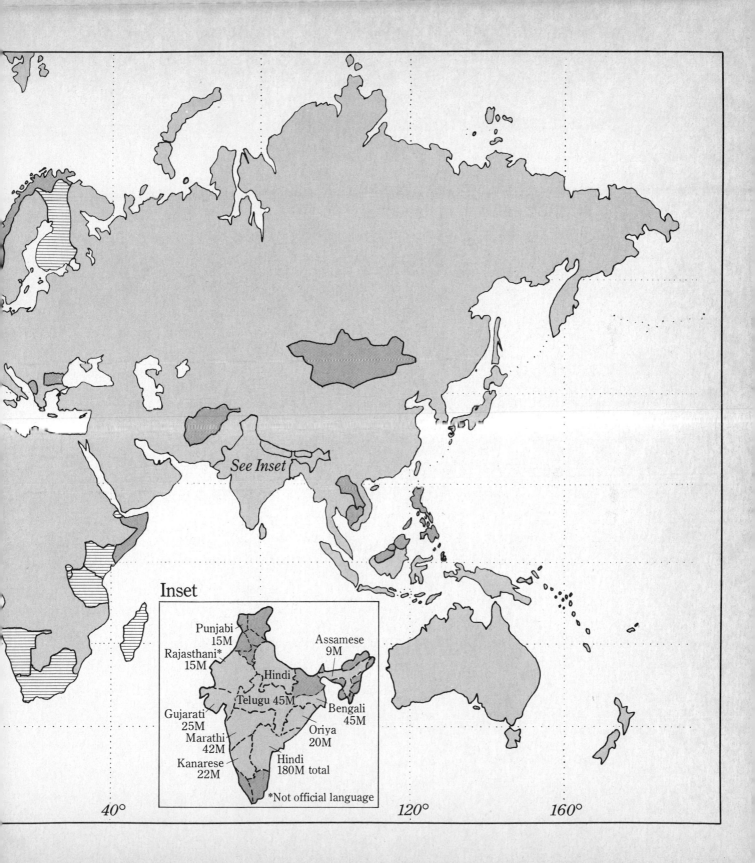

See Inset

Inset

Punjabi
15M

Rajasthani*
15M

Assamese
9M

Hindi

Telugu 45M

Gujarati
25M

Bengali
45M

Marathi
42M

Oriya
20M

Kanarese
22M

Hindi
180M total

*Not official language

40°   120°   160°

VOYAGER LANGUAGE MAP
(prepared by Susan S. Lang)

The following is a list of the countries whose official language is *not* represented on the Voyager space-craft.*

Country	Language	Population Millions	Thousands	Percent of World's Population
Afghanistan	Pashto (Pushtu)	16		0.4
	Dari-Persian	5		0.1
Albania	Albanian	3		0.07
Andorra	Catalan		30	7×10^{-4}
Bulgaria	Bulgarian	9		0.2
Iceland	Icelandic		220	5×10^{-3}
Kampuchea (Cambodia)	Khmer	8.3		0.2
Laos	Lao	3.3		0.08
Malaysia	Malay	12.3		0.3
Maldives, Republic of	Tiveli (Sinhal)		120	2.9×10^{-3}
Mongolia	Khalka Mongolia	2.0		0.05
Norway	Norwegian	5.0		0.12
Philippines	Pilipino	43.7		1.07
Swaziland	siSwati [sic]		500	0.01
			TOTAL	2.6

*More than 87 percent of the world's population is represented by the languages aboard the Voyager spacecraft. In the case of fourteen countries that have more than one official language, Voyager has one of the languages but not the other (with the exception of Singapore, which has four—Voyager has two of them; and India, which has fifteen—Voyager has nine of them plus one language that is not official). From this table, it can be seen that about 3.6 percent of the world's population is not represented on Voyager. Thirteen countries with only one official language, amounting to 2.6 percent of the world's population, are not represented at all. The 6 percent of the world's population not reflected by the figures on the three tables are peoples whose language is not an official language of their country and not one of the unofficial languages on the Voyager record. The figures on the tables represent the number of persons that speak a language as their mother tongue, and do not reflect the millions that can speak second and third languages.

VOYAGER LANGUAGE MAP

The following is a list of countries that have more than one official language, and are partially represented on the Voyager spacecraft.

Country	Language Represented	Language Not Represented	Millions of People Not Represented	Percent of World's Population (Not Represented)
Burundi	French	Kirundi	4	0.09
Djibouti, Rep. of	French	Somali	0.15	3.6×10^{-3}
Finland	Swedish	Finnish	5	0.1
India	Bengali	Assamese	13	0.3
	Gujarati	Kashmiri	3	0.07
	Hindi	Malayalam	27	0.7
	Kannada	Sanskrit		
	Marathi	Sindhi	10	.2
	Oriya	Tamil	55	1.7
	Punjabi			
	Telugu			
	Urdu			
	Rajasthani (not official)			
Kenya	English	Swahili	country is almost entirely bilingual	
Madagascar	French	Malagasy	8	0.2
Malta	English	Maltese	country is bilingual	
Namibia	English	Afrikaans	0.5	0.01
Nauru	English	Nauruan	8×10^{-3}	2×10^{-3}
Rwandi	French	Kinyarwandu	4	0.09
Samoa	English	Samoan	0.15	0.003
Singapore	Chinese	Samoan	0.15	0.003
	English	Malay	0.3	7.3×10^{-3}
South Africa, Rep. of	English	Afrikaans	4	0.1
Tanzania	English	Swahili	most speak English	
			TOTAL	3.57

5

THE SOUNDS OF EARTH,

by Ann Druyan

Be not afeard. The isle is full of noises,
Sounds and sweet airs, that give delight,
and hurt not.

— *Shakespeare,* The Tempest

The twelve-minute sound essay was conceived for two audiences: the human and the extraterrestrial. In the former, we hoped to evoke smiles of recognition, and in the latter, a sense of the variety of auditory experiences that are part of life on Earth. We wanted to use the microphone as the ear's camera in further enhancing Voyager's portrait of our planet and ourselves.

The world of our imagined extraterrestrials would be the result of a vastly different pattern of what Darwin described as "life's ever-branching and beautiful ramifications." The murmurs of such a place would be very unlike our own, and we might reasonably expect to share with its inhabitants only a few of the most fundamental geological, meteorological and possibly technological idioms. Indeed, the very idea of distinguishing between "musical" and "nonmusical" sounds posed a problem. We realized that elsewhere in the universe such a distinction would be even more blurred that it is here; perhaps cricket songs, a gavotte and the harbor-filling bray of an ocean liner's foghorn would seem of a piece to alien senses. Because we could not know how the message would be perceived by them, we decided to risk some fairly flagrant localisms in the interest of presenting as much about ourselves as possible.

The process of selecting the sounds began outside of Ithaca, New York, on a bright spring day that was auspiciously abuzz with wild May country noises. Timothy Ferris, Wendy Gradison and I joined the Sagans at their dining-room table for a vigorous round of group onomatopoeia. We tried to think of every sound we'd ever heard, and I wrote most of them down. On the following day I returned to New York City and set about trying to locate the best examples of each. I started by phoning sound libraries and universities all over North America.

"I understand that you have the finest recordings of croaking frogs" or "the meanest hyenas" or "the most devastating earthquake. How would I go about obtaining a copy?"

"For what purpose?" was the standard response.

"We're sending a record into interstellar space," I'd reply in what I judged to be my least manic voice. "And I'm trying to put together a suite of the sounds that we hear on Earth." This usually meant some empty long-distance static while I reeled off the corroborative phone numbers of federal agencies and well-known scientists. A great deal of skepticism was duly expressed, but not one person hung up before they'd heard the whole story.

And some of them were instantly engaged by the notion of Voyager's grand reach across space and time. Dr. Roger Payne of Rockefeller University was such a person. He was very excited by our desire to extend whale greetings on the record. When I told him that as a long overdue gesture of respect for these intelligent co-residents of Earth, we wished to include their salutations among those of the statesmen and diplomats, he was thrilled.

"Proper respect!" he cried. "Who is this? Oh, at last! Wonderful! You can have anything I have. I'll bring it to you myself. The most beautiful whale greeting was one we heard off the coast of Bermuda in 1970. That's the one that should last forever. Please send that one."

When we heard the tape, we were enchanted by its graceful exuberance, a series of expanding exultations so free and communicative of another way of moving and being on Earth. We listened to it many times and always with a feeling of irony that our imagined extraterrestrials of a billion years hence might grasp a message from fellow earthlings that had been incomprehensible to us.

Alan Botto of Princeton, New Jersey, was another friend of the project. Fred Durant of the Smithsonian Institution's National Air and Space Museum told me to call Mr. Botto for the "best rocket launch you ever heard." It turned out to be a rousing Saturn 5 lift-off recorded in a highly passionate Mission Control room, with a countdown, ignition roar, cheers, applause and the heartfelt wish "Fly, bird" blurted out by a man momentarily overwhelmed by what people can do. Botto also supplied us with a great hurtling freight train.

When I reached Mickey Kapp, president of Warner Special Products, he was in Rome on his vacation. A space enthusiast for many years, Mr. Kapp spoke of Jupiter and Saturn as if they were stations on an old commute. "Why, sure," he said from his room at the Excelsior to mine on West 74th, "you're welcome to all our sounds. Take as many as you want." He placed the entire Elektra Sound Archives at our disposal and hand-delivered the cuts we selected. It would have been impossible to complete the sound essay in such as short time without his very kind cooperation.

Some of the people who declined to participate cited their mistrust of any endeavor sponsored by the government. Others wanted substantial amounts of money in return for a moment's whoosh of the breeze through the trees or the rush of a river. We couldn't afford to give them much more than the cost of a reel of tape and return postage. One man who was reputed to have a wonderful collection of children's street cries threw me out of his office, shouting after me that NASA "had some nerve sending a little girl to talk to a big soundman like me." But almost everyone else was very nice and eager for a dab of the immortality that Voyager's unique passage to millions of years from now seemed to confer.

Timothy Ferris and I went to Washington, D.C., to meet with the Sagans and Murry Sidlin for a series of late-night musical repertoire conferences. During the day we visited the headquarters of the National Geographic Society, where we found some huffy orangutan grunts. We also went to the Library of Congress' Archive of Recorded Sound. It was there that we heard a terrible sound.

When we arrived, an engineer was waiting for us with a supermarket shopping cart full of records, some in jackets and others in torn manila sleeves. The engineer told us not to touch them. As he went through them, we were to point to the cuts that we wished to hear. Somewhere in among the wolves and the brine shrimp was a heavy lacquer disc of what is believed to be the first field recording ever made during a battle: an ugly repeating loop of a World War I skirmish in France with an American soldier urging a mustard-gas grenade launcher to fire. The soldier's voice seems horribly cheerful and thoughtless, as mechanical a sound as the answering hiccup of the poison canister. It drones at us from across sixty years, and Tim and I try to see what this man must have been seeing, but all we can manage is bits of war stolen from movies and some smoke.

We try to stop hearing it all day long. It's so tainting that we both hesitate before mentioning it to the others at dinner. This leads us into a discussion of just exactly how realistic a picture of life on Earth we wished to convey. Was the Voyager message to be a historical gesture or merely a social one?

Murry was adamant that we should send only the best of ourselves. And while none of us was absolutely convinced that the record would be incomplete without so vivid a demonstration of our imperfection as our violence, there was a feeling that being truthful was important in ways that might be momentarily obscured by culture. Most of the cherished beliefs of the previous decade turned flimsy in this one. And even now the prejudices of this particular moment lose their currency and change into something else. When we contemplated Voyager's inconceivable future, composed of maybe a million times ten years or sixty years, we despaired at knowing what the citizens of that age would understand or prize. If we showed ourselves as we really are, a species involved with struggle, wouldn't we at least be assured of the record's value as an accurate document?

We failed to come to any conclusion that evening. Instead, we drifted back into the debate about the musical repertoire. The next day Tim and I flew back to New York City and took my father to a Mets game. There were roughly sixty thousand people making noise at Shea Stadium. Several times I found myself shutting my eyes as tightly as I could to see what I could hear.

A week later, we had the fifty sounds we'd been looking for and we were ready to begin our work in the studio that CBS had provided for us. Our sound engineer was a calm, rusty-haired man in his early fifties named Russ Payne. He is a very patient man, a student of the Jain philosophy who speaks with a cowboy acccnt. During our breaks he would eat a piece of fruit, smoke a cigarette and talk about the life of the spirit. When we got to the part of the tape with the locomotive on it, he told us that his daddy has been an engineer and had taken him on some trains that sounded just like that onc.

A rock-and-roll sound prodigy from Brooklyn named Jimmy Iovine showed up a couple of times to raise the levels on the elephants and to check out the surf. He was very anxious to have a photograph taken of himself in front of the rocket ship. He said he wanted to give it to his mother. But the task of engineering the sound essay fell entirely to Russ and Tim. They used a sixteen-track Ampex.

There were many helpful suggestions made, most notably Tim's and Jon Lomberg's, as to how the sounds should be organized within the essay. I felt that it would be most informative to arrange them chronologically. We took many liberties within that very broad structure, but the fundamental direction of the montage is evolutionary: from the geological through the biological into the technological.

Since horsecarts, chopping wood, the hiss of bus brakes, and other sounds of our era take up as much time on the record as the rippling of primeval ponds, the sequence is open to the criticism that it, like our written history, vastly overemphasizes the last few thousand years at the expense of the millions that preceded them in the chronicle of our species. But if the sounds in the essay accurately reflected the time scale of Earth's four-and-a-half-billion-year story, all but the last few moments would have been only the gurgle of waves and the whisper of wind across barren plains; mammals would have to roar out all they had to roar in a few seconds, and the proud accomplishments of all human civilization would have expired in a single beep of Morse code. If the denizens of a distant planet can make sense of the essay—and arguably it may be the easiest part of the record for an alien intelligence to relate to—perhaps they will not be wholly unacquainted with the paradoxes time engenders, and will listen in a tolerant spirit.

Here are the Sounds of the Earth in sequential order:

1. *Music of the Spheres*

The essay begins with the giddy whirl of tones reflecting the motions of the Sun's planets in their orbits—a musical readout of Johannes Kepler's *Harmonica Mundi,* the sixteenth-century mathematical tract whose echoes may still be found in the formulas that make Voyager possible. Kepler's concept was realized on a computer at Bell Telephone Laboratories by composer Laurie Spiegel in collaboration with Yale professors John Rogers and Willie Ruff. Each frequency represents a planet; the highest pitch represents the motion of Mercury around the Sun as seen from Earth; the lowest frequency represents Jupiter's orbital motion. Inner planets circle the Sun more swiftly than outer planets. The particular segment that appears on the record corresponds to very roughly a century of planetary motion. Kepler was enamored of a literal "music of the spheres," and I think he would have loved their haunting representation here.

2. *Volcanoes, Earthquakes and Thunder*

A series of rumblings to signify the dramatic upheavals of our planet's early history, including a rare tape of a 1971 Australian earthquake, obtained from Dr. David Simpson of the Lamont-Doherty Geological Laboratories. Most of the Earth's atmosphere is thought to have been outgassed through volcanoes, fumaroles and cracks in the surface of our planet in the first few hundred million years of geological time. Chemical reactions induced by solar ultraviolet light and electrical storms initiated a sequence of chemical reactions that led eventually to the origin of life.

3. *Mud Pots*

Geological gurgling sounds similar to the glub-glub of chocolate pudding on a stove—suggestive, we hoped, of simmering life.

4. Wind, Rain and Surf

A momentary evocation of the hundreds of millions of years when these were the only Sounds of Earth, with special emphasis on the oceans as the scene of our origins. The oceans themselves were out-gassed from the Earth's interior.

5. Crickets, Frogs

Intended to betoken the debut of vociferous life on earth, most of these sounds were taken from the CBS library, with the exception of one adult male cricket, *Teleogryllus oceanicus,* who is performing a solo serenade to the females. He was recorded by Dr. Ronald R. Hoy at the Langmuir Laboratory at Cornell University.

6. Birds, Hyena and Elephant

A chorus of creatures to suggest the developing varieties of fauna as Earth gets really busy with life.

7. Chimpanzee

The voice of a lone primate rises above the others and seems to screech its mad announcement of a new consciousness.

8. Wild Dog

A lonely baying that reverberates with the dangers and uncertainties of our beginnings.

9. Footsteps, Heartbeats and Laughter

A human being makes its first appearance, walking erect with its hands free to change the world.

10. Fire and Speech

Humans begin to use fire to alter their environment, and the hearth becomes, perhaps, the site of the birth of language and culture. The words are those of Professor Richard Lee of the University of Toronto extending greetings in the !Kung language of the Kalahari Bushmen, one of the last representatives of the hunter-gatherer societies that sus-tained the human endeavor for almost all our several-million-year history. A photograph of Bushman hunters is included as item 60 of the picture sequence.

11. *The First Tools*

Our upright posture left our hands free for manipulating the environment. A critical moment in human history occurred when the first stone tools were made out of soft rock more than two million years ago. Enormous numbers of stone-cutting, flaking, penetrating and pounding tools are found in many paleolithic sites. We wished to include the sound of stone on stone, of stone tools in the course of being fashioned. Carl walked the streets of midtown New York in a poignant effort to find two suitable rocks; not only were there no suitable rocks, there were no rocks of any sort to be found. He called Alexander Marshack of the Museum of Comparative Zoology at Harvard for recommendations on a source of soft rock and a short description of the method of manufacturing stone tools. Linda Sagan then obtained appropriate flint samples from Dr. Ralph Solecki of the Department of Anthropology, Columbia University, who also provided thick gloves and goggles: flint is sharp, and there must have been many accidents attendant to the ancient manufacture of tools. The record includes this satisfying sound of flint fracturing and crumbling when struck sharply with another rock. Some of the results would have made adequate, although rudimentary, knives and spears.

12. *Tame Dog*

The dog is heard to bark again, but this time all traces of menace are gone; animals have been domesticated. Almost every sound that follows on the essay is the result of human activity. Dogs are represented as items 43, 61 and 68 of the picture sequence.

13. *Herding Sheep, Blacksmith Shop, Sawing, Tractor and Riveter*

A suite of agricultural and construction sounds. We tested several roosters and cows, but they all sounded terribly stagy.

14. *Morse Code*

When it came time to decide what message within the message we would be sending in Morse code, Carl immediately suggested *Ad astra per aspera*—To the stars through difficulties. William R. Schoppe, Jr. (WB2FWS), a ham radio operator at CBS, was kind enough to tap it out for us.

15. *Ships, Horse and Cart, Train, Truck, Tractor, Bus, Automobile, F-111 Flyby, Saturn 5 Lift-Off*

A great many human miles are covered in this transportation sequence. The horse and cart start out on a dirt road and end up on a paved one. The transition modes from there on come very quickly and reflect accurately the astonishing pace of progress in the development of transportation over the last hundred years. The train and the supersonic aircraft convey in stereo a satisfying sense of motion. This sequence roughly parallels pictures 102, 105, and 113.

16. *Kiss*

This wonderful sound proved to be the most difficult to record. We were under strict orders from NASA to keep it heterosexual, and within such a constraint we tried every permutation we could think of without success. Jimmy Iovine happened to show up that day, and he was most anxious to produce a believable kiss by sucking his arm. But this was to be that impossible thing, a kiss that would last forever, and we wanted it to be real. After many unusable kisses that were either too faint or too smacky, Tim kissed me softly on the cheek; it felt and sounded fine.

17. *Mother and Child*

The very first cries of an infant and the stilling of a six-month-old's cries by his mother were provided for us through the courtesy of Dr. Margaret Bullowa and Dr. Lise Menn of M.I.T.

18. *Life Signs*

We know that EEG patterns register some changes in thought. Would it be possible, I wondered, for a highly advanced technology of several million years from now to decipher my thoughts? On the chance that it might be, I contacted Dr. Julius Korein of the New York University Medical Center, and with Tim's help we set up a recording session for my innermost self. Using a medical-data recorder attached to an audiotape recorder, I was left to meditate alone in a room for an hour while the workings of my brain, heart, eyes and muscles were being re-corded. A short segment of the graphs of my vital signs appears below.

Despite the fact that there was only a tiny chance that my mind would ever be read in this way, the course of my thoughts seemed to me to be worthy of serious consideration. I made a sort of mental itiner-ary of the ideas and individuals of history whose memory I hoped to per-petuate, and with the exception of a couple of irrepressible facts of my own life, I managed to stick to it pretty well. The hour was electronically compressed into a minute, and it is a fierce sound, something like a string of exploding firecrackers.

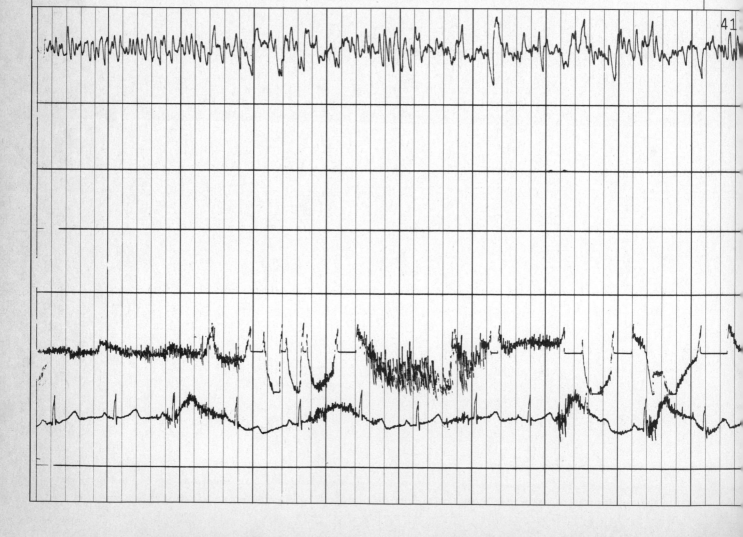

41

19. *Pulsar*

The concluding moment of the essay sounds ironically like the rasp of a phonograph needle left to languish unattended at the end of a record. It is in fact a recording of a quickly varying natural radio source some 600 light-years away from us and designated CP1133. It was provided for us by Frank Drake and Amahl Shakhashiri of the National Astronomy and Ionosphere Center. The regularity of the pulsar beat was considered, when the first pulsar was discovered, to be a sign of intelligent life (although we now know that pulsars are rapidly rotating neu-

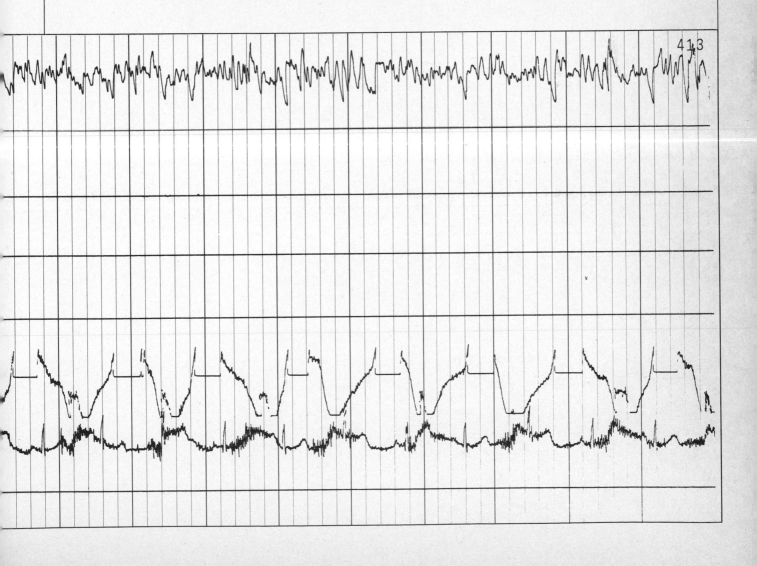

413

tron stars). My recorded life signs sound a little like recorded radio static from the depths of space. The electrical signatures of a human being and a star seem, in such recordings, not so different, and symbolize our relatedness and indebtedness to the cosmos.

Nineteen hundred years ago Horace wrote that "words challenge eternity." The fact that we recall his epigram proves him right. We have no way of knowing how much of this beautiful planet will have been obliterated long before Voyager ceases its wandering; how many of the voices celebrated on this record will have been silenced forever by our carelessness or merely by time. Voyager moves among the stars, bearing its cargo of echoes and images, and, in the logic of such distances, it keeps us alive.

6
VOYAGER'S MUSIC,
by Timothy Ferris

As the eyes are framed for astronomy so the ears are framed for the movements of harmony.

—*Plato,* Republic

Music is the harmony of heaven and earth.

—*Chinese musical text*
Yueh-chi, second century
B.C.

I. Choosing the Music

The world's music—from the sun chants of ancient Egypt and the "celestial orchestras" of the Buddhists to the frequency with which the words "moon" and "stars" crop up in Western popular songs—is dotted with themes inspired by the sights of the night skies, when the sun withdraws and we are permitted to view the broader scheme of things. Now eighty-seven and a half minutes of music have been dispatched to the stars, aboard Voyager, as if in token payment against that debt of inspiration. We wanted to send music of a quality compatible with the elegance of such a heritage, and with enough variety to hint at something of the diversity of Earth's peoples.

In the service of this ambition, we established two criteria. First, contributions from a wide range of cultures should be included, not just music familiar to the society that launched the spacecraft. Second, nothing should be included out of merely dutiful concerns; every selection should touch the heart as well as the mind. As the musicologist Robert Brown wrote early in the project, "If we don't send things we passionately care for, why send them at all?"

We recognized that we could hope to meet the first criterion imperfectly at best. In addition to our own cultural biases and the time constraints of the record, we had to contend with the sharp drop in information that imposes itself when one looks beyond one's own culture. Thousands of recordings of Bach's music are available in the West, but only a few recordings of Georgian choruses or African pygmy songs; we have the benefit of many examples of the virtuosity of Glenn Gould, but almost none of the work of the Chinese ch'in player Kuan P'ing-hu; our appreciation of Stravinsky is aided by his writing, but the words of the composers of Javanese gamelan music are lost. Earth may be one of many worlds, but it also contains many worlds.

To the extent that we succeeded in presenting music of non-Western cultures—half of the Voyager record is theirs—we owe our success to the cooperation of Brown, Alan Lomax and other friends and advisers. Only a handful of persons devote themselves to recording and understanding the music of societies remote from their own. Most work with inadequate funds, in a climate of indifference born of the misapprehension that the art of one's own culture is better than that of others.

The second criterion, that we feel deeply about all we put on the record, naturally produced differences of opinion. Some of us were more moved by classical music, East and West, than by what is called "folk" music. Others felt the opposite way. All those involved in selecting the music—the core personnel were Carl and Linda Sagan, novelist Ann Druyan and me, but at various times the committee involved a number of others—lost some favorite piece along the way: Carl had championed a piece by Debussy, Alan Lomax a quiet song by a Sicilian sulfur miner, I Bach's Passacaglia and Fugue. The latter two lost out because of time problems, the former by virtue of a decision in the case of Western classical music to concentrate on several compositions by the same composers, Bach and Beethoven, in hopes of facilitating "decoding" by extraterrestrial listeners. Any disappointment over music excluded was compensated by excitement over music included; to select from all the world's music is to realize dreams of harmless plunder.

The decision to cut the record at $16^2/_3$ revolutions per minute rather than $33^1/_3$, tripling the amount of time available for music, came rather late in the project, with the result that everything had to be chosen and assembled within less than two months. In soliciting suggestions, we found ourselves in the position of saying we were putting together a record that would last a billion years, but needed ideas *today*. People proved understanding, and proffered hundreds of recordings. Some of these promptly established themselves in the repertoire—for example, Surshri Kesar Bai Kerkar's performance of the Indian raga, recommended independently by two musicologists, and the ch'in composition "Flowing Streams." We were still making choices hours before the record was cut. At the last minute Carol Kulig had located the Georgian chorus "Tchakrulo," which everyone recognized would be an excellent substitute for a far more derivative piece of Soviet music that had persisted in the repertoire for weeks. The problem was that "Tchakrulo" is sung in Georgian. None of us could understand the words. Lomax located a Georgian living in Queens, a gracious gentleman named Sandro Baratheli, who came to the studio on the morning when the lacquer masters of the record were to be cut. He listened to the song. Lighting a cigarette, he discoursed on the folk music of East Georgia. It

Music on Voyager
(prepared by Susan S. Lang)

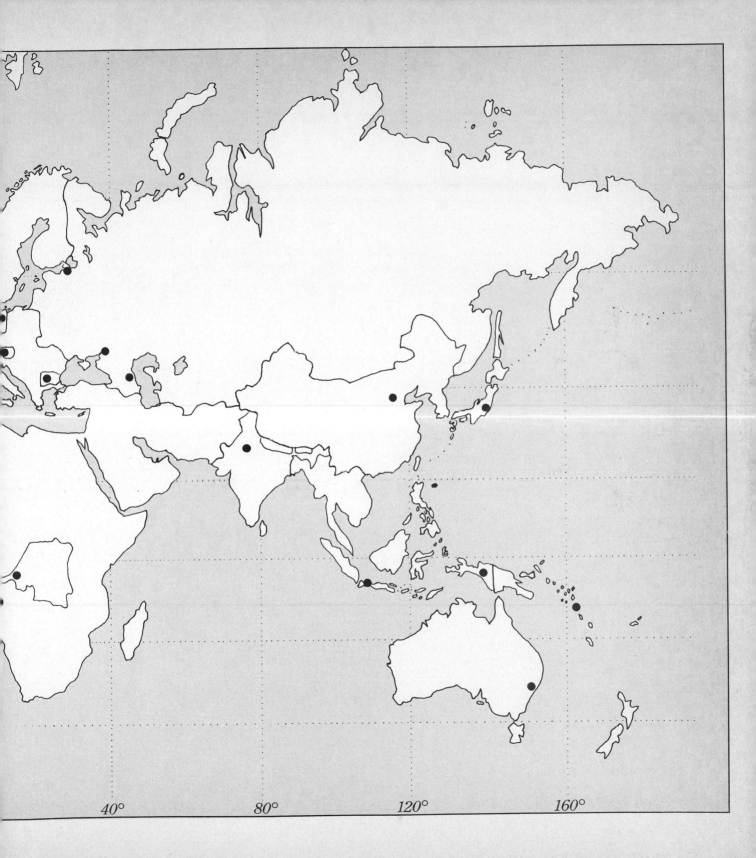

was fascinating, but engineers were waiting upstairs in the cutting room, and when they were through, the masters had to be flown immediately to Los Angeles to be made into metal discs to go on the spacecraft.

"Yes, Mr. Baratheli," we interrupted, "but what do the words *say*?"

Baratheli was not to be rushed. He had a healthy Georgian disdain for American urgency. Eventually he explained that the words constituted a protest by peasants against a local landowner. The song was spirited and undoctrinaire, in the Georgian tradition of tough-minded independence. We jumped up with signs of relief—it was an old song, and for all we knew could have celebrated bear-baiting—the engineer spliced the tape onto the master reel and we went upstairs.

The record imposed unusual demands on engineers in the cutting studio. To inscribe the data of the photographs into the grooves with minimum distortion, a Honeywell data recorder was plugged directly into the cutting board. The day before, it had been discovered that the photographic data ran ten minutes longer than expected. The problem was solved in telephone calls with Frank Drake and Honeywell engineers, during which we worked out a method of inscribing two channels of picture data simultaneously, one on either wall of the record's stereo groove. Even with this improvement, timings were close, and not until the first lacquer was complete were we certain that the computer-driven cutting lathe, reprogrammed to work at half speed, could squeeze everything onto the disc.* When the masters had been cut, an engineer etched into the space between the lead-out grooves near the center a dedication written a month before on the back of a manila envelope during one of our listening sessions: "To the makers of music—all worlds, all times."

---

*The outcome of cutting the record at $16^2/_3$ r.p.m. is respectable, if not superlative, fidelity. Frequency response over most of the disc is 20–15,000 Hertz, plus or minus two decibels, falling off six decibels by about 17,000 Hertz; in the crowded inner grooves the roll-off by 15,000 Hertz reaches six decibels. Channel separation averages forty decibels. Extraterrestrial students might note, among the other quaint charms of the recording, that some of its selections are monophonic, some stereophonic. This state of affairs is open to the correct interpretation—that sound recording is a recent development on Earth—but also to incorrect interpretations—e.g., that some of the music was composed by a species having only one ear.

Sometimes I wonder whether other spacecraft with artifacts aboard, the products of other civilizations, are drifting among the stars. It would be rather surprising if in the ten or fifteen billion years of our galaxy's history we were the only creatures ever to have launched interstellar spacecraft. In any event it is pleasing to think that ours was the planet, or one of the planets, that chose to dispatch music.

We don't know whether human music will mean anything to nonhuman intelligences on other planets. But any creature who comes across Voyager and recognizes the record as an artifact can realize that it was dispatched with no hope of return. *That* gesture may speak more clearly than music. The record says: However primitive we seem, however crude this spacecraft, we knew enough to envision ourselves citizens of the cosmos. It says: However small we were, something in us was large enough to want to reach out to discoverers unknown, in times when we shall have perished or have changed beyond recognition. It says: Whoever and whatever you are, we too once lived in this house of stars, and we thought of you.

II. The Music

Bach

The musical culture of which Bach was beneficiary and greatest exemplar arose from the codification of music, the organization of institutions to train and support musicians, the perfection of such major instruments as church organs and the violin, and the successful incorporation, within this structure, of musical influences arriving from as far away as Asia. Its roots were to be found in a folk music that had sprung up almost as naturally as, and not independently of, the harvests of European farms. From the Middle Ages to the Renaissance, music was channeled and refined and put to the service of human edification, almost as we today garner and refine oil from wells. The result was one of the most musically organized societies the world has ever seen. Every court, church and university of any consequence in Bach's day proclaimed itself in music.

We see through the lens of Bach's art both his and older times.

Looking backward, Bernard Jacobson writes: "What really lies behind Bach's writing is a whole polyphonic tradition rooted in the choral masterpieces of the sixteenth century, of Palestrina and his school. These in turn have their origin, on the liturgical side, in the ancient system of Georgian tomes and, on the secular side, in the medieval manifestations of European folk-music." Looking forward, we find that Bach's sense of analysis and organization, his desire to get at the root of everything in music and set it down on paper, precursed strains that run through our art and our whole society today. He was so coolly calculating in theory that his music still sounds modern, and a piano player today can get away with the parlor trick of representing a Bach composition as something new.

The two strains, new and old, represent themselves today in a seesaw preference for the "mind" as against the "heart" of Bach. The mind is championed regularly, in musicological analyses that might have pure mathematics as their subject rather than music. The heart is championed in more emotional language, as in these words by the harpsichordist Wanda Landowska: "Let us not be afraid of the supreme contrapuntal sciences of the fugues, nor be overawed by the stern appearance and heavy wig of Father Bach. Let us gather around him, feel the love, the noble goodness that flow from each one of his phrases and that envigorate and bind us by ties strong and warm."

The process of consolidation that made Bach's music possible goes on today, not only in art but in other fields, including the technology that made Voyager possible. Humans have yet to decide whether it is a good thing. The rise of art music in Germany gave the nobility Haydn, Telemann, Bach, Mozart and Beethoven, but nearly killed off the folk music of the untitled. Today one branch of technology (radio and the phonograph record) has made art music available to ordinary people, while other branches exploit natural resources of the many in the service of a few. It may not be too far-fetched to suggest that those who think this a worthwhile bargain are inclined toward Bach's "mind," while those who suspect we are on the wrong path look to Bach's "heart." From either perspective he is a nearly universal composer, at least in earthly terms. Three of his compositions went aboard Voyager.

Prelude and Fugue in C from The Well-Tempered Clavier, *Book 2*
By Bach's day, the capacities of the system of tuning traditionally in

use had come to be strained by refinements in musical instruments and by the practice of assembling growing numbers of musicians to perform works of increasing complexity. Pythagorean tuning, a legacy of the Greeks, worked well for melodies and for harmonies played in a few keys, but the more ambitious Baroque composers found it fettering.

The problem was that some disharmony is intrinsic to the octave, the basic unit of Western music. Every method of tuning has to put it somewhere. In Pythagorean tuning, certain intervals, the major thirds and major sixths, were sacrificed to disharmony so that others, the fifths, could be tuned perfectly. Composers avoided writing harmonies in the dissonant intervals. By the early sixteenth century, composers had begun to experiment with parceling out the inherent disharmony more equitably, all along the octave. No one interval would sound with Pythagorean purity, but music could be written in a full range of harmonies and in any key, without having to avoid the dangerous shoals of the major thirds and sixths. Few listeners noticed the disharmonies when they were spread thin.

Various systems were proposed to deploy the disharmonies more or less equally along the octave. All were called "tempering," meaning that they moderated the dissonance by diluting it. The secondary tones generated by the harpsichord, clavichord and piano tended to mask the moderate inequities that resulted, suiting these instruments for displays of the virtues of tempering. It is not known which system of tempering Bach favored, or for which instruments he wrote *The Well-Tempered Clavier,* but the work clearly was intended to show the freedom and flexibility tempering had to offer.*

Book 1, twenty-four preludes and fugues in keys climbing up through the octave, was published in 1722. More than twenty years later, Bach repeated the task with twenty-four more preludes and fugues. By this time the question of tuning had been settled in favor of the even-tempered approach, and composition of the second book was probably motivated less by didactic purpose than by Bach's passion for design. The second set of compositions has come to be designated Book 2 of *The Well-Tempered Clavier,* although Bach himself did not so title it.

---

*Tempering appears to have been discovered independently in some other cultures, notably by Hsu Tsai-yu in China in about 1596.

The prelude developed from the interval prior to a concert when musicians tune their instruments. From it came the overture and the prelude employed in church organ music, and the prelude associated with the fugue in secular works. Bach elevated the form to a new prominence, exploring new comparisons between a prelude and its fugue. In the C Major, the prelude, intricate and subtle, is attached to a fugue of contrasting simplicity. Bach had borrowed the subject of the fugue from an earlier composer, halved its time, and expanded upon its subject. The four voices of the prelude and the three of the fugue work at close quarters, dashing out in displays of freedom while retaining a discipline pleasing for being so obviously voluntary. Wanda Landowska compared the fugue's gait to that of a well-trained thoroughbred, able to run but prepared to draw up short at a command.

Gavotte en rondeaux from the Partita No. 3 in E Major for Violin

Here is an example of art music arising from folk music. The gavotte was a traditional French dance. Polyphonic fiddle-playing was an old German custom; the fiddler often sat at a small organ, working the foot pedals as accompaniment. Bach employs the gavotte as a round and elaborates the simple dance melody polyphonically. The effect of multiple voices is achieved by what has been called "implied polyphony." Snatches of bass line are posted like signs along a roadway, with such skill that the listener's mind fills in the line well beyond what is actually being played. On a less analytic level, the piece reveals that Bach remained sensitive to the uncomplicated pleasures associated with this old dance. The melody itself has great charm.

Like the ch'in composition on the Voyager record, Bach's six sonatas and partitas for solo violin challenge a solitary musician working with a somewhat recalcitrant instrument to create music that opens out to the horizons. In the success of composer and performer, national boundaries fade, so that in this piece, for example, the influences of French music upon the theme, and of Italian technique upon the method of playing, are absorbed and transformed into music that almost supersedes nationality.

The Gavotte en rondeaux is highly compressed, a characteristic it shares with several other selections on the Voyager record, among them "El Cascabel," "Johnny B. Goode," the New Guinea men's house song, "Flowing Streams," the first movement of Beethoven's Fifth

Symphony, and Bach's Prelude and Fugue. The Voyager spacecraft is a compact object, designed with weight a major consideration, and the music on the record seems to reflect some of the same imperatives. There is something satisfying about an artist's making stringent demands upon time.

Brandenburg Concerto No. 2 in F, First Movement

The music section of the Voyager record begins on this note of energetic optimism. We have no grounds to suppose that an extraterrestrial listener would recognize human optimism or pessimism, or for that matter human "music" as such, and so to permit ourselves emotional considerations in choosing music for an interstellar artifact represents an act of faith. But what else could we do? We began the music with Bach.

He wrote the Brandenburg concertos at the age of thirty-six, during one of the happiest periods of his life, when he enjoyed the friendship of a sympathetic patron, Prince Leopold, and when the death of his wife Maria Barbara still lay in the future. Bach was familiar with the concerto grosso form as it had developed in the hands of Corelli, Vivaldi and others, but as usual he was ill content to work entirely within existing boundaries, and viewed the commission as an opportunity to both innovate and sum up. Bach's taste in innovation lay not in shattering existing forms, but in demonstrating unexpected resources within them, in the manner of a haiku poet.

Bach's talent for polyphony, demonstrated in two voices in the violin partita and in three and four voices in the Prelude and Fugue in C, is exemplified here in the tonal richness of the orchestra. Albert Schweitzer was prompted to call the Brandenburg concerti "the purest product of Bach's polyphonic style."

In the opening eight bars, the recorder, oboe, solo violin and first violins play in unison beneath trills from the trumpet and viola to introduce the theme of the concerto, announced by the solo violin. The oboe and then the recorder take up the theme. A variation on the trumpet follows, in the onset of one of those hill-and-valley chases that make Bach's allegro movements invigorating. A semiquaver bass accompaniment of the early bars has meanwhile been transformed into a solo theme on the trumpet, and a harmonic line that appeared originally on the viola has descended to become the bass. This is the sort of effect that we get throughout the movement, and it is pure Bach—diversity within order, wit within discipline, the music passing like a caravan of dancing acrobats reciting poetry.

The second Brandenburg pressed the art of trumpet playing to its limit, and considerable scholarship has been expended to determine just how trumpets of the time were constructed if, without the aid of valves, they were to play it. Bach was forced to concede that some trumpet figures he would have liked could not be played; the concerto theme is altered in bars 21 and 22 of the first movement as a concession to the limitations of the instrument. This departure from plan, detectable to anyone who analyzes the music, might prove interesting to musical scholars in remote times or places.

Javanese Gamelan

"Kinds of Flowers"

At first sight, a gamelan—the word means orchestra—looks like a vision of the Industrial Revolution gone off in a joyful direction. The chief material is bronze. The instruments are percussive. They describe shapes suggestive variously of cooking pots, steam boilers, oil drums and railroad engines. A full gamelan looks as if it could haul a dozen freight cars through a mountain pass if the cosmos were put together a little differently. The gamelan has been put together, however, not to make time but music.

The sound, chiefly bell and gong tones, resembles rain in slow motion. Increase the tempo and the rain turns to wind. The singing is full and unaffected, the work of people with both eyes on the present. Rhythms sound in accordance with tone, shorter intervals on high instruments, longer intervals on deeper instruments; some big brass gongs, larger than a man, are struck rather rarely. Once assembled, orchestras are named and an effort is made to keep them together for some time. Gamelans a century or more old are not uncommon.

Western interest in gamelan dates from at least 1899, when Claude Debussy heard one in Paris. The music is beautiful but can take some getting used to. The nineteenth-century Dutch East India Company ambassador who reported that "music in the East is still in its cradle and is practiced only upon very simple and monotonous instruments" was echoed by a NASA attorney who in 1977, upon hearing "Kinds of Flowers," a piece in which rhythm plays something of the role that prophecy plays in *King Lear,* volunteered, "I can detect no *rhythm* in this piece whatsoever."

How this unique music sprang up in Java and in its neighboring island Bali is not fully understood. Hindu colonists brought bronze percussive instruments with them to Java, but bronze drums had been in use on the island before the Hindus arrived. Chinese and Indian musicians reached Java, but no one is certain how they might have generated music so markedly different from their own. The popularity of pentatonic (five-tone) tuning in gamelan has been offered as evidence of Chinese authorship, but pentatonic tuning turns up all over the world.

"Kinds of Flowers" is a *ketawang,* or short, gamelan piece, performed here with an orchestra of about thirty-five players and perhaps a dozen singers. It was recorded January 10, 1971, in the reception hall of one of the four major royal courts of central Java by Robert Brown, now director of the American Society for Eastern Arts, Center for World Music, in Berkeley, California. The words, sung with unstrained gusto, refer to two of nine sorts of flowers symbolic in Javanese Hinduism of the nine *rasas,* or moods. The piece ends with a flex in rhythm, a short acceleration followed by a ritard.

Pygmy Girls' Initiation Song

The pygmies of the Ituri forest in Zaire, Africa, constitute one of nature's many examples that strength can wear the cloak of weakness. A friendly people, they have welcomed Sudanese, Bantu, Arab and Western travelers. They have no government and settle differences by friendly discussion, say anthropologists who have lived with them. They discourage competition and encourage cooperation. In one pygmy game, half a dozen children climb a young sapling until the top bends to the ground, then all jump off at once. If one child jumps too soon, it spoils the game. If one holds on too long, attempting to demonstrate a superior bravery, he or she is launched through the air. The pygmies have no priests and display little formal religion beyond a reverence for the rain forest. Their philosophy is one of acceptance. In a song about night in the forest, they remind themselves that "if darkness is, then darkness is good." Nomads, they rarely occupy any one site for more than a few months. Living in this fashion, they have occupied the Ituri forest since at least the twenty-fifth century B.C., when their presence was recorded by Fourth Dynasty Egyptians.

Today, as when the Egyptians wrote of them, the Mbuti (as Ituri pygmies collectively are called) erect no monuments, show little interest in the visual arts, and rarely play musical instruments. Their joy lies in storytelling, song and dance.

Not surprisingly, these arts have become highly refined. The Mbuti sing some songs by assigning one note to each singer in a circle, so the melody spins around at a dizzying rate. Others are done as rounds, the parts sometimes orbiting in opposite directions. Close harmony in parallel seconds is common, sometimes sung by dancers who dance very close together, almost touching, as if to illustrate the structure of the music. The Mbuti sing polyphonically and have been observed to incorporate into songs the echo of their voices bouncing off the trees of the rain forest.

The Voyager selection comes from an *alima,* or girl's puberty initiation rite. The word is derived from *lima,* the Bantu term for moon, as the rite marks a girl's first menstrual period. (The pygmies appear to have lost their original language, and they incorporate words adapted from their neighbors.) This *alima* song was recorded by the anthropologist Colin Turnbull, who lived with the Mbuti for six years. As Turnbull describes the ceremony: "For the pygmies it's a time of enormous joy when a young girl gets her first menstrual period. It's announced to the whole world. Her family is congratulated, because now she can be a mother, and what greater joy for a girl? At the same time they recognize the increased responsibility, because among the Mbuti, no child may be born out of wedlock. In fifty years of field work, anthropologists have found no documented case of any child being born out of wedlock there. When a girl first menstruates, she will sometimes wait for a friend to also have her first period, and then the two of them invite their friends, both older and younger, to join them in an *alima* house where they live for a month.

"During this time, boys who come to court them may enter the *alima* house and sleep with the girls of their choice, but only with the approval of both the girls and their mothers. The mothers guard the house and prevent any undesirable youths from entering; they will give any such youth a good fight. Once inside, a youth may sleep with one or a number of girls by mutual agreement. It's considered a time of experimentation, with long-range marriage in view. Until this time sexual intercourse was merely pleasurable; now it is also a responsibility.

"The boys and girls talk and think in terms of both physical and emotional satisfaction, and usually, though not always, a marriage results from the *alima* experience. Divorce is a rarity. . . . Once a couple is absolutely certain that they are fitted as life partners, the boy makes a nominal gift to the girl's parents—it may be a bow and arrow— and if this is accepted he will then present a large antelope he has killed himself as an indication of his ability to fill the role of hunter. If the girl's parents accept these gifts, the boy and the girl then set up a household together.

"The *alima* is one of the most joyous festivals in the Mbuti culture because it concerns itself with life and with the responsibilities of parenthood.

"These people are among the most primitive in the world," Turnbull adds. "They have no stone tools. They use only bamboo and other forest products. Yet in terms of human relationships and their ability to control those relationships for the benefit of society as a whole, I very soberly, out of both personal experience and academic judgment, believe them to be vastly more advanced than we are. I mean no criticism of ourselves. It merely shows that as civilization has progressed, our problems have become so complex that we can't afford the human considerations that to the Mbuti are foremost."

Senegalese Percussion

The music of Africa displays the imprint of a people who migrated south some two thousand years ago, whose language presaged Bantu, and whose influence on all the arts lent the continent a semblance of unity. We find it today in the regular company of travel and labor, the rhythms of music and motion—an old tapestry still being woven.

The African emphasis on rhythm in music has been interpreted, even by some relatively sympathetic students, as evidence of primitivism. The argument, which satisfied political as well as aesthetic predispositions, was that African percussion betokened a culture that had yet to discover the superior charms of refined melody and harmony. This misapprehension can be laid to rest on at least two grounds. First, African music contains plenty of melody and harmony, some of it extremely sophisticated; the pygmy song on Voyager offers one of many examples. Second, studies using electronic data-processing techniques to analyze hundreds of recordings of African music indicate that it evolved as a matter of preference, in the hands of people who experimented with a wide variety of the world's music; in other words, ignorance of alternatives appears to have played no important role in African musical history.

This recording, made in Senegal in 1963 by Charles Duvelle, is of music played to accompany field work. The instruments are drums, bells, and three flutes, the flutes employed exclusively for punctuation. Listening to it calls to mind a line from the *Li Chi,* the first century A.D. Chinese book on music: "Music creates joy. . . . Man cannot exist without joy, and joy cannot exist without movement."

Mexican Mariachi

"El Cascabel"

This express-train rendition of a popular old Mexican song is performed by Lorenzo Barcelata and the Mariachi México. Barcelata comes from Michoacán, a state on the central Pacific coast of Mexico whose black population has influenced music of the region. The swapping of solos is characteristically Mediterranean, but the rapidity of the trade-off and the overlapping of the parts is African. It is also characteristic of American jazz and rhythm and blues. Its effect in "El Cascabel" is energetic. Barcelata's mariachi orchestra, despite its impressive size and full tone, seems agile as a school of flying fish.

After an opening flourish on fiddles and horns to establish the theme, Barcelata sings with Spanish bravura. The song is based on a double entendre ("What a pretty bell, my dear/Who gave it to you?/ . . . If you want to sell it to me, I'll give you a kiss"), but the words, familiar to most Mexican listeners, have only secondary importance.

Barcelata's voice quickly gives way to a soaring fiddle run full of rhythmic variations and punctuated by trumpets. The back-up vocalists take a turn, with flutes above; then comes a seesaw set of fiddles in a descending run. Guitars and gitarrones pump out rhythm with the energy of men shoveling coal to save a sinking ship. Cornets and fiddles join in a rapid exchange. The voices, all male, end on a ritard in the descending figure described by the fiddles and trumpets. It seems to be over almost as quickly as it began.

Blind Willie Johnson

"Dark Was the Night"

Out of the enslavement of Africans arose a strain of music in America that has captured the affection of the twentieth-century world. Specialists debate where the seams of definition lie between blues, jazz, jitterbug, and rock-and-roll, but all are cut from the same cloth, three bolts of which are aboard Voyager.

If we wished to challenge Gertrude Stein's assertion that "one does not in one's heart believe in mute inglorious Miltons," a good place to start would be the Depression-era South and its music called, for good reason, the blues. Nearly every Southern city supported—if that is the word—black blues singers whose music could be heard on street corners and in churches and bars. For these singers, the critical assessment of passers-by could mean the difference between shelter and sleeping in the street; it is no accident that of the handful whose songs were recorded, the best were very good indeed, and that their legacy of poetry and music has been drawn upon by Western popular composers ever since.

Johnson was born in Marlin, Texas, within a year or two of the turn of the century. He was blinded by his stepmother, who in a rage dashed a pan of lye in his face when he was seven years old. His mid-twenties found him surviving on the streets of Dallas on the strength of his guitar playing and powerful voice. Like several other accomplished blind blues singers, he managed through his music to attract and marry a devoted woman. Her name was Angeline. They married in 1927 and remained together until his death in the winter of 1949.

Johnson was a master of slide guitar playing, a technique in which the guitar is tuned to an open chord and the strings stopped by sliding a bottleneck or other hard object over them; Johnson used a pocketknife. Slide playing gave the guitar a melodic flexibility reminiscent of a fiddle's, and lent it a metallic edge that helped it cut through street noise.

"Dark Was the Night" is based on an old Scots long-meter hymn. For this version, recorded in Dallas, December 3, 1927, Johnson altered the melody and replaced the lyrics with a wordless moan. The result, I feel, is one of the most fundamentally moving pieces of music ever recorded.

Johnson died of pneumonia in Beaumont, Texas. His house had burned, obliging him and Angeline to sleep on a waterlogged bed. In Angeline's words, "We had a—we burnt out there in the North End . . . and when we burnt out, why, we didn't know many people, and so I just, you know, drug him back in there, and we laid on the wet bed covers—with a lot of newspaper. It didn't bother me, but it bothered him. Yes. You see, he'd turn over. And I just lay up on the paper. And I thought if you put a lot of paper on, you know, that it would, you know, keep us from getting sick. We didn't get wet, but just the dampness. You know, and then he's singing, you know, and his veins opened, and everything. And it just made him, you know, sick. . . . [The hospital] wouldn't accept him. He'd-a been living today if they'd accepted him. 'Cause he's blind. Blind folks has a hard time—you can't get in the hospital. . . ."

Johnson's song concerns a situation he faced many times, nightfall with no place to sleep. Since humans appeared on Earth, the shroud of night has yet to fall without touching a man or woman in that same plight.

Louis Armstrong

"Melancholy Blues"

The year that Blind Willie Johnson recorded "Dark Was the Night," Louis Armstrong made a series of recordings in New York that were to transform jazz. Music is no monarchy, and Armstrong evidenced no pleasure in the title "King of Jazz" bestowed on him by critics, but it is difficult to find a more influential twentieth-century musician in any field.

His persistent optimism and his latter-day success encouraged us to forget that his childhood was harsh. His father left home when Louis was five, and the boy was brought up partly in the New Orleans Waif's Home. In his autobiography Armstrong writes that his first girlfriend, his first wife and possibly his mother were prostitutes. As to the level of violence in the community, he recalled cheefully, "I ain't never seen so much knife wailing. Toe-to-toe. One take a slice there, the other take a slice here. Man! Mary Jack died of it."

The solvent was music. "Music all around you," Armstrong said. "The pie man and the waffle man, they all had a little hustle to attract the people. Pie man used to swing something on the bugle and the waffle man rang a big triangle." There were men's lodge bands, marching bands, dance bands, and on Saturday and Sunday afternoons, jazz bands rolled through the streets playing from flatbed wagons. (Armstrong speculated that the phrase "on the wagon" to designate sobriety dated from the New Orleans musicians' decision whether to accept a wagon gig or drink all weekend.)

Alan Lomax describes his view of the evolution of New Orleans jazz this way: "The late 1800s were hard times for blacks in the South, especially in New Orleans, because that's where blacks had nearly seized power. There had been a lot of killing done. What little was left of their power was concentrated in early New Orleans black lodges. They organized marching bands to play at funerals. How could people stop you from holding a funeral? Everybody's got to have a funeral.

"The interesting thing is that horns in a polyrhythmic relation to drums is the principal orchestral form in Africa, and in putting together these lodge bands the New Orleans blacks went back to their ancestral roots. Their bands were full of horns and drums. They seized upon curved horns and straight horns and trombones, and they *spoke* through them. It was a language, and also an assertion of male strength and power. Black males were marching again, as if they were back in Africa. They hadn't been able to do that during the whole of slavery.

"The Africans were accustomed to using their instruments in a talking fashion, making them speak, and Louis, of all the great musicians, was the one who actually *sang* through his horn. And he changed the whole technique of instrumental playing in the West forever."

Listening to "Melancholy Blues," it is difficult to argue with Lomax's contention that we are hearing a musical people in the act of rediscovering their voice. The song's roots, straight blues, harken back to black country music, but now the blues take on a bold new rhythm, handled on this track by banjo and tuba; recording engineers in 1927 had trouble with drums and the drummer here plays only cymbals. Over this come exuberant solos on trombone, clarinet and Armstrong's horn.

Chuck Berry

"Johnny B. Goode"

When jazz rose up out of the blues and went to the cities, the rural soil from which blues had sprung was left behind. By the late 1950s, Armstrong found modern jazz just about the only type of music he didn't like. It was only a matter of time until somebody returned to the countryside.

Chuck Berry, an automobile assembly-line worker who moonlighted with pick-up bands in St. Louis, considered himself a blues singer. He especially liked slow blues, which he punctuated with elaborate electric-guitar playing. But he discovered that he was no crooner; audiences grew impatient with his slow tunes and responded only when the tempo picked up. Searching for upbeat material, Berry began writing songs that incorporated guitar riffs long employed in black and white country music, but now syncopated, sped up, and amplified. Audiences jumped to their feet and danced. Berry was helping to invent rock-and-roll, music that was to go around the world as had jazz a generation before. "Johnny B. Goode," released in 1958, is about a poor boy in the country who makes the same discovery that Louie Armstrong and others made—that music might deliver him from obscurity and gain him respect. Its first verse sets the scene with the orderliness of an English ballad or a nineteenth-century novel—a log cabin in Louisiana where Johnny lives and learns to play the guitar. The second verse is remarkable for effortlessly shifting its perspective three times in four sentences. We first see Johnny alone, then from the point of view of the engineer on a train (Berry, born about 1926, was one of those Americans who still regarded trains as symbols of escape to the big city), then as the subject of praise from listeners, anticipating that of the crowds who will bathe him in admiration once he becomes a star. The third verse centers on Johnny's mother's prophecy that "maybe some day your name will be in lights." The story ends there. Rock-and-roll songs normally have, as F. Scott Fitzgerald said of American lives, no second act.

The vivid imagery in Berry's lyrics helped establish an idea that had been glimpsed by jazz musicians, that popular music could be a vehicle for poetry. But Berry himself, after a spate of writing that lasted only a few years, showed a lack of interest in innovation commensurate to that of the Homeric bards. At age fifty he was still performing the same songs, arguing rather persuasively that they emerged differently each time they were played. He traveled with a small suitcase and his guitar, hiring equipment and back-up musicians locally wherever he played. "I'm proud to say that if you call me in the morning, and there's a plane going to where you're at," he liked to say, "I'll play and please you in the evening."

Japanese Shakuhachi

"Cranes in Their Nest"

The bamboo flute called shakuhachi came to Japan, as did many things, from China.

Chinese imperial court orchestras maintained large pitchpipes used to tune the instruments, in the service of an admonition that uniform pitch was essential to preserving order in Heaven and on Earth. Bamboo tubes of various lengths, banded together, formed a large version of the panpipe, an instrument that keeps cropping up in Voyager music. At some point Chinese musicians took apart the pitchpipes and began playing them individually, with fingerholes drilled in the bamboo. Flutes came to be designated by their length, as this determined their fundamental pitch. The word *shakuhachi* is believed to be a corruption of the measurement of one such flute in Chinese as pronounced by the Japanese—*isshaku hassun,* meaning one *shaku* and eight *sun,* or about twenty-two inches.

The shakuhachi became popular in Japan during the Edo, largely as the result of the intrigues of a group of *komuso,* wandering priests who wore wicker baskets on their heads that covered their face and concealed their features. Many of the late-sixteenth and early-seventeenth-century komuso were ex-samurai who had been stripped of rank and privilege, including the privilege of carrying swords. Membership in the masked order enabled them to avoid potentially embarrassing confrontations with those they had bullied in the days when they were armed. In case these precautions proved insufficient, a number of the samurai-turned-priests took to carrying a shakuhachi that could be used as a club in a pinch. For these purposes, a larger and heavier version of the flute was preferred, one cut from the base of the bamboo, and it is from this model that the modern shakuhachi evolved. William Malm, a musicologist at the University of Illinois to whose scholarship we owe reconstruction of this story, writes: "This is perhaps the only instance in music history in which the practical necessity of self-defense was a major factor in instrument construction."

The shogun government reacted by requiring licenses of shakuhachi players. The samurai priests forged licenses. The authorities, rather than further anger what was, after all, a band of trained fighting men, offered the priests sanction if they would become government spies. They agreed and set up a series of headquarters from which they could, in Malm's words, "fan out along the avenues and back alleys . . . playing a few soft melodies and overhearing equally intimate conversations," from behind their wicker masks. "One finds today that the wandering komuso of Tokyo still have many acquaintances on the police force," Malm adds.

One of these ex-samurai, Kinko Kurosawa (1710–1771), traveled around the country gathering flute compositions of the *fuke* zen monks. His collection of thirty-six shakuhachi pieces is known today as the *honkyoku,* or "Original Pieces." "Cranes in Their Nest" is one of these.

The modern shakuhachi closely resembles the seventeenth-century samurai's cudgel. It is a bamboo flute with fingerholes, one thumbhole, and no mouthpiece. It is played through a gash cut in the bamboo near the top. In trained hands it is capable of an impressive musical vocabulary. To construct a shakuhachi requires careful selection of a length of bamboo of appropriate thickness and size, as nearly circular as possible. In some cases the bamboo may be bent in the workshop to improve on nature. The interior is lacquered to improve the tone.

Tradition dictates that original pieces be played with frequent dynamic rises and falls, frail rivulets of notes trailing off at the end of most phrases. The sound has been well described by Malm: "From a whispering, reedy *piano,* the sound swells to a ringing metallic *forte* only to sink back into a cotton-wrapped softness, ending with an almost inaudible grace note, seemingly an afterthought. It is a combination of all these musical idioms that produces feelings of vagueness and melancholy in the mind of many a listener." Rhythm is not fixed and may be varied at the discretion of the soloist. Pitch is set in accordance with the resonance of the flute being played.

The ideal of Japanese solo music is to produce a broad range of effects from a minimum of ingredients. The music is not annotated, and there is ample room for improvisation. Titles frequently are programmatic, but listeners are invited to allow their imaginations to roam beyond the indicated subject matter. In this piece, the titular subject is the affection of cranes for their offspring. Some listeners find the flute's birdlike cry appropriate to Voyager's lonely flight through space.

Mozart

Queen of the Night aria, No. 14, from The Magic Flute

The Magic Flute, Mozart's last opera, premiered September 30, 1791, less than three months before Mozart's death at age thirty-five. The Queen of the Night aria has been called "one of the most extraordinary depictions of character ever achieved in music," and the character depicted is evil: "The vengeance of Hell boils in my heart; death and despair flame round me!" sings the queen, who rules from a throne decorated with stars. Upon completing the opera, Mozart resumed work on his Requiem, commissioned by an anonymous patron whom Mozart, as his health began to fail, suspected of having poisoned him with the ironic intent that the requiem become Mozart's own. Before he could complete the work Mozart was dead, destined for a pauper's grave. These grim circumstances have prompted some to view the opera in as tragic a light as the Requiem, but there is reason to think that the composer felt more cheerful about it.

The opera had been commissioned by Emmanuel Schikaneder, who was then staging popular opera in a theater in the Vienna suburb of

Wieden. Schikaneder enjoyed theatrics, drinking and womanizing, pleasures to which Mozart was not entirely a stranger. The production was something of a family affair. Schikaneder wrote the libretto and played the part of the bird-catcher Papageno, ad-libbing and mugging for the audience. Mozart's sister-in-law Josefa Hofer played the Queen of the Night. Mozart described Josefa as "a lazy gross perfidious woman, and as cunning as a fox." He thought her suitable to play the queen. The performances were successful, punctuated by applause and laughter, some of the latter occasioned by jokes Mozart played on his friends on stage. (In one scene, Schikaneder as Papageno was to play a set of prop chimes while a musician backstage provided the music; Mozart took over the chimes and dashed out a rainbow of improvisations while the audience laughed watching Schikaneder try to keep up.)

Aficionados of Italian opera may be placated to consider that although this sole Voyager operatic selection is, of course, Austrian, Mozart learned to compose opera in Italy and wrote this aria specifically in the Italian bravura style. Readers not tired of hearing about panpipes may be interested to learn that Mozart too was charmed by them, having heard Indonesian pipes, imported during a general awakening of European interest in Asian music, and he incorporated them in much of *The Magic Flute*. They are not, however, heard in The Queen of the Night aria.

I do not recall to what degree the choice was conscious, but in selecting music to go aboard a spacecraft that would sail in interstellar darkness, we found that we had included four pieces on the theme of night—Blind Willie Johnson's "Dark Was the Night," the Navajo Night Chant, the aboriginal song of the morning star, and this Mozart.

Georgian Chorus — "Tchakrulo"
Azerbaijan Bagpipes — "Ugam"

Voyager's two musical selections from the Soviet Union come from a ganglionic zone, the Caucasus. Since deep prehistoric times the valleys of this mountain range between the Black and the Caspian seas have witnessed shifting tides of migration to and from Asia, the Mideast and the Mediterranean. The region's location subjected it to these migrations; its mountain barriers discouraged their frequency and helped distill the cultures of those who remained. The results have arrested the attention of travelers for centuries. Jason sought the Golden Fleece in the Caucasus. The Arabs called the region a "mountain of languages," and when Roman legions reached the Caucasus, they found it necessary to employ the services of interpreters in eighty languages. Many travelers commented on the sophistication of the music they heard there.

The Azerbaijanis are a Turkic people who migrated from the East in historical times. Their religion is Islam. The solo bagpipe piece on Voyager displays a haunting series of variations played over a drone rich with subdominants, in which may be heard hints of both the lands where they arrived and lands left behind; the music holds something recognizable for listeners from Spain to Afghanistan.

It was collected by Henry Cowell, the American composer and pianist who in his middle years became increasingly interested in world folk music, to the extent that he altered his own path of composition to pursue a course he termed "neoprimitive."

The Georgian song was recorded by Radio Moscow as part of a national program intended to encourage folk musicians. Appropriate to an area that has been called a "polyphonic island," the song is performed in three voices, exchanged among a chorus and two soloists. In Georgian, the word *"tchakrulo"* means both "bound up," like a bundle of hay, and "hard" or "tough." The song accuses a regional prince of injustice to the peasants, then asserts that the ordinary people will set things right—so both meanings of the title are explored. In the subtle authority of the music may be heard strains that run through Western classical music today, evidence supportive of the argument that Georgians were the inventors of Western polyphony.

Bulgarian Shepherdess' Song—"Izlel je Delyo Hagdutin"

The presence of two bagpipe pieces, Bulgarian and Azerbaijani, aboard Voyager prompts the reflection that astronomy and music unite in the history of the shepherd. The need to attend to flocks each night turned shepherds into students of the stars and authors of constellations. In several parts of the world they employed bagpipe music to soothe the sheep and keep them together in the darkness. Alan Lomax points out that the sound of early bagpipes resembled the baaing of sheep, as did the bagpipe itself, which often was made of sheepskin with the hooves still on it. "My guess is that the bagpipe is a shepherd's instrument because the sheep responds to it as if it were one of them," Lomax says. "The instrument lies in the shepherd's arms like a sick lamb—often in Bulgaria it's covered in wool—and it produces a kind of bleating sound. The sheep follow the sound and stay close to the shepherd. In that way a shepherd can keep his flock together at night even while they are grazing. I've been with Spanish shepherds who played all night long. Some know hundreds of tunes. I suspect that shepherds created much of our European tune-stock; they had plenty of time, and a captive audience."

In this song, recorded in the isolated mountain village of Arda, the bagpipe music closely resembles a shepherd's call. The words celebrate a familiar folk figure, the outlaw who harasses occupation troops. Delyo is his name and *"hagdutin"* describes his calling as an outlaw-bandit of the variety of Robin Hood or Brennan on the Moor. Delyo sides with the peasants and warns Turkish officials not to try to convert them to Mohammedanism. The Turks ruled Bulgaria for five centuries, and while the words of this song express resistance to that situation, the melody shows signs of Turkish influence. The bagpipes play with a terrific force more than matched by the singing of Valya Balkanska, who manages to retain an air of charm while sounding as if she could make herself heard three valleys away.

The quality of Bulgarian folk music is matched by its quantity. One collector, Vasil Stoin, had transcribed 12,000 folk songs by the time of his death in 1939. At the suggestion of the composer Béla Bartók, the emphasis then shifted from transcription to tape-recording in the field. Today the archives of the Bulgarian Institute of Music hold over 100,000 songs.

Stravinsky

Sacrificial Dance from The Rite of Spring

The Rite of Spring represents a raid by a keen intellect upon a zone of the imagination that developed when our ancestors lived in societies resembling those we now elect to call primitive. The idea for the piece came to Stravinsky in a dream, "a scene of pagan ritual in which a chosen sacrificial virgin danced herself to death," as he recalled it. "Being a Russian," he added, "for me this image took form as the epoch of prehistoric Russia." Stravinsky's opening theme was borrowed from a folk tune rooted in a Carpathian shepherd's song of unknown antiquity, and throughout the piece he exercised an option that would most closely associate him with the primitives: he emphasized rhythm.

The reception afforded the work at its premiere at the Théâtre de Champs-Elyseés in Paris in 1913 is history. The dancers couldn't hear the orchestra for the catcalls. The musical press termed the composition "hideous" and "barbaric." Seven years later the New York critic Deems Taylor wrote: "It sounds like cacophony because I am not used to it, and it probably sounds all alike for the same reason that Chinamen all look alike to me; I'm not well acquainted."

Still later, the Rumanian composer and music writer Roman Vlad, who had been born six years after *The Rite of Spring* was composed and so grew up in a musical world that had long ago reassured itself that the work was perfectly acceptable, wrote: "Here, *perhaps for the first time in musical history,* rhythm plays a major role in the musical discourse, sweeping all the melodic and harmonic elements wholesale into the vortex." (Italics added.)

It may seem remarkable that such a sentence could be written in a world where rhythm had been playing "a major role in the musical discourse" for thousands of years, but the remark offers a clue to understanding the shouts of rage on the night of its premiere. The Western world finds it convenient, in this season of its predominance, to imagine that because our voices speak most loudly, nobody else has much to say. *The Rite of Spring* threatened this false assumption by introducing into the concert hall a replica of the music of our denigrated prehistoric ancestors and of their contemporary kin, the citizens of the "underdeveloped" world. To the degree that the work succeeded as music, it was bound to engender anger. It reminded us of how much we owe to people we have forgotten.

The outrage soon abated and *The Rite of Spring* was absorbed by our civilization with a quiet gulp, like a rabbit swallowed by a snake; what happens in concert halls never really changes the world. Stravinsky wrote nothing like it again, declining to make a career of mining the neolithic. The composition built no bridges between cultures. It was more like a shout across the river.

Navajo Night Chant

The Navajos, today the most populous group of American Indians, are related to the Apaches. They migrated to the Southwestern United States a thousand years ago as hunters, later to adopt agriculture and sheep-herding under the influence of the Pueblos.

The Night Chant belongs to Grandfather of the Gods, one of thirty-five major Navajo ceremonies. It lasts nine days. Its purpose is to initiate boys and girls into the tribe's ceremonial life. The dancers conducting the ceremony wear masks which—like the horns of the New Guineans and the Australian aborigines and the bagpipes of the Solomon Islanders—are prepared over a period of weeks or months under strict control and to the accompaniment of ritual. The singing is in unison. Singers rehearse for months beforehand, striving to introduce new songs and variations the appeal of which might lead to their being adopted as a permanent part of the ceremony. An innovation in this particular song is that the normal male voice alternates with an eerie falsetto.

The sole accompaniment to the voices on the Night Chant is provided by gourd rattles, shaken in dance motion by the dancers as they move; as a beguiling consequence one can almost see the dance by listening to the recording.

The Night Chant was recorded by Willard Rhodes, then of Columbia University, who made more than a thousand recordings of American Indian music.

Anthony Holborne
"The Fairie Round," from Paueans,
Galliards, Almains, and Other Short Æirs

Constraints of time permitted few efforts on Voyager to depict the history of music. This short piece for recorder consort marks one exception. Listen to "The Fairie Round" in conjunction with the New Guinea men's house piece or the Melanesian panpipes, and the recorder's ancestry in wooden horns and panpipes is apparent. Listen to it next to Bach and it sounds connected forward in time as well.

This snatch of Renaissance music was recorded under the direction of David Munrow, whose death May 15, 1976, at age thirty-three was mourned on both sides of the Atlantic by enthusiasts of Middle Ages and Renaissance music. In his short career, Munrow organized the Early Music Consort of London and gave concerts of all-but-forgotten music that both exhilarated and instructed audiences. He released thirty-three record albums of early music and appeared as a bassoonist on many recordings of the standard repertoire as well, including five versions of the Brandenburg concerti. Informed of Munrow's death, his associate John Currie, chorus director of the Scottish Opera, said: "Happily he lived long enough to establish with a very wide public that there is no such thing as music which is dead simply because it is old."

Peru

Wedding Song
Panpipes and Drum Song

The Spanish invaders found Peruvian musicians playing many sorts of instruments made of wood, stone, bone and metal. The efflorescence of their music then and now may allow us, without at all disparaging the music of other South American peoples, to agree with the musicologist Robert Stevenson that "musically speaking, the Andean peoples outstripped all other New World enclaves." As we might expect from people whose high-altitude home has given them the largest thoracic capacity in the world, Peruvians like to sing and play wind instruments.

The wedding song, sung in pure, unaffected tones by a Peruvian village girl of about fifteen, was recorded in 1964 by John Cohen, a popular American folk singer. "Karen Bundy, a Peace Corps volunteer, said she knew some little girls who knew some nice songs and would sing them for us," Cohen recalls. "As we were recording, the girl's mother knocked on the door and wanted to know what was going on. Fortunately the knocking didn't turn up on the tape." This was in Huancavalica, high in the Andes.

The words of this Inca song represent a young girl's lament for having married when too young to know what she was doing. "You took me to church on Sunday; I thought it was time for mass. . . ." she sings. "The band played, I thought it was your birthday. [I was a] fool." The girl Cohen recorded had endured no such experience herself, and this, I think, adds to the charm of the recording—as it has been said, at the other end of the spectrum, that the effectiveness of Billie Holiday's wishful "The Man I Love" derives from the fact that the singer doesn't believe the words.

Signal evidence that men navigated the Pacific in prehistoric times is to be found in similarities of musical instruments in South America with their counterparts in China, India and the South Pacific. Few of the similarities are more striking than the construction of panpipes on both sides of the Pacific. The scales and pitches customarily employed are the same, and ancient Chinese and South American musicians alike sometimes constructed their instruments in two joined sets of six pipes each.

The Voyager selection is played on one of these two-row panpipes. Hollow wood sticks are cut to different lengths, open at the top; sound is produced by blowing across the opening. The ramshackle, irregular tempo of the drum accompaniment is intentional and evidences no lack of expertise; the player deliberately manipulates the rhythm in favor of the unexpected. It may be played here by a one-man band. Musicians playing panpipes and drum simultaneously can be seen on pottery painted in Peru prior to the Inca conquest, and on the streets of Peruvian cities today.

Melanesian Panpipes

The principal music of Malaita, a 115-mile-long island in the Solomon Islands of the Pacific, is the panpipe ensemble. The pipes are made with great care and beautifully ornamented. Of the two types of panpipes used in the Solomons, single-row and double-row, the inhabitants of Malaita prefer the single-row variety.

Their songs concern the sights and sounds of nature, and are accompanied by stories elaborating on their emotional tone and the lessons they can teach. The stories are not normally revealed to audiences, but are conveyed privately among musicians, as in a guild.

When a panpipe group gets together to play, they normally rehearse the tune once through by playing it softly to themselves—this in itself can be quite lovely—then play it twice at full volume. Counterpoint is common, although the tune on Voyager is played in simple harmony.

The traditional music of Melanesia is disappearing, a sad story echoed in many parts of the world. For years Christian missions discouraged its performance and encouraged younger islanders to think of it as "old-fashioned," a doctrine that persists in some quarters. "This astonishing attitude is still defended today," reports a French musicologist who has recorded Melanesian music, "by the missionaries of the two Protestant churches of Malaita, the South Sea Evangelical Mission (SSEM) and the Seventh-Day Adventists (SDA). . . . For decades the colonial power has repeated to the Melanesians that any ancestral customs are scornful. And in 1970, the Solomon Islands radio devoted to traditional music and oral literature together, all in all, fifteen minutes a week."

The Reverend D. A. Rawcliffe of Pawa warns that unless this trend is reversed the instruments themselves will disappear along with the music they play. Panpipes "used to be common in most islands," he writes, but "are now found only in a few, notably in Malaita. . . . And even there a mere handful of men know how to make them now."

Australian Horn and Totem Song

Sandra LeBrun Holmes, a respected collector of aboriginal music, dance and visual arts, was born on a small sheep station near Broken Hill in western New South Wales, at the hands of an aboriginal midwife. She has lived and worked amongst the aborigines for over thirty years. Her arms and chest bear the scars of slashes made in ceremonies to initiate her into their tribes.

"Since childhood I have regarded aborigines as my own people," she writes. "I have sought to preserve and record their songs, their dances, and—*them*. I always felt a deep compassion for them and as I grew up became more and more identified with them, and so my deep interest, love, and life's work has deepened until it is all that is meaningful to me and gives me happiness. I am seeking to save some of their visual and recorded history and their sacred places and their pride. Inevitably I have come up against harsh racism and am called either an eccentric or a 'white nigger.' My great dream is to establish a teaching museum somewhere, to teach whites to understand aborigines and to recognize them as human beings who have their own religions and identity."

The two song excerpts that appear on the Voyager record were recorded by Holmes in 1958 on the Crocodile Islands of Arnhem Land, the largest of Australia's aboriginal reservations, an expanse of 31,200 square miles in the Northern Territory. The instruments are ironwood clap sticks and the didgeridoo, a large wooden drone trumpet. The didgeridoo lacks fingerholes, and getting sound out of it requires massive volumes of air. To meet its demands, musicians develop their lungs and lower back muscles over the years. A solo voice chant is heard on the second song.

Life in Arnhem Land is not particularly harsh by aboriginal standards—there are tribes in the central regions that subsist entirely on insects—but it is sufficiently unrelenting that music of the region reflects a preoccupation common to aboriginal art, anxiety over the caprice of nature. In a subsistence society, vicissitudes of climate can spell hardship or death. Many aboriginal rites seek to placate nature, to ask that the days and seasons proceed in a reasonably moderate and pre-dictable fashion.

In one of these excerpts, a singer of the Millingimbi tribe imitates a devil bird, a pancultural symbol of fate's dangers that was no stranger to Sophocles. In the other excerpt, the morning star, Barnumbirr, is ceremonially lifted up into the eastern sky from the land of the dead; its rising will be followed by the warmth of dawn. The gravity of the music fits the concerns from which it springs.

New Guinea

From the island of New Guinea comes another sample of ancient tribal music, this played on two large hardwood horns. Listeners will notice the beauty of the alto theme sounded at the beginning and end. The intervening duet may at first sound repetitious. Closer listening reveals that the same figure is never played twice in quite the same way. The variations prove to follow a structure of their own, and attending to them—an exercise something like attempting to reconstruct an un-sounded voice in a Bach fugue—introduces the listener to a music the nature of which I would call hypnotic. The closest parallel in nature I can think of is the interlocking call of crickets—a sound that, once you attend to it, displays patterns of bottomless variety.

New Guinea has been inhabited by humans since prehistoric times, sustaining that interplay of people from surrounding cultures we so often find at the roots of accomplished music. Most natives of Papua, New Guinea, live in male-dominated societies led, as elsewhere in Melanesia, by a "big man" who owes his leadership not only to heredity but also to his demonstration of appropriate abilities. He and his fol-lowers spend much of their time in the men's house, an elaborately constructed dwelling whose carved hardwood roof beams may tower thirty or forty feet over the village. Prior to important ceremonies, the village males gather in the big man's house and play this trancelike music on large horns. The horns, a male symbol, may not be played, or in some cases even viewed, by women.

Alan Lomax, in what may not be too great a leap of analogy, sees this way of life echoed in the New Orleans black men's lodges whose horn music produced Louis Armstrong. Lomax describes a New Guinean ceremony: "In New Guinea the men's music plays an important part in the yam/pig economy. There is great pressure to acquire more land to raise more yams to feed more pigs and people. Ceremonial feasts are held to cement alliances—and incidentally to slaughter some of the pigs that are eating the tribe out of house and home. At these feasts the men put on displays of aggressive singing and dancing. The thunder of their choirs and stamping feet can be heard miles away. The dancers wear elaborate shoulder and head decorations of leaves and feathers sometimes rising ten or fifteen feet into the air, like trees waving in the wind. The design of these costumes match Picasso or Matisse, but they fade after a day or so and are thrown away. Days and weeks of planning and work in the men's house go into creating these ceremonial displays. One group in western New Guinea carves images of alligators, many of them eighteen to twenty feet long. When the ceremony is over, all are discarded, thrown in the river, to make way for the next year's creations. These people are fantastic artists."

The recording was made by Robert MacLennan.

Chinese Ch'in

"Flowing Streams"

"Flowing Streams" calls to mind the great Chinese landscape painters of the Sung Dynasty, who executed hand scroll paintings of rivers after preparing themselves by memorizing miles of those rivers. They felt that they could begin painting only after they knew the river so intimately that they could *feel* its contours, as Mark Twain in our time was to describe a river pilot's knowledge. Only then could the painting hold in balance two equally mysterious forces—those that created the river (the Chinese geomancers called rivers "the veins of the Earth") and those that produced the artist's perceptions of it.

"Flowing Streams" originated as part of a longer piece, "Towering Mountains and Flowing Streams," said to have been composed by Yü Po-ya between the eighth and fifth centuries B.C. Mountains and rivers are the object of prayers and religious rites still performed today, and they endure as symbols in Chinese art, poetry and philosophy—as in

Lao Tsu, who writes that the ocean and river hold dominion over mountain streams because they lie beneath them, an idea of importance to Taoism and to Chinese thought in general. "Towering Mountains and Flowing Streams" was split into two compositions during the T'ang Dynasty. Each piece has since evolved into several regional variations. The one on the Voyager record comes from the Szechuan school.

Ch'in are often elegantly constructed, and it is customary before a recital to rest the instrument face down so that the audience may examine the inlays on its wooden back. Turned upright, it reveals seven silk strings set over a lacquered boxlike body. Mother-of-pearl inlays indicate positions for playing harmonics. The strings, tuned to a five-tone scale, are plucked with the right hand and stopped with the left. There are no frets. Great variety of tone is possible.

Ch'in notation lists over a hundred ways to stop the string with the fingers of the left hand; each has acquired poetic ornamentation accumulated over a hundred generations of teachers. One medium-slow vibrato known as "the fading sound of a temple bell" is annotated to remind the musician that his finger on the string should oscillate like "fallen blossoms floating downstream." A particular three-fingered chord followed by a flourish is known as the "sound a fish makes when leaping out of the water." A technique of stopping a string with the back of the first joint of the fourth finger is "a panther grasping something." Harmonics are to be played as lightly as "dragonflies alighting on the water," and a staccato plucking on a single string is called "cold ravens picking at the snow."

The Chinese philosophy of solo performance emphasizes approaching the act of playing in the proper spirit. Chou Wen-chung of the Columbia School of the Arts, who recommended inclusion of "Flowing Streams" on the Voyager record, cites the Confucianist *Record of Music* to the effect that "The greatness in music lies not in perfection of artistry but in the attainment of *te*—a term which is often translated as 'virtue' or 'spiritual power' but should be understood as referring to 'that by which things are what they are.' In other words, the emphasis is on the single tones and their natural virtue or power by which these tones are what they are." Chou suggests that Eastern and Western music derived from the same source, the West having since diverged toward polyphony, the East toward *te*.

"Flowing Streams" calls to mind the sight of a river, as "La Mer" suggests the sea, but its importance lies in territory beyond the representative. As with a river or any other sight in nature, we are always aware of something beyond what we perceive, something whose nature we can barely discern. I consider this awareness healthy medicine for those of us who are guilty of using words like "universe" as if we knew what we were talking about. The visions that open up within a piece like "Flowing Streams" prompts us to reflect upon their kin in our perception of nature, and that for me is what art is about. As the Chinese *Record of Rites* says, "The Chin . . . creates humility."

Raga "Jaat Kahan Ho"

One of my favorite transitions on the Voyager record comes when "Flowing Streams" ends and we are transported, quick as a curtsy, across the Himalayas to the north of India, and from the sound of one musical genius, Kuan Ping-hu, to another, Surshri Kesar Bai Kerkar. Born in 1893 in the province of Goa, she was awarded the honorific title Surshri in 1938 by Rabindranath Tagore on behalf of the residents of Calcutta, and subsequently was presented with the same title by the president of India on behalf of the nation as a whole. The warm tone of her voice invites comparison with Valya Balkanska of Bulgaria, and her effortless three-octave range does not suffer from comparison with Edda Moser's. These gifts she combines with deep resourcefulness in improvisation. It adds little to our appreciation of this raga, but may add something to our delight over Kesar Bai's abilities, to note that she made this recording when past the age of seventy.

The word *raga* means "color," "mood" or "passion," and in the classical music of India, as in that of other societies, considerable thought has been devoted to how music can be preserved for posterity without losing its passion and immediacy. The Hindu approach has been to evolve a scale of twenty-two tones, of which five, six or seven main tones are selected for any given raga. The intervening tones are employed for improvisation or embellishment. The Hindu word for musical fundamentals means "ancestor," while the microtones between are known as "successors" or "descendants." The performing musician works within the precepts of his ancestors, as is appropriate for a dutiful son or daughter, but improvises and elaborates within that framework. In this way both past and present are honored.

The standard of performance is rendered more complicated by the fact that many of the forms of improvisation have taken on specific emotional and intellectual meanings in Indian culture and even within regional cultures; the sophisticated listener, acquainted with the significance of these variations, receives messages from the performer, to which the performer may add further comment.

Something of this sort occurs in music all over the world, as when an African raps a drum tattoo that reminds his fellows of the day the elephant was killed, or an aborigine sounds a set of flute notes associated with the spirit of his great-grandfather, or a Canadian pianist assails a romantic keyboard tradition by doubling his tempo. But for complexity of dialogue between performer and audience, and between tradition and innovation, no music surpasses that of India.

The raga heard on Voyager is formally designated for morning performance, but its popularity has led to its use as a closing number, a kind of encore, for concerts day or night. Sitar, drum and drone are employed, but the featured instrument is Kesar Bai's voice. She sings in seven primary tones, with soaring excursions into secondary tones at almost every phrase. The drum accompaniment is in the *dipachandi,* a stately 14/4 rhythm that arouses the sense of timelessness valued in Hindu art. The words are those of a mother asking her child not to go to a festival because she is still too young. Kesar Bai sings them in a tone that indicates she thinks the child will go anyway.

Despite her obvious virtuosity, Kesar Bai sings with no apparent self-importance. The music sounds humble. Indian virtuosos presumably are as susceptible to egoism as anyone else, but their professional ideal is summed up in an old story about the Mogul emperor Akbar, who asked his famous court musician Tan Sen, "How much do you know of music?"

Tan Sen replied, "My knowledge is like a drop in a vast ocean of promise."

Beethoven

It was Beethoven's fate to have been portrayed by his immediate successors in terms of his role as a founder of the Romantic movement.

At least two Beethovens resulted, both prettified. One is Beethoven the defiant rebel, fighting with his music to tear down an unjust world as Joshua with his trumpet brought down Jericho. Of this Beethoven we are told such stories as the famous deathbed scene in which, hearing a thunderclap, he shakes his fist at the storm. The other romantic Beethoven is a kind of woeful lap dog, forever being misunderstood and kicked out into the cold. Both Beethovens share the staginess with which posterity afflicts the great.

Whoever the real Beethoven may have been, he lived in a world rather closer to that of the "primitive" musicians who accompany him on Voyager than the romantic profiles suggest. Consider that Beethoven, an easygoing conductor, premiered the Fifth Symphony with an orchestra so poorly rehearsed that at one point he had to bring them to a halt, shout "Once again!" and start over. (Afterward he wrote blandly to his publishers, "The public showed its enjoyment of this.") Or consider this story by the violinist Louis Spohr, an account of Beethoven conducting a new concerto from the pianoforte keyboard: "[He] forgot at the first *tutti* that he was a solo-player, and springing up, began to direct in his usual way. At the first *sforzando* he threw out his arms so wide asunder that he knocked both the lights off the piano upon the ground. The audience laughed, and Beethoven was so incensed at this disturbance that he made the orchestra cease playing and begin anew. Seyfried, fearing that a repetition of the accident would occur at the same passage, bade two boys of the chorus place themselves on either side of Beethoven, and hold the lights in their hands. One of the boys innocently approached nearer and was reading also in the notes of the piano part. When therefore the fatal *sforzando* came, he received from Beethoven's outthrown right hand so smart a blow on the mouth, that the poor boy let fall the light from terror. The other boy, more cautious, had followed with anxious eyes every motion of Beethoven, and by stooping suddenly at the eventful moment he avoided the slap on the mouth. If the public were unable to restrain their laughter before, they could now much less, and broke into a regular bacchanalian roar."

Beethoven loved puns and coarse humor. Bad music made him laugh out loud. He could be tender and warm with people he cared for, but in general he displayed atrocious manners. He was sarcastic and sardonic. He was clumsy. His sloppiness prompted housekeepers to quit, and when they had quit and dirty dishes and decaying food threatened to overwhelm him, he would pack up and move to another flat. He wore the same clothes until they fell apart or until friends took an interest and replaced them with new ones, whereupon he would emerge in sudden splendor without apparently noticing the difference. Goethe called him an "utterly untamed personality."

His life was saturated with misfortune. His mother named him after a previous child who had died in infancy, and seems to have reminded him of that fact often enough that by his own testimony he regarded himself as a "false child." He left school when he was eleven. At nineteen he was given financial responsibility for the family by his father, an alcoholic musician unable to find work. Afflicted by chronic dysentery and by deafness, he became convinced he would die before he reached thirty. He retired to the countryside and wrote his will.

"What a humiliation, when anyone standing beside me could hear at a distance a flute that I could not hear, or anyone heard the shepherds singing, and I could not distinguish a sound!" he wrote in a letter. "To become a philosopher in my twentieth-eighth year is not easy—for the artist, more difficult than for any other. O God! thou lookest down upon my misery: thou knowest that it is accompanied with love of my fellow-creatures and a disposition to do good! O men! when ye shall read this, think that ye have wronged me: and let the child of affliction take comfort on finding one like himself, who, in spite of all the impediments of nature, yet did all that lay in his power to obtain admittance into the rank of worthy artists and men." At the peak of his creative powers, Beethoven could not hear a note; musicians in orchestras he conducted were instructed to ignore him, and guests at his home nodded politely when Beethoven played *piano* passages so softly that no sound emerged at all.

Beethoven told his friends that he longed for marriage and a family, but his nearest approach to that ideal was his tyrannical guardianship of his nephew Karl, who responded by failing in society, in school and even in suicide, when in 1826 he put a pistol to his head and pulled the trigger, wounding himself. Beethoven proposed marriage to various women, among them Magdalene Willmann, who later explained that she refused him "because he was so ugly and half crazy." When marriage did seem attainable, he shied away. A fact sometimes overlooked about the famous letter to his "Immortal Beloved," declaring his love and apologizing profusely for not having written sooner, is that Beethoven never mailed it.

Despite his misfortunes Beethoven found the courage to produce astounding work. This may be why we find him mysterious, and why each age, impatient with mystery, is anxious to view him by its own lights. Courage itself is mysterious. By virtue of its survival value, it has been bequeathed us by millions of our ancestors at the expense of millions of others more timid or more foolhardy. Whatever share is bequeathed each of us, we know it to be a quality we cannot create, but can hope to discover. This old story runs back through the history of our struggle to achieve dominance of our planet, and we are its subjects, not its authors. But we find it transcribed in the music of Beethoven. He *composed* it.

The word "compose" means to place things in their proper order, to fix them, and—further up the tree of etymology—to take a stand on behalf of the result. This, I think, is what Beethoven meant when, leaving a performance of a work by another artist, he remarked, "I must compose that." He meant there was something there, but the composer had failed to assemble it, hold it up, stand by it. For Beethoven there was as much *there* as for any composer we know of—more tenderness and exuberance, more grief and loneliness, more rage and humor than we would will upon anyone—and he composed those emotions with grace, strength and ingenuity. His sketchbooks offer little to support the romantic notion of the composer who hears a bird call or the clang of a blacksmith's forge and rushes home to spew out a symphony in a fit of inspiration. Instead, we find an artist whose imagination was harnessed by a tenacious intellect. Themes such as the opening bars of the first movement of the Fifth Symphony, which seems spontaneous as a cry of pain, are revealed in the sketchbooks to have been refined laboriously from earlier ideas. However "crazy" Beethoven may have been as a man, as an artist he was balanced.

Nor did Beethoven, however rebellious, develop independently of his times. He grew up in a musical stew that had been cooking for generations. He studied under Haydn and possibly Mozart, and learned fugal structure by poring over *The Well-Tempered Clavier*. His music arose from a musical society. Vienna, where he lived and died, had been a settlement since early paleolithic times. Its inhabitants had included Celtic tree worshipers, Roman invaders, German tribespeople, Christian crusaders, migrants from the Balkans, Slavs, Franks—and all these people brought music. Of the rules and principles by which Beethoven learned to write music, Sir George Grove reminds us that "they are no *dicta* or *fiat* of any single autocrat, which can be set at naught by a genius greater than that of him who ordained them. They are the gradual results of the long progress of music, from the rudest of *volkslieder,* from the earliest compositions of Josquin des Pres and Palestrina —gradually developing and asserting themselves as music increased in freedom and as new occasions arose, as instruments took the place of voices, as music strayed outside the church and allied itself to the world; but as absolute and rigorous and imperative as the laws which governed the production of an oak or an elm, and permits such infinite variety of appearance in their splendor and beautiful forms."

Symphony No. 5 in C minor, First Movement

Schoolchildren sing the theme of the first movement of Beethoven's Fifth, the Allies used it in propaganda broadcasts during the Second World War, and it has been made into a best-selling pop record. But its familiarity cannot be expected to trouble the extraterrestrial listeners for whom the Voyager record was intended, and it doesn't much bother us here on Earth either. It may be possible to drain the life out of a piece of Beethoven's music by popularizing it, but no one yet has succeeded at that feat. The Fifth Symphony sounds at least as compelling to us today as it did to Beethoven's contemporaries. It "has been the harbinger of the Beethoven religion," writes Grove. "It introduced a new physiognomy into the world of music. It astonished, it puzzled, it even aroused laughter; but it could not be put down, and in time it subdued its listeners. . . ."

Beethoven wrote the Fifth while, as usual, immersed in personal tumult. He began it in 1805, was interrupted by his engagement to the Countess Theresa Brunswick—a happy interlude that produced the "Eroica" Symphony—then completed it in 1807–1808, after they had separated and broken off the engagement. Its first performance was the mitigated disaster that had Beethoven shouting, "Begin again!" A more successful second performance followed, and the Fifth soon received the acclaim it has enjoyed ever since. The composer Hector Berlioz was to say of the first movement that it went "both beyond and above anything which had been produced in instrumental music." A dissenting voice was cast by Goethe, who, after having had the Fifth played for him by Felix Mendelssohn, said, "That causes no emotion, it's only astonishing and grandiose," but later complained that he was unable to keep the theme from running through his mind.

Beethoven himself seems to have been impressed by the theme, for he chose to reintroduce it, as a kind of echo, at the conclusion of the symphony—a highly unusual step that has been called unprecedented, though he may have borrowed it from Haydn's Symphony No. 14. The English essayist and musician Sir Donald Francis Tovey described this reprise of the scherzo as a "memory," and speculated, in a remarkable sentence, that Beethoven decided not to elaborate on the memory because "if you cannot recover the sensations you felt during an earthquake, it is not much use telling as your own experience things about it that you could not possibly have known at the time."

In the first movement of the Fifth, we hear a full symphony orchestra functioning in the service of passion within constraints seemingly as bald as those of natural law. Whether the laws that lend grace to this cataclysm are best considered inventions of Beethoven, or of his musical tradition, or of the natural world itself, are matters that will be debated as long as the symphony survives. It is a work sufficiently subtle that scholars remain divided on the question of exactly where its theme leaves off and its variations begin, and so symmetrical that its score is beautiful just to look at. Beethoven seems immune from a central deficiency of Western classical music, its underdeveloped rhythms; as in much of Beethoven's music, the rhythmic constituents of the Fifth stand on equal footing with its thematic and harmonic constituents. "It is astonishing," writes Tovey, "how many of Beethoven's themes can be recognized by their bare rhythm without quoting any melody at all."

In addition to its other virtues, the first movement of the Fifth recommended itself for the Voyager record because of its brevity. It has been called "the most concise representation that has ever been accomplished in music."

Cavatina from the String Quartet No. 13 in B flat, Opus 130

Beethoven's late quartets are like the islands of Polynesia, whose allure turned their inhabitants into navigators. You could spend a lifetime exploring them, and when you were gone, they would remain to tantalize subsequent explorers. The Voyager record offers, in the Cavatina, a lagoon of one island, the Thirteenth quartet.

The word "cavatina" refers to an operatic song characterized by clarity, even tempo and simplicity. In Beethoven's Cavatina, the first violin substitutes for the singer. Threads of characteristic Beethoven technique run through the piece, notably the rising phrase from B♮ to F found also in his piano sonatas Opus 106 and Opus 109, in an echo technique that recalls the woodwinds in the adagio of the Ninth Symphony, and in the structure of the movement as a whole, forecast in the andante of Florestan's aria in *Fidelio.* But it emerges sounding like nothing else in his music.

Most listeners would agree that here Beethoven stirs deep emotions—one student, Joseph Kerman, writes that "the Cavatina is his *most* emotional slow movement"—but the question is, which emotion? Certainly it is sad. Beethoven wrote it at a heartbreaking time, less than two years before his death, and he inscribed below the eight bars of its most wrenching passage the word *beklemmt,* meaning "afflicted" or "oppressed." Charles Holtz, a constant companion of Beethoven's in those years, said Beethoven remarked that he could move himself to tears simply by thinking about the Cavatina. The music scholar Joseph De Marliave described the movement as "an agonized entreaty, an intolerable longing for happiness and peace, a longing broken with sobs that break from the music with deeper intensity of feeling than even the living voice of the musician could express." But sadness alone can't define the Cavatina. Strains of hope run through it as well, and something of the serenity of a man who has endured suffering and come to terms with existence perceived without illusion.

It may be that these ambiguities make for an appropriate conclusion to the Voyager record. We who are living the drama of human life on Earth do not know what measure of sadness or hope is appropriate to our existence. We do not know whether we are living a tragedy or a comedy or a great adventure. The dying Beethoven had no answers to these questions, and knew he had no answers, and had learned to live without them. In the Cavatina, he invites us to stare that situation in the face.

Voyager Record Music

(in sequence)

1. Bach, Brandenburg Concerto No. 2 in F, First Movement, Munich Bach Orchestra, Karl Richter, conductor. 4:40.
2. Java, court gamelan, "Kinds of Flowers," recorded by Robert Brown. 4:43.
3. Senegal, percussion, recorded by Charles Duvelle. 2:08.
4. Zaire, Pygmy girls' initiation song, recorded by Colin Turnbull. 0:56.
5. Australia, Aborigine songs, "Morning Star" and "Devil Bird," recorded by Sandra LeBrun Holmes. 1:26.
6. Mexico, "El Cascabel," performed by Lorenzo Barcelata and the Mariachi México. 3:14.
7. "Johnny B. Goode," written and performed by Chuck Berry. 2:38.
8. New Guinea, men's house song, recorded by Robert MacLennan. 1:20.
9. Japan, shakuhachi, "Cranes in Their Nest," performed by Coro Yamaguchi. 4:51.
10. Bach, "Gavotte en rondeaux" from the Partita No. 3 in E major for Violin, performed by Arthur Grumiaux. 2:55.
11. Mozart, *The Magic Flute,* Queen of the Night aria, no. 14. Edda Moser, soprano. Bavarian State Opera, Munich, Wolfgang Saivallish, conductor. 2:55.
12. Georgian S.S.R., chorus, "Tchakrulo," collected by Radio Moscow. 2:18.
13. Peru, panpipes and drum, collected by Casa de la Cultura, Lima. 0:52.
14. "Melancholy Blues," performed by Louis Armstrong and his Hot Seven. 3:05.
15. Azerbaijan S.S.R., bagpipes, recorded by Radio Moscow. 2:30.
16. Stravinsky, *Rite of Spring,* Sacrificial Dance, Columbia Symphony Orchestra, Igor Stravinsky, conductor. 4:35.
17. Bach, *The Well-Tempered Clavier,* Book 2, Prelude and Fugue in C, No. 1. Glenn Gould, piano. 4:48.

18. Beethoven, Fifth Symphony, First Movement, the Philharmonia Orchestra, Otto Klemperer, conductor. 7:20.
19. Bulgaria, "Izlel je Delyo Hagdutin," sung by Valya Balkanska. 4:59.
20. Navajo Indians, Night Chant, recorded by Willard Rhodes. 0:57.
21. Holborne, *Paueans, Galliards, Almains and Other Short Aeirs,* "The Fairie Round," performed by David Munrow and the Early Music Consort of London. 1:17.
22. Solomon Islands, panpipes, collected by the Solomon Islands Broadcasting Service. 1:12.
23. Peru, wedding song, recorded by John Cohen. 0:38.
24. China, ch'in, "Flowing Streams," performed by Kuan P'ing-hu. 7:37.
25. India, raga, "Jaat Kahan Ho," sung by Surshri Kesar Bai Kerkar. 3:30.
26. "Dark Was the Night," written and performed by Blind Willie Johnson. 3:15.
27. Beethoven, String Quartet No. 13 in B flat, Opus 130, Cavatina, performed by the Budapest String Quartet. 6:37.

References

Arnold, Denis, and Fortune, Nigel, eds. *The Beethoven Reader.* New York: Norton, 1971.

Batley, E. M. *A Preface to* The Magic Flute. London: Dennis Dobson, 1969.

Blom, Eric. *Grove's Dictionary of Music and Musicians,* 5th ed. New York: St. Martin's, 1955.

Boyden, David. *The History of Violin Playing from Its Origins to 1761.* London: Oxford University Press, 1965.

Brown, Robert. Private communication re "Kinds of Flowers."

Bukofzer, Manfred. *Music in the Baroque Era.* New York: Norton, 1947.

Burk, John. *The Life and Works of Beethoven.* New York: Modern Library, 1943.

Carrell, Norman. *Bach's "Brandenburg" Concertos.* London: George Allen and Unwin, 1963.

Chailley, Jacques. *The Magic Flute: Masonic Opera.* New York: Knopf, 1971.

Charters, Samuel Barclay. "Blind Willie Johnson," liner notes to Folkways Album FG3585.

Cho Wen-chung. Private communication re "Flowing Streams."

Cohen, John. Liner notes to the album *Mountain Music of Peru,* Folkways Records FE4539.

————. Private communication re Peruvian wedding song.

Colodin, Irving. *The Critical Composer.* Port Washington, N.Y.: Kennikat Press, 1969.

Courlander, Harold. *Negro Folk Music USA.* New York: Columbia University Press, 1963.

Cowell, Henry. Notes to *Folk Music of the USSR,* Folkways Record FE4535.

Craft, Robert, and Stravinsky, Igor. *Expositions and Developments,* Garden City, N.Y.: Doubleday, 1962.

Daniélou, Alain. *A Catalogue of Recorded Classical and Traditional Indian Music.* New York: UNESCO, 1966.

David, Hans, and Mendel, Arthur, eds. *The Bach Reader,* rev. ed. New York: Norton, 1966.

Emsheimer, Ernst. "Georgian Folk Polyphony." *The Journal of the International Folk Music Council,* vol. XIX, 1967.

Feather, Leonard. *The New Encyclopedia of Jazz.* New York: Bonanza Books, 1955.

Forbes, Elliot, ed. *Beethoven: Symphony No. Five in C Minor.* New York: Norton, 1971.

Goffin, Robert. *Jazz: From the Congo to the Metropolitan.* Garden City, N.Y.: Doubleday, 1944.

Goldovsky, Boris. *Accents on Opera.* Freeport, N.Y.: Books for Libraries Press, 1953.

Graham, Desmond. "Cool Command," *Opera News,* vol. 35, no. 21, March 20, 1971.

Gray, Cecil. *The Forty-Eight Preludes and Fugues of J. S. Bach.* London: Oxford University Press, 1937.

Grew, Eva Mary, and Grew, Sidney. *Bach.* New York: Collier, 1947.

Grove, Sir George. *Beethoven and His Nine Symphonies.* New York: Dover, 1962.

Harris, Rex. *Jazz.* London: Pelican.

Holmes, Sandra LeBrun. Private correspondence.

Holroyde, Peggy. *The Music of India.* New York: Praeger, 1972.

Hood, Mantle. "Music of the Javanese Gamelan." Paper presented at the Festival of Oriental Music and the Related Arts, UCLA, May 8–22, 1960.

Horgan, Paul. *Encounters with Stravinsky.* New York: Farrar, Straus, 1972.

Hutchings, Arthur. *The Baroque Concerto.* London: Faber and Faber, 1961.

Iliffe, Frederick. *The Forty-Eight Preludes and Fugues of Johann Sebastian Bach.* London: Novello and Company.

Kalischer, A. C., ed. *Beethoven's Letters.* New York: Dover, 1972.

Kaufmann, Walter. *Musical References in the Chinese Classics.* Detroit Monographs in Musicology, Information Coordinators, 1976.

———. *The Ragas of North India.* Bloomington: Indiana University Press, 1968.

Keller, Hermann. *The Well-Tempered Clavier by Johann Sebastian Bach.* New York: Norton, 1976.

Kerman, Joseph. *The Beethoven Quartets.* New York: Knopf, 1971.

Kishibe, Shigeo. *The Traditional Music of Japan.* Tokyo: Japan Cultural Society, 1969.

Kunst, Jaap. *Music in Java: Its History, Its Theory and Its Technique.* The Hague: Martinus Nijhoff, 1973.

———. *Music in New Guinea.* The Hague: Martinus Nijhoff, 1967.

Landon, H. C. Robbins. *Beethoven: A Documentary Study.* New York: Collier, 1974.

Lao Tsu. *Tao Te Ching.* New York: Knopf, 1972.

Lentz, Donald. *The Gamelan Music of Java and Bali.* Lincoln: University of Nebraska Press, 1965.

Lomax, Alan. *Cantometrics: A Method for Musical Anthropology.* Teaching cassettes and a handbook, by Extension Media Center, University of California, Berkeley, California.

———, and the Cantometrics Staff. *Folk Song Style and Culture.* Washington, D.C.: American Association for the Advancement of Science, 1968; 2nd ed., New Brunswick, N.J.: Transaction, 1978.

———. Private communication and conversations re Voyager music.

Lydon, Michael. *Rock Folk.* New York: Dial, 1971.

Malm, William. *Japanese Music and Musical Instruments.* Rutland, Vt.: Charles E. Tuttle Company, 1959.

————. "Practical Approaches to Japanese Music," from *Readings in Ethnomusicology,* David McAllester, ed. New York: Johnson Reprint, 1971.

Marcuse, Sibyl. *A Survey of Musical Instruments.* New York: Harper & Row, 1975.

de Marliave, Joseph. *Beethoven's Quartets.* New York: Dover, 1961.

Meryman, Richard, ed. *The Life and Thoughts of Louis Armstrong—A Self Portrait.* New York: Eakins Press, 1971.

Miles, Russell. *Johann Sebastian Bach: An Introduction of His Life and Works.* Englewood Cliffs, N.J.: Prentice-Hall, 1962.

Moberly, R. B. *Three Mozart Operas.* New York: Dodd, Mead, 1967.

Morgenstern, Sam, ed. *Composers on Music.* New York: Pantheon, 1956.

Munrow, David. *Instruments of the Middle Ages and Renaissance.* London: Oxford University Press, 1976.

David Munrow obituary, *Musical Times,* vol. 117 (July 1976).

Nettl, Paul. *Mozart and Masonry.* New York: Philosophical Library, 1957.

Orito, Hizan. "Shakuhachi." Distributed at the October 17, 1971, meeting of the Koto Music Club of New York.

Needham, Joseph. *Science and Civilization in China,* vol. 4, pt. 3. New York: Cambridge University Press, 1970.

Panassié, Hugues. *Louis Armstrong.* New York: Scribner's, 1971.

Radcliffe, Philip. *Beethoven's String Quartets.* New York: Dutton, 1968.

Raim, Ethel, and Koenig, Martin. Liner notes to *Village Music of Bulgaria,* Nonesuch Records.

Rawcliffe, Reverend D. A. "'Notes on a Set of Records of Solomon Islands Music," mimeographed letter, undated.

Rhodes, Willard. Liner notes to the album *Music of the Sioux and the Navajo,* Folkways Records FE4401.

Sachs, Curt. *The History of Musical Instruments.* New York: Norton, 1940.

Sackheim, Eric. *The Blues Line.* New York: Grossman, 1969. (Mrs. Johnson's account of Blind Willie Johnson's death comes from here, p. 459).

Sadie, Stanley. *Mozart.* New York: Grossman, 1970.

Schweitzer, Albert. *J. S. Bach.* New York: Dover, 1911.

Seaman, Jerald. "Russian Folk Song in the Eighteenth Century." From *Music and Letters,* vol. 40, Oxford University Press, July 1959.

Siegmeister, Ellie. *The New Music Lovers' Handbook.* Irvington-on-Hudson, N.Y.: Harvey House, 1973.

Sonneck, O. G., ed. *Beethoven: Impressions by His Contemporaries.* New York: Dover, 1967.

Spitta, Philipp. *Johann Sebastian Bach.* London: Novello & Company, 1889.

Stevenson, Robert. "Ancient Peruvian Instruments." *Galpin Society Journal,* vol. XII (June 1959).

———. *Music in Mexico.* New York: T. Y. Crowell, 1952.

———. *The Music of Peru.* Washington, D.C.: Pan American Union, General Secretariat of the Organization of American States, 1960.

Stravinsky, Igor. *An Autobiography.* New York: Simon & Schuster, 1936.

Taylor, Deems. "Review of 'The Rite of Spring.'" *The Dial,* September 1920.

Tovey, Donald Francis. *Essays in Musical Analysis.* London: Oxford University Press, 1935.

"Tributes to David Munrow." *Early Music,* vol. 4, no. 3 (July 1967).

Turnbull, Colin. Liner notes to *Music of the Ituri Forest,* Folkways Records FE4483.

———. Private communication re pygmy girls' initiation song.

Vlad, Roman. *Stravinsky.* London: Oxford University Press, 1960.

Wilkinson, Charles. *How to Play Bach's Forty-Eight Preludes.* London: New Temple Press.

Yurchenco, Henrietta. Private communication re "El Cascabel."

7

THE VOYAGER MISSION TO THE OUTER SOLAR SYSTEM,

by Carl Sagan

Look here, upon this picture, and on this . . .
the front of Jove himself.

—William Shakespeare,
Hamlet, *Act 3, Scene 4*

Our Earth is a worldlet, a tiny ball of rock with a heart of liquid iron and an astonishingly thin skin that contains atmosphere and ocean, mountains and abyssal trenches, microbes and men. It orbits the Sun in the inner solar system along with a few other similar objects: Mercury, Venus, the Moon, Mars, and the asteroids. There are minor differences—largely in the details of the thin exterior layers—but these small planets, rocky and metallic, are essentially all the same. They are called the terrestrial planets, after their prototype, Earth.

Beyond Mars and the asteroid belt we enter a different regime of the solar system. It is farther from the Sun, and things are colder. We encounter terrestrial-sized objects that may be at least partly rocky. In the outer solar system there are four planets that dwarf the Earth and that clearly represent an entirely different sort of object. Jupiter, Saturn, Uranus and Neptune are composed largely of hydrogen gas. In the case of Jupiter, the gas is compressed to a liquid, and toward its interior, to a metal. The mass of Jupiter is 317 times the mass of Earth. A half-dozen Earths could fit into a single storm system on Jupiter, its Great Red Spot.

Despite their gargantuan sizes, these four jovian or Jupiter-like planets spin very rapidly, Jupiter rotating once every nine hours and fifty-five minutes. When such a large, gaseous object spins so rapidly we are sure to have interesting patterns of motion; and we see in Jupiter an array of bands and belts parallel to the planet's equator, regions of falling and rising air, vaporizing and condensing volatiles. In addition, Jupiter and Uranus and perhaps Saturn are constantly giving off more radiation than they are receiving from the Sun. The distinction between a star and a planet is this: a star shines by its own emitted light, while a planet shines by light reflected from its star or sun. By this definition the jovian planets are planets in the visible part of the spectrum to which our eyes are sensitive; but in the infrared or heat part of the spectrum a case may be made that they are starlike. The excess energy may come from the fact that these worlds are imperceptibly, slowly, gravitationally contracting, as stars are thought to do in their earliest histories. The interior temperatures of Jupiter and its fellow jovian planets cannot possibly be high enough to drive the thermonuclear reactions that make the Sun shine. But there is a real sense in which Jupiter may be described as a star that failed. The jovian planets certainly occupy some middle ground between terrestrial planets and stars.

1. Launch of the Voyager 2 spacecraft from the Kennedy Spaceflight Center, Cape Canaveral, Florida, on August 20, 1977. Courtesy NASA.

1

2

3

2. The Voyager Record in its aluminum cover mounted on the spacecraft. Courtesy NASA.

4

3. Crescent Earth, right, and crescent Moon, left, photographed by Voyager 1 on its way out of the solar system. This is the first photograph ever taken of the Earth-Moon system together. Most of the features seen on the Earth are clouds. The Moon is so much dimmer because it reflects about five times less light per unit area than does the Earth.

4. The Voyager spacecraft as it would appear if well-illuminated in interplanetary or interstellar space. An alien spacecraft approaching Voyager a billion years from now, and directing a great searchlight on it, would see something like this—although the spacecraft very likely would have accumulated a number of bumps and bruises in the interim. Courtesy NASA.

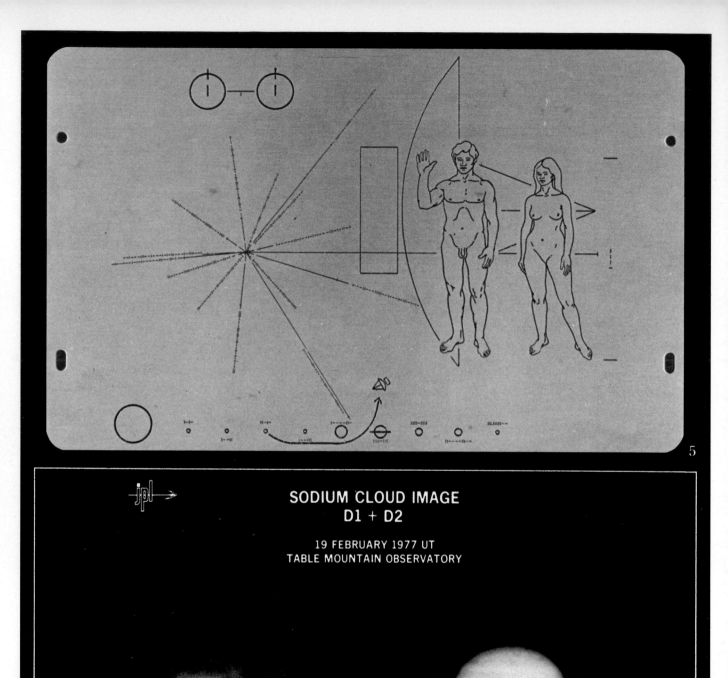

SODIUM CLOUD IMAGE
D1 + D2

19 FEBRUARY 1977 UT
TABLE MOUNTAIN OBSERVATORY

DIAMETER OF Io: 3640 km

|—————| 10 arc sec

|—————| 30,000 km

5

6

5. A photograph of the Pioneer 10 and 11 plaque.

6. A photograph taken at the Table Mountain Observatory of the Jet Propulsion Laboratory through a sodium filter, showing the extensive sodium cloud near the Jovian moon Io. Io's orbit around Jupiter is also shown. Courtesy of T. V. Johnson, Jet Propulsion Laboratory.

7. Schematic diagram of the Voyager spacecraft with some of the spacecraft properties listed. The scanning platform, which contains most of the planet-oriented instruments, is shown at top. Courtesy NASA.

8. Relative sizes of the large satellites of Jupiter and Saturn, compared with Mercury and the Earth's Moon. The colors and surface features are schematic only.

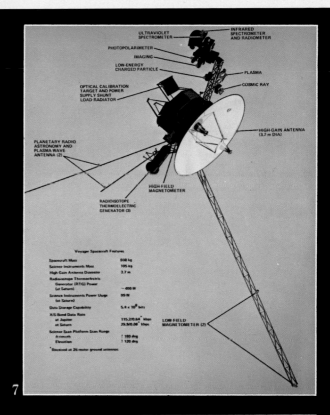

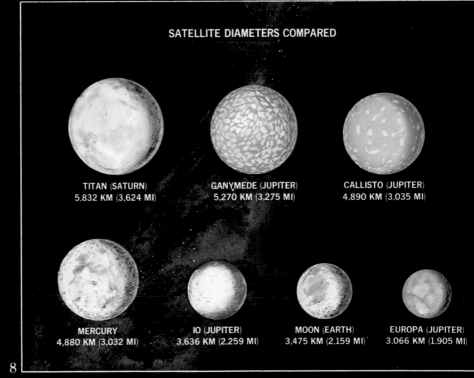

SATELLITE DIAMETERS COMPARED

TITAN (SATURN)
5,832 KM (3,624 MI)

GANYMEDE (JUPITER)
5,270 KM (3,275 MI)

CALLISTO (JUPITER)
4,890 KM (3,035 MI)

MERCURY
4,880 KM (3,032 MI)

IO (JUPITER)
3,636 KM (2,259 MI)

MOON (EARTH)
3,475 KM (2,159 MI)

EUROPA (JUPITER)
3,066 KM (1,905 MI)

9. Photograph of Saturn and its rings obtained at New Mexico State University, Las Cruces, New Mexico. Courtesy of Dr. Bradford A. Smith.

10. Pioneer 11 photograph of Jupiter with the Great Red Spot at center.
Courtesy NASA.

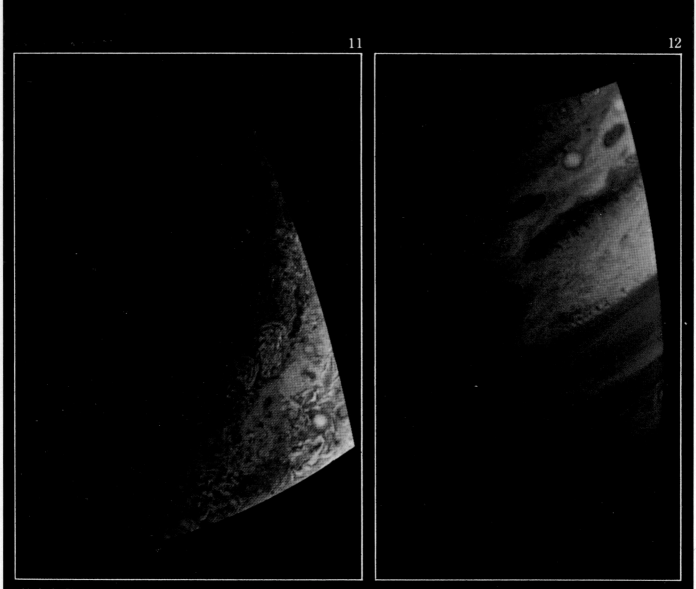

11. Left, Pioneer 11 photograph toward the Pole of Jupiter, with details computer-enhanced at the Image-Processing Laboratory, JPL. These graceful details in the Jovian clouds had never been suspected to exist before the Pioneer 10 and 11 missions. 12. Right, comparable enhancement of the region around the Great Red Spot, at center. Many of these smaller features have as yet no clear explanation in terms of the meteorology of the atmosphere of Jupiter.

The Sun, the stars, the interstellar medium, the other galaxies—indeed, the universe as a whole—are made chiefly of hydrogen. So are the jovian planets. But the terrestrial planets are anomalous. This difference is thought to be derived from those days in the earliest history of our solar system when the Sun and planets were condensing out of a vast cloud of interstellar gas and dust composed primarily of hydrogen. As the sun turned on, the inner solar system warmed up and the small low-gravity objects that were destined to become the terrestrial planets could not retain hydrogen, the lightest and fastest-moving gas, which trickled away into interplanetary space. In the outer solar system, however, temperatures were low and the forming planets were massive. Hydrogen did not have escape velocity and therefore was retained.

The jovian planets are therefore in some sense similar to the early Earth. If there is a solid, rocky surface to Jupiter it is in the very core, so far below the region we can view as to be permanently inaccessible. We see nothing on Jupiter, Saturn, Uranus or Neptune but atmosphere and clouds. Those atmospheres and clouds may be in some respects similar to Earth near the dawn of its history. It is therefore interesting that regions of bright coloration exist on Jupiter and Saturn. Reds, browns, yellows and oranges as well as blues are in evidence. The white clouds are probably condensed ammonia, condensed water, and their compounds. The highest white clouds are probably a kind of ammonia cirrus on Jupiter. But what could the source of the coloration be? Besides hydrogen, the principal constituents of the atmosphere of Jupiter are helium, ammonia, methane and water. There is some evidence for very small quantities of other materials, some of which (like germane, GeH_4, the hydride of germanium) are very exotic. But none of these materials by themselves are colored. Phosphine, PH_3, has been spectroscopically detected on Jupiter and red phosphorous compounds may make some contribution to the color of the Great Red Spot—although there are problems with phosphorous as an explanation of the general brownish coloration of the planet. Sulfur and its compounds have not been detected directly, but they must be there—if hydrogen cannot escape from Jupiter, the much more massive sulfur certainly cannot. But the details of the colorations do not seem to be matched by sulfur and its compounds, at least according to the best present studies.

However, if we take a mixture of hydrogen, helium, methane, ammonia, and water and supply energy—ultraviolet light as simulated sunlight, or an electrical discharge as simulated lightning—we can make in the laboratory a range of complex organic molecules that have many of the properties of the jovian coloring material. Among these molecules are the amino acids, the building blocks of proteins, and a wide range of other organic molecules employed in life on Earth. Such experiments are highly relevant to the question of the origin of life because Earth's early environment was hydrogen-rich, and Earth's early atmosphere probably included methane, ammonia and water vapor. The fact that the stuff of life can be made so readily under such general hydrogen-rich conditions has been an encouragement to those concerned about the possibility of life elsewhere. The possibility that organic matter is readily made on Jupiter and the other jovian planets today is a very exciting prospect. The amount of organic matter that is there must, however, be very small, because the atmosphere of Jupiter is extremely convective and organic matter made high in the atmosphere will in a relatively brief period—say, a month—be carried down to great depths where the temperatures are elevated and the organic matter will be fried. An important and unsolved problem is whether the steady-state abundance of organic matter—the equilibrium between what is made and what is destroyed—can be enough to explain the jovian coloration.

An even more speculative point concerns the possibility of life in the clouds of Jupiter. We have so far made no searches of Jupiter's environment in enough detail even to begin to investigate such a possibility, but it is not, in my opinion, entirely out of the question. There is a place in the atmosphere of Jupiter—and when the high clouds clear we can sometimes see down to it—where the temperature is about that of the surface of the Earth, where there is probably abundant liquid water in the clouds, and where organic molecules fall from the skies like manna from heaven. Whether life could have arisen and maintained itself in the convective circumstances of Jupiter's atmosphere is an open question; but the fact that there are such apparently pleasant places on Jupiter encourages us to keep our minds (and our eyes) open.

Jupiter is a source of continuous radio emission and radio bursts, both of which are received by radio telescopes on Earth. It was deduced many years ago that this emission is the result of charged particles— protons and electrons—from the solar wind trapped in a vast radiation belt about Jupiter by an intense jovian magnetic field. When Pioneers 10 and 11 flew through the jovian radiation belts this proposition was dramatically verified. The strong magnetic field on Jupiter may be due to its spinning metallic hydrogen interior; and the details of the trapped radiation belts, the configuration of the magnetic field, and particularly the interaction between the trapped particles and the moons of Jupiter are of very great interest. Here, as with the question of the weather on Jupiter, studies of another planet may significantly illuminate our knowledge of our own. Leakage from Earth's radiation belts produce the auroras in both polar zones and are strongly connected with such practical matters as radio propagation on Earth and possibly even with the weather.

Jupiter has fourteen or more moons, but only four large ones, called the Galilean satellites after Galileo, their discoverer. The innermost Galilean satellite is called Io, and its orbit constrains it to plow through the great radiation belt of trapped charged particles that surrounds Jupiter. This circumstance somehow enables Io's position to control the emission of radio bursts toward the Earth. Io itself seems to be trailing a vast cloud of sodium, sulfur, potassium and other atoms in a kind of truncated doughnut trailing the moon in its orbit about Jupiter. It has been suggested that Io once had salty oceans; that because of its low gravity the water in those oceans has long since escaped to space; and that the salts remaining behind are being sputtered or splayed off the surface of Io by the charged particles in the jovian radiation belts, thus producing the doughnut-shaped cloud.

The possibility of dried-up ocean basins on Io immediately suggests that the moons in the outer solar system will not be close copies of our own dead and battered hulk of rock which—with, I suppose, a certain affection—we call *the* Moon. The moons in the outer solar system are very different. Many of them have such low densities that they cannot possibly be composed primarily of rock and must instead be essentially icy. Some have atmospheres. Some—like Iapetus, the ninth moon of Saturn—have enormous differences in brightness between the hemisphere that is pointing in the direction of the satellite's motion around its planet and the hemisphere facing the other way; in Iapetus' case, the brightness difference between the leading and trailing hemispheres is a factor of six. There is no even semi-plausible explanation of this circumstance.

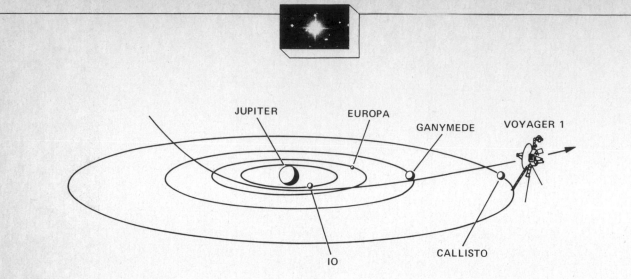

Schematic diagram of the passage of the Voyager 1 spacecraft through the Jupiter system. Notice the close encounters with the moons Io and Ganymede.

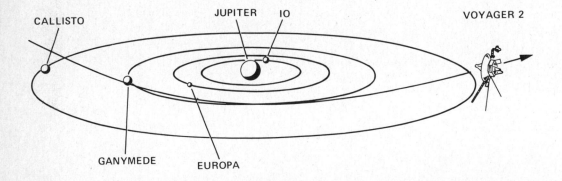

Passage of the Voyager 2 spacecraft through the Jupiter system. Note the close encounters with Callisto and Ganymede.

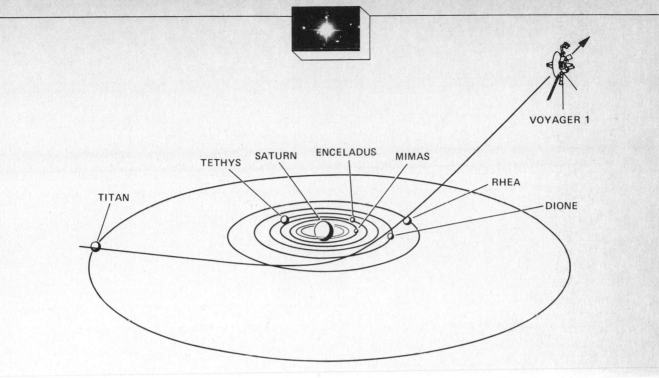

Passage of the Voyager 1 spacecraft through the Saturn system. Note the close encounters with the moons Titan, Dione, and Rhea.

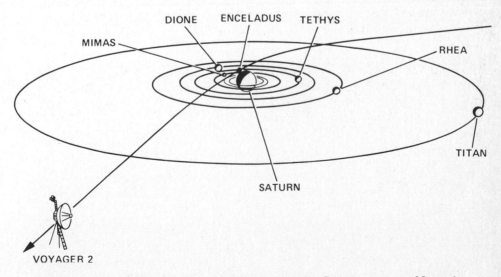

Passage of the Voyager 2 spacecraft through the Saturn system. Note the close encounter of the spacecraft with the moons Enceladus and Mimas and with the rings of Saturn.

What will the surface of a rocky or icy moon that has spent four billion years plowing through an intense radiation belt look like? Nobody knows. The radioactivity in the rocks of a partly rocky, partly icy moon will melt the subsurface ice, producing a kind of slush. But the ice in the outer solar system should be not merely water-ice but also methane-ice and ammonia-ice. What is the long-term geology of such a place? Can there be methane seas and ammonia volcanos? Nobody knows. The craters on the Moon are produced by small asteroids colliding with its surface. They are preserved for billions of years because there is no wind or water, no weathering on the Moon. But when a small asteroid collides with an icy object, the ice should melt. Will that "heal" the crater scar? When we look close up at the moons of the outer solar system, will we find them cratered or not? In particular, will the icy parts be cratered? Will there be new categories of surface features unknown among the terrestrial planets? Nobody knows.

And what of Titan? Titan is the largest moon of Saturn and the largest moon in the solar system. It seems to be too warm for its distance from the Sun, perhaps because it traps heat in its atmosphere. Titan has a significant atmosphere—one much denser than that of Mars. It is composed of methane and perhaps hydrogen and other gases. It seems to be surmounted by a brownish cloud layer which, if it exists, almost everyone believes to be composed of organic matter. The irradiation of the methane alone should produce a complex array of hydrocarbons, perhaps related to asphalt and petroleum. The surface temperature of Titan is so low that organic molecules produced there over its evolutionary history have not been instantly fried like organic molecules in the atmosphere of Jupiter. The surface of this moon may therefore be littered with some of the molecules that on Earth, 4 billion years ago, led to the origin of life. In detail, what is the surface of Titan like?

From the surface of Titan, through a break in the clouds, one might be able to see Saturn, looming and magnificent, pale yellow set in a blue sky, its magnificent rings casting a shadow on the clouded globe of the planet itself. There are several rings of Saturn—no one knows how many. But a number of circumplanetary breaks in the rings have been seen, the most famous of which is the Cassini division separating the A and B rings. The rings of Saturn are astonishingly thin, far thinner rela-

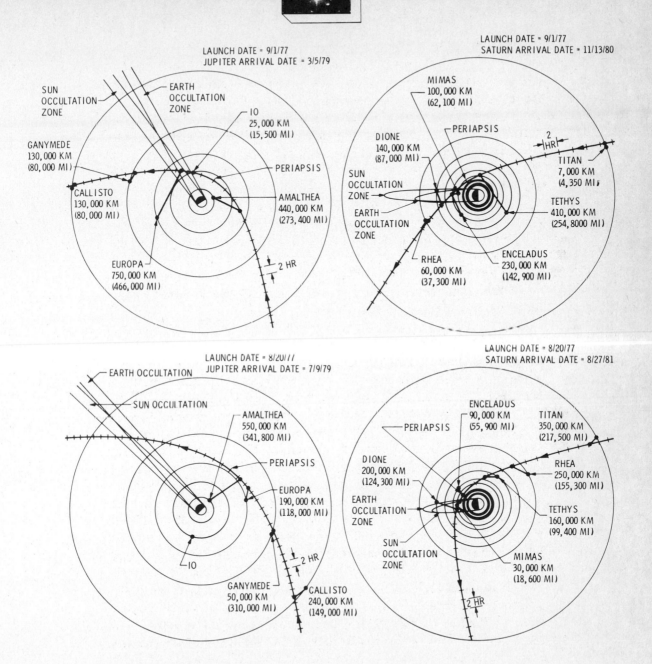

More detailed views of the trajectories of the Voyager 1 and Voyager 2 spacecraft through the Jupiter and Saturn systems. Voyager 1 was launched later than Voyager 2.

tive to their lateral dimensions than a piece of paper. But the rings are not gas or solid sheets, as is sometimes depicted in television or motion pictures. Rather, the rings of Saturn are an immense horde of orbiting snowballs, each perhaps meters across, with bumps, facets and irregularities of much smaller dimensions. However, this conclusion is inferential, and no one has yet seen close up any of the constituent boulders, snowballs or particles that comprise the Saturnian rings.

In 1976 an important discovery was made: that the planet Uranus as well as Saturn is surrounded by rings, although the rings of Uranus appear to be composed of extremely dark objects quite unlike the bright snowballs of the rings of Saturn. Such rings may possibly arise when a weakly coherent moon wanders so close to its planet that the planet's tidal gravitational influence tears it apart. Alternatively, the rings may indicate places where the planetary tides have prevented the formation of satellites; if this is the case, the rings represent residua from the epoch of formation of satellites in the early history of the solar system. The discovery of the Uranus rings was in some sense a relief to many of us in planetary astronomy; we no longer have to worry about why it is that only Saturn has rings. The phenomenon evidently is to some degree a general one.

Uranus and Neptune are so far from Earth that we know very little about them. Even their periods of rotation are still subject to some debate. Almost all the planets in the solar system rotate with axes of rotation to some extent perpendicular to the plane of their orbits about the sun. But Uranus is quite different; its axis of rotation lies almost in the plane of its orbit, as if it is rolling around the Sun on a surface, like a billiard ball. In the 1980s the axis of rotation of Uranus will be pointed toward the inner solar system—that is, toward Earth and the Sun. In that period the Sun's rays, feeble as they are at Uranus' great distance from the Sun, will be beating down more or less directly on one of the planetary poles, a situation quite different from our familiar one in which the sunlight is more intense at the equator than at the pole. A study of the weather on Uranus would be exceedingly interesting.

The five moons of Uranus revolve around the planet in the plane of the planet's equator, so that in the middle 1980s the orbits of the Uranian moons will circle the planet like the rings of a bull's-eye from the vantage point of a spacecraft approaching from Earth. Uranus and Neptune are significantly more dense than Jupiter and Saturn, which means that they must have less hydrogen, the least dense gas, and more of the heavier elements. But how hydrogen could have been depleted in the icy darkness of the outer solar system during the early flickering history of the Sun is an almost total mystery.

There are at least two other denizens of the outer solar system about which we know even less than we do about Uranus and Neptune: these are Pluto, the outermost known planet, and Chiron, a newly discovered small planet or large asteroid that circles the Sun between the orbits of Saturn and Uranus. We are not even sure of the sizes of these objects, much less such matters as composition or interior structure. Beyond Pluto is a realm of outer darkness from which the Sun appears merely as a bright star and which is inhabited by billions of slowly orbiting snowballs, each about a mile across. When these snowballs occasionally enter the inner solar system and heat up, the snows vaporize and a great tail is ejected by the solar wind away from the Sun. The snowball is then called a comet. But in their usual realm these objects are much less exuberant.

The distance from Earth to the Sun is called, immodestly by astronomers from the planet Earth, one "astronomical unit." It is 93 million miles or 150 million kilometers and is abbreviated A.U. The main belt of asteroids extends out to about four astronomical units. Thus the terrestrial planets extend from Mercury at about 0.4 A.U. from the Sun to the asteroids at about 4 A.U. from the Sun. But Neptune is 30 A.U. from the Sun, and the comets extend to 100,000 A.U. The inner solar system where we live and about which we know most is an insignificant province in the vastness of the Sun's empire. No one knows just where the solar system ends. The distance from Earth to the nearest star is a few hundred thousand A.U., and it is even conceivable that there are distant comets that are simultaneously in orbit—perhaps in figure-eight trajectories—both about our Sun and about one or more of the stars in the nearby Alpha Centauri system. But interplanetary space is filled with the solar wind and associated magnetic fields. Interstellar space has its own charged particles and magnetic fields. One useful definition of the boundary of the solar system is the place where the pressure exerted on the interstellar gas by the solar wind is compensated for by the interstellar magnetic field. Such a place is called the heliopause, the place where the Sun's influence—at least in this regard—stops. But no one has at yet measured where the heliopause is or the very interesting character of the interplanetary particles and fields at that transition.

It is clear, to paraphrase Isaac Newton, that in our spacecraft exploration of the inner solar system we have been playing on the seashore when the vast ocean of the solar system lay all undiscovered before us. But that situation is about to change dramatically. The Voyager spacecraft are scheduled to take the first systematic close-up looks at Jupiter and its fourteen or so moons in 1979; at Saturn, its ring system and its ten or so moons in 1980 and 1981; and perhaps at Uranus in 1986. Controlled by its own onboard computer as well as subject to instructions from the Earth, and crammed with an array of scientific instruments, the two Voyager spacecraft should revolutionize our knowledge of the outer solar system. The spacecraft are accelerated by Jupiter's gravity to reach Saturn in much less time than would otherwise be possible, and Saturn's gravity—if this option is ultimately adopted—is similarly utilized to reach Uranus. It is because of these gravity-assisted trajectories that the Voyager spacecraft eventually will leave the solar system, an accident of celestial mechanics that led to the Voyager records being placed aboard the spacecraft.

There are eleven separate scientific investigations on board each Voyager spacecraft. Each investigation corresponds to a specific scientific instrument designed for the purpose, and each instrument has associated with it a team of scientists and engineers who, in most cases, have been working on the investigation for nearly a decade. Their names are listed in Appendix E. The degree of dedication as well as skill required for such missions is very great.

The trajectories that have been chosen through the Jupiter and Saturn systems are the result of complex and often painful compromises between competing scientific objectives. Voyager is at closest approach to Jupiter and booming through its system of inner satellites for only a few hours. In that period of time only so many scientific measurements can be made. Shall we orient our mission to fly through the Io flux tube and examine the charged particles and magnetospheric interactions and radio bursts; or shall we concentrate on flying behind some of the satellites to use radio occultation techniques to search for atmospheres; or shall we concentrate on imaging and spectroscopy of the moons; or on a study of Jupiter itself? The optimum trajectories through the Jupiter system for some of the scientific objectives will not permit us to do all we want to do in the Saturn system, such as fly behind the rings or take a close look at Titan. The best trajectory through the Saturnian system will not permit us to get to Uranus at all.

The accompanying six figures show typical trajectories through the Jovian and Saturnian systems for Voyagers 1 and 2. From these diagrams we see that close encounters will be made with a large number of satellites in both systems, with the rings of Saturn, and, of course, with the planets themselves. The table on pages 226 and 227 gives some basic data on the Jupiter and Saturn systems. The lovely and exotic names of the moons are all taken from Greek mythology. They may have been unpronounceable in the past, but some of them are shortly to be household words. Before Voyager, the best images of the moons of Jupiter were obtained by Pioneers 10 and 11, which showed disks of a few of the Galilean satellites with barely discernible smudges. But we see from the table that Voyager will—assuming there are no engineering failures—obtain photographs of the Galilean satellites with resolution (the ability to make out fine details) of a few kilometers and coverage of the satellite surfaces of several tens of percent. We will move from being vaguely aware that the satellites have surface features to being able to photograph objects the size of a small city on the planet Earth. Mariner 10 was an entire mission that obtained the first close-up photographs of the planet Mercury—at a surface resolution of a few kilometers and a coverage of some tens of percent. Voyager will obtain comparable data for two or three planets and eight or ten moons. There is little doubt that the results will be spectacular.

From about 100 days before encounter, the Voyager imaging systems will obtain photographs of Jupiter superior to the best such photographs obtained through the largest telescopes on Earth. In the following weeks, the planetary image will steadily grow, many color photographs will be taken, and motion pictures of the weather on Jupiter, rotating under our cameras, will be put together. At the closest approach to Jupiter, cloud features or other objects in the atmosphere as small as a hundred meters (three hundred feet) across will be made out. A few hours from Jupiter, a mosaic of photographs will be taken filling the Great Red Spot, thought to be an immense cyclonic weather disturbance initiated perhaps a million years ago in the earlier history of Jupiter. The half-dozen or so photographs that will on this occasion fill the Great Red Spot will each be composed of about a million dots like those in a newspaper wirephoto. When Voyager arrives in the Saturn system, we will be able to place a dozen such photographs, one after another, across the rings while looking down upon the ring plane. The rings of Saturn have engaged, fascinated and tantalized even amateur astronomers with small telescopes since the time of Galileo. The Voyager photographs of the Saturnian rings should deliver a new dimension not only of scientific but also of aesthetic imagery.

While much of the public attention on the Voyager mission may be directed to the imaging science investigations, the other experiments are of very great interest and importance. Since Jupiter, Uranus and possibly Saturn radiate more energy to space than they receive from the Sun, the study of the planetary heat budgets by infrared instruments will be interesting. But these same instruments are also capable of determining something of the chemistry, perhaps even the organic chemistry, of the atmospheres of the jovian planets and Titan; a little about the mineral and ice composition of the surfaces of the moons and the rings of Saturn. They will also study the vertical structure and weather in those objects with atmospheres. A complementary investigation will be made by an ultraviolet spectrometer to study the composition and structure of the atmospheres of Jupiter, Saturn, Uranus, Titan and the Galilean satellites (where some evidence exists for extremely diffuse atmospheres), as well as a study of the doughnut-shaped clouds of sputtered atoms in the orbits of Io and perhaps other Galilean satellites. Another instrument, called a photopolarimeter, will measure the polarization of the sunlight reflected from planets and satellites as the viewing angle from the spacecraft changes. This will permit studies of the physical and chemical properties of atmospheric aerosols and the surfaces of the satellites and the rings of Saturn.

VOYAGER FLIGHT PATHS

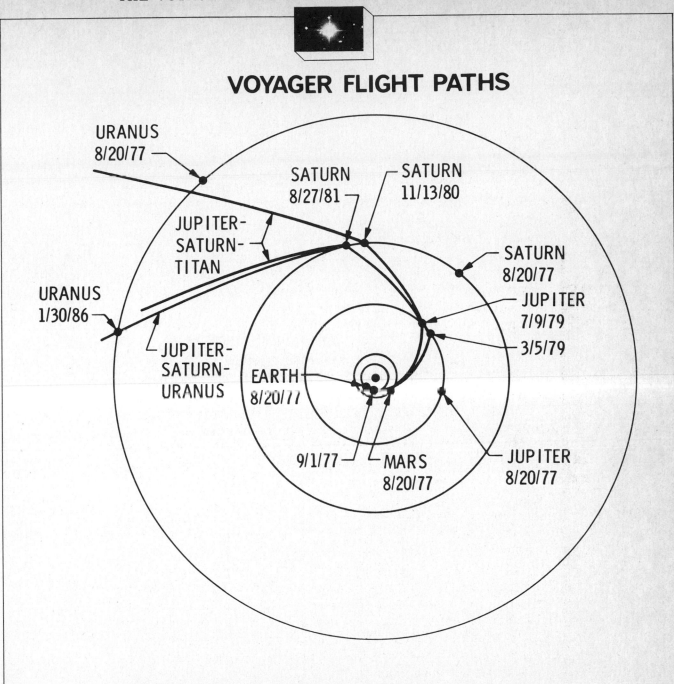

Schematic diagram of the trajectories through the outer solar system of the Voyager 1 and Voyager 2 spacecraft. The dates given are for the positions of the planets shown in their orbits. Voyager 1 is described as "Jupiter-Saturn-Titan" and Voyager 2 as "Jupiter-Saturn-Uranus."

THE SATELLITES OF JUPITER AND SATURN AND THEIR COVERAGE BY THE VOYAGER IMAGING SYSTEM

Planet	Satellite		Diameter in km	Distance from Sun in millions of km	Distance from planet in thousands of km
Earth			12,756	149.6	
	Moon		3,476		384.4
Jupiter			142,800	778.4	
	Amalthea		240		181.3
	Io	The Galilean satellites	3,640		421.6
	Europa		3,050		670.9
	Ganymede		5,270		1,070
	Callisto		5,000		1,880
	Leda		~10		11,110
	Himalia		170		11,470
	Lysithea		~20		11,710
	Elara		80		11,740
	Ananke		~15		20,700
	Carme		~25		22,350
	Pasiphae		~30		23,300
	Sinope		~15		23,700
Saturn			120,000	1,424.6	
	Janus		?		168.7
	Mimas		400		185.8
	Enceladus		550		238.3
	Tethys		1,200		294.9
	Dione		1,150		377.9
	Rhea		1,450		527.6
	Titan		5,800		1,222.6
	Hyperion		~500		1,484.1
	Iapetus		1,800		3,562.9
	Phoebe		~200		12,960

~means "very roughly." Satellites are almost exactly as distant from the Sun as their planet. Periods of revolution of planets (about the Sun) or satellites (about their planets) are given in Earth days and Earth years. Most moons have periods of rotation equal to their periods of revolution.

Planet	Satellite		Period of revolution	Typical Voyager best surface resolution in km	Coverage of surface as viewed by Voyager
Earth			1 year		
	Moon		27.32 days		
Jupiter			11.86 years	0.1	
	Amalthea		0.49 days	9	35%
	Io	The Galilean satellites	1.77 days	1	50%
	Europa		3.55 days	5	40%
	Ganymede		7.16 days	2	40%
	Callisto		16.69 days	3	35%
	Leda		240 days		
	Himalia		251 days		
	Lysithea		260 days		
	Elara		260 days		
	Ananke		617 days		
	Carme		692 days		
	Pasiphae		735 days		
	Sinope		758 days		
Saturn			29.46 years	0.1	
	Janus		0.82 days		
	Mimas		0.94 days	2	30%
	Enceladus		1.37 days	7	30%
	Tethys		1.89 days	5	30%
	Dione		2.74 days	3	30%
	Rhea		4.52 days	3	30%
	Titan		15.95 days	3	50%
	Hyperion		21.28 days	11	15%
	Iapetus		79.33 days	22	15%
	Phoebe		550.45 days		

Each Voyager spacecraft is powered by a radioisotope thermoelectric generator, and communicates all its scientific and engineering information to Earth via a large parabolic radio antenna, broadcasting at two different frequencies. But the Voyager trajectory will take it through clouds of interplanetary gas, through the charged particles in the magnetosphere of Jupiter, behind the rings of Saturn, and behind (as viewed from Earth) the atmosphere and clouds of Jupiter and Titan. Each time material passes between the spacecraft transmitter and the receiving stations on Earth, the signal fades in a characteristic way and important information can be obtained about the interposed object. For example, we expect to learn, for the first time, from the Titan occultation experiment what the pressure and temperature is at the surface of Titan, rather than up near the cloud tops to which our present instruments are restricted. In addition, the radio science investigations will determine the precise trajectory of the Voyager spacecraft as they pass close to the various planets, satellites and ring systems, and this will permit us to derive important information about the masses of these objects and—in the case of Jupiter and Saturn—about the structure of their deep interiors, data vital for understanding their origins. In addition to using the existing radio antenna for sending radio waves past planets, there are special radio-wave detectors on Voyager to study the bursts and other radio emission from Jupiter, and possibly from Saturn and Uranus, with particular attention to the influence of the satellites of Jupiter on the jovian radio bursts.

Finally, there are four investigations of the charged particles and magnetic fields in interplanetary space and around the jovian planets and their satellites. Two devices for measuring very low strength magnetic fields are attached to an extremely long girdered boom, projecting from the spacecraft so as not to be confused by the magnetic fields established by electrical circuitry in the other instruments. Among the many investigations that these instruments will carry out will be a search for the heliopause, although it is possible that the Voyager transmitters will have died long before the spacecraft traverses this magnetic boundary between the solar system and interstellar space.

The main objective of the Voyager mission is clearly this extremely rich harvest of scientific information. Voyager represents the first in-depth reconnaissance of the outer solar system, and I believe it will change our view of the planetary family of the Sun forever—as well as have a profound influence on our aesthetic sense of our surroundings in space.

But there is something else aboard the two Voyager spacecraft. Long after its transmitters have died, far beyond the heliopause, in the remote future two phonograph records containing greetings from the planet Earth will be inexorably speeding on.

References

Gehrels, T., ed., *Jupiter*. University of Arizona Press, 1976.

Sagan, Carl, in *The Solar System*, A Scientific American Book. W. H. Freeman and Company, 1975.

————, and Salpeter, E. E., "Particles, Environments and Hypothetical Ecologies in the Jovian Atmosphere." *Astrophysical Journal Supplement*, vol. 32 (1976), 737–755.

Smith, B., et al., "Voyager Imaging Experiment." *Space Science Reviews*, vol. 21 (1977), 103–128.

EPILOGUE,

by Carl Sagan

A dense field of stars in the constellation of the Little Bear. One of these may be AC+79 3888. Photograph courtesy of National Geographic Society—Palomar Observatory Sky Survey. Copyright, California Institute of Technology.

It was impossible to view the last tongues of flame from Voyager's Titan booster as it departed from Cape Canaveral without contemplating the fate of the record. The record is affixed to the exterior of the spacecraft. While cosmic rays and radiation from the Sun and stars could cause some damage, the main threat to it is micrometeorites, tiny microscopic particles of fluff, probably the debris of comets, that fill interplanetary space. These microplanets are in orbit about the Sun and have their own velocities, but as the spacecraft ventures farther into the outer reaches of the solar system, those velocities become less and less. The spacecraft's own speed of about fifteen kilometers a second as it plows through this horde of micrometeorites poses the chief hazard. The most conservative estimate of damage is based on the assumption that the spacecraft will be traveling record first. If the record were not encased in its aluminum cover, all particles that could produce tiny pits or craters larger than about half a record groove could cause damage to the sound quality. In this case, all micrometeorites heavier than about a hundredth of a microgram (equivalently, larger than about 0.007 centimeters in diameter) could cause such damage.

There are probably many more micrometeorites in the inner solar system, where comets are vaporized by the Sun's heat and disintegrate, than in the outer solar system, where they are still in deep freeze. Again, a conservative calculation of damage might assume that micrometeorites are as abundant far beyond the orbit of Pluto as they are in the vicinity of the Earth. If this is the case, tiny pits destroying about 10 percent of the record will be accumulated by the time the spacecraft has traveled one light-year, about a quarter of the distance to the nearest star. This calculation applies only to the face of the record oriented outwards.

Ten percent damage is clearly too much even for an extraterrestrial civilization easily able to do some reasonable interpolation on the missing bits of information. It is for just this reason that the Voyager records are encased in an aluminum cover 0.08 centimeters (0.03 inches) thick. Only micrometeorites more massive than about five micrograms can penetrate the cover, and there are far fewer big micrometeorites than little ones. Employing the same conservative assumptions as before, we calculate that less than 2 percent of the record should be micropitted by the time the spacecraft reaches a distance of one light-year. This corresponds to about 4,000 tiny impacts before it leaves the cloud of cometary debris. Thereafter, in interstellar space, the abundance of micrometeorites should be much less, and the outward face of the record will degrade at the very slow rate of about 0.02 percent of its area for every fifty light-years traveled. An additional 2 percent of damage will not occur until the spacecraft has traveled an additional five thousand light-years, which is one-sixth of the distance between the Sun and the center of the Galaxy. It will take the Voyager spacecraft about a hundred million years to traverse such a distance. If Voyager were by chance to enter the planetary system of some other star, similarly endowed with comets and micrometeorites, then the record might acquire as much additional damage on the way into such a planetary system as it acquired here on the way out. But the chance of such an accidental entry is very small.

In all of these calculations—which are mainly due to Paul Penzo of the Jet Propulsion Laboratory—the damage applies only to the outward-facing side of the record. The inward-facing side, protected by the record itself and by the spacecraft, suffers essentially no damage at all. A rough estimate of a billion years for the average lifetime of the record therefore seems reasonably safe. The records were mounted with Side 1 inwards. Therefore all of the pictorial information, human and cetacean greetings, and "The Sounds of Earth" (as well as the first third of the music—from the First Movement of the Second Brandenburg Concerto to the Partita No. 3 for Violin) will survive essentially forever.

And toward where are the Voyager spacecraft destined? Are they likely under any circumstances to encounter another planetary system? The directions in the sky toward which the spacecraft eventually will be headed depend very much on the precision of maneuvers near Jupiter, Saturn, and Uranus during the strictly scientific phase of the mission. Voyager 1 is tentatively planned to arrive at Saturn on November 13, 1980, and to leave the solar system toward a point in the sky with a declination of 10.1 degrees and a right ascension of 260.0 degrees. It is in the constellation Ophiuchus. Voyager 2, if all goes well, will arrive at Uranus on January 30, 1986, and leave the solar system with a declination of −14.9 degrees and a right ascension of 315.3 degrees, in the direction of the zodiacal constellation Capricornus. This Voyager 2 direction assumes that the spacecraft will not, as it is currently not planned to, encounter Neptune on its way out.

Stars have their own, so-called proper, motions. The Voyager spacecraft are moving so slowly that in many tens of thousands of years the stars in the solar neighborhood will have reassorted themselves into quite different relative positions than those they now occupy. It is a difficult computer task to calculate what stars might by chance be along the Voyager spacecraft trajectories 50,000 or 100,000 years from now. Mike Helton of the Jet Propulsion Laboratory has attempted to make such a calculation. He calls attention in particular to an obscure star called AC+79 3888, which is now in the constellation of Ursa Minor—the Little Bear, or Little Dipper. It is now seventeen light-years from the Sun. But in 40,000 years it will by chance be within three light-years of the Sun, closer than Alpha Centauri is to us now. Within that period Voyager 1 will come within 1.7 light-years of AC+79 3888 and Voyager 2 within 1.1 light-years. Two other candidate stars are DM+21 652 in the constellation Taurus and AC-24 2833 183 in the constellation Sagittarius. However, neither Voyager 1 nor Voyager 2 will come as close to these stars as to AC+79 3888.

Astronomers classify this star as a red dwarf of spectral type M4. It is substantially smaller and cooler than the Sun. It may also be much older. The nearest M dwarf star which is not a member of a double or multiple star system is called Barnard's Star. It is about six light-years away. Our ability to detect planetary systems around other stars is at present extremely limited, although it is rapidly improving. Some preliminary evidence suggests that there are one or more planets of about the mass of Jupiter and Saturn orbiting Barnard's star, and general theoretical considerations suggest that planets ought to be a frequent complement of most such stars.

If future studies of AC+79 3888 demonstrate that it indeed has a planetary system, then we might wish to do something to beat the odds set by the haunting and dreadful emptiness of space—the near certainty that, left to themselves, neither Voyager spacecraft would ever plummet into the planet-rich interior of another solar system. For it might be possible after the Voyager scientific missions are completed—to make one final firing of the onboard rocket propulsion system and redirect the spacecraft as closely as we possibly can so that they will make a true encounter with AC+79 3888. If such a maneuver can be effected, then some 60,000 years from now one or two tiny hurtling messengers from the strange and distant planet Earth may penetrate into the planetary system of AC + 79 3888. Since this star is probably much older than the Sun, it may be that intelligent life evolved there long ago. But the evolution of intelligence does not proceed at a uniform pace. Perhaps in 60,000 years intelligence and technical civilizations will have only recently emerged on a planet of this system. The inhabitants will of course be deeply interested in the Sun, their nearest star, and in its retinue of planets. What an astonishing finding the Voyager record, this gift from the skies, would then represent!

They would wonder about us. They would know that 60,000 years is a long period of time in the history of civilizations. They would recognize the tentativeness of our society, its tenuous acquaintance with technology and wisdom together. Had we destroyed ourselves or had we gone on to greater things? Some of the Voyager music intentionally expresses a kind of cosmic loneliness, which would perhaps communicate itself across the expanse of light-years and the differences in evolutionary histories. We, too, were time-capsuling, searching the skies and seeking another civilization with which to communicate.

But one thing would be clear about us: no one sends such a message on such a journey, to other worlds and beings, without a positive passion for the future. For all the possible vagaries of the message, they could be sure that we were a species endowed with hope and perseverance, at least a little intelligence, substantial generosity and a palpable zest to make contact with the cosmos.

ACKNOWLEDGMENTS

ACKNOWLEDGMENTS
Carl Sagan

The Voyager record project is deeply indebted to literally hundreds of people who generously contributed their time, dedication, hard work, and expert knowledge. Many of them—for example, those who sent greetings into space and the photographers who were responsible for the 118 pictures—are acknowledged elsewhere in this book. Others—such as many of the support people at CBS Records—are too numerous to mention. But here are some acknowledgments I feel are essential; others are made in the acknowledgments by the other co-authors of this book. John Casani of the Jet Propulsion Laboratory, the Voyager project manager, conceived, following the Pioneer 10 and 11 precedent, the desirability of a Voyager message and provided both material and moral support. At NASA Headquarters the help of A. Thomas Young, director of lunar and planetary programs and Noel Hinners, associate administrator for space science, was critical. Alan Lovelace, then acting administrator of NASA, and Gerald Mossinghoff, NASA deputy general counsel, were, considering the peculiar political and legal problems which this project raised, very supportive. Arnold Frutkin, NASA associate administrator for international affairs, played a key role in unclogging the United Nations logjam. Frank Press, director of the office of Science and Technology Policy in the Executive Office of the President, secured Mr. Carter's statement on Voyager. On the actual record production, critical roles were played by Herbert Schlosser, then president of the National Broadcasting Company; Tom Shepard of RCA Victor; Arthur Taylor, formerly president of the Columbia Broadcasting System; Bruce Lundvall, president of CBS Records; Joe Agresti and Al Shulman of CBS Records, who secured worldwide copyright releases on the music; and Russ Payne of CBS, who with exemplary patience and skill mixed the record. The lacquer masters were cut at CBS Records by Vladimir Meller. The pictures were recorded at Colorado Video, Inc., Boulder, Colorado; and the copper mothers cut at James G. Lee Record Processing, Gardena, California. The aluminum covers were etched at Litronic Industries, Irvine, California. Minneapolis Honeywell generously lent us their Model 5600-C recorder. Copyright releases for the flight pictures were obtained by Wendy Gradison, Laboratory for Planetary Studies, Cornell, Amahl Shakhashiri, National Astronomy and Ionosphere Center, Cornell, and Nina Laurence at NASA Headquarters. The same releases for this book were obtained by Susan Lang of the Laboratory for Planetary Studies at Cornell, who also prepared the two maps and organized the final form of the table of greetings in 55 languages. I am extremely indebted to Shirley Arden of the Laboratory for Planetary Studies, who provided major assistance in the preparation of all phases of this book and who, in particular, organized much of the recording sessions for the spoken greetings at Cornell University. Paul Penzo and Mike Helton of the Jet Propulsion Laboratory performed important calculations on the erosion and interstellar trajectories of the Voyager spacecraft at our request. We are grateful to those individuals at NASA's Office of Public Affairs, the U.S. Mission to the United Nations, the United Nations Outer Space Committee, and the Office of the Secretary General of the United Nations who provided assistance; as well as to President Carter and Secretary General Waldheim for their statements. We also thank Martin Williams, the curator of jazz at the Smithsonian Institution; Daniel J. Boorstin, the Librarian of Congress; Phyllis Morrison of the Children's Museum, Boston; Frank Oppenheimer of the Exploratorium, San Francisco; Frederick C. Durant III of the Smithsonian Institution; Harry Levin, dean of the College of Arts and Sciences, Cornell University; Steven Soter and Bishun Khare, Laboratory for Planetary Studies, Cornell University; many people at the National Astronomy and Ionosphere Center at Cornell; Fred Eggens, University of Chicago; as well as my coworkers and consultants on the Voyager Record Committee mentioned in the text, including Robert E. Brown, A. G. W. Cameron, Arthur C. Clarke, Frank D. Drake, Ann Druyan, Timothy Ferris, Wendy Gradison, Robert Heinlein, Alan Lomax, Jon Lomberg, Philip Morrison, B. M. Oliver, Leslie Orgel, Linda Sagan, Murry Sidlin, and Stephen Toulmin.

ACKNOWLEDGMENTS
F. D. Drake

I wish I could list the names of everyone who helped us make this project successful. But the names are too numerous, the occupations too diversified, and the locations span a continent. I wouldn't know where to draw the line. Their contributions ranged from small to very large, although I am most reluctant to rank their efforts by these criteria. Each and every bit of cooperation we received was monumental at the time it was given us. I fear I couldn't begin to do justice to all those colleagues and friends across the nation were I to attempt to list, even in alphabetical order, their names, for I might forget someone, or worse, I may not even know of the input of others who contributed through their work in outside organizations.

Nevertheless, a few individuals, in addition to the ones mentioned throughout the book, stand out among them. These include:

Roscoe Barham. He is an employee of the National Academy of Sciences in Washington, D.C. On his own time, he consented to play messenger and drive between such locations as George Washington University, the National Geographic Society, and Washington National Airport in order to assure that we received a certain slide of a human embryo in time. He sent us the slide PDQ! Without his help, we would have been hard put to arrange for a substitute, since the only other possible alternative to the embryo slide was available only in Sweden!

Barbara Boettcher. She is the NAIC draftsman. She spent countless hours sketching specific objects for us. She got caught up in the excitement of the project, and she often said that for her no reward could be more meaningful than the fact that her penmanship has been immortalized.

Valentin Boriakoff. A research associate with NAIC, Val devoted considerable time and effort to locating the proper electronics needed for recording the picture signals. His dedication to the success of this project was heartwarming. He sacrificed his own research time by taking many trips to Colorado, often via circuitous routes and often on last-minute call, where he also advised and participated in the recording session. Val's contributions were rewarded amply, according to him, when he was chosen to perform for one of our special pictures. For the next billion years, he will represent humanity in the matter of the way in which we eat sandwiches.

Herman Eckelmann, NAIC staff photographer. I do mention "Eck" in my chapter, and so does Jon Lomberg. However, his relentless, self-sacrificing pursuit of the success of the project was a thing to marvel at. Many were the nights when he was in his darkroom until past midnight. Occasionally he had a quick sandwich, usually dry by the time he got to it, while clicking away his camera as he was taking pictures from magazines, books, and so forth. Days of personal leave, planned on as a family venture, were postponed while Eck spent the days running around Ithaca taking pictures of highways, supermarkets, airports, hospitals, and so on. Without his determination the picture sequence on the record would not have been done on time.

Wendy Gradison. Wendy took to this project with a fantastic zeal. Many of her days and nights fused to become one inseparable working session. Initially she did most of the legwork with Jon Lomberg, gathering the huge ensembles of photos from which selections were to be made. Finally, on behalf of NASA, she undertook the challenging but unrewarding task of securing permissions from the picture contributors for the use of all photos selected to appear on board the spacecraft. Hers is the only human image to appear twice in the pictures, thereby outdoing Alfred Hitchcock!

Jon Lomberg. Jon is one of those unique individuals whose creative talents seem to propel him into a constant state of energy and zip. He set aside his normal life completely for the sake of the picture sequence. He took up residence in Ithaca, worked thirteen to fifteen hours each day, and got so wrapped up with this task that all his being, for the duration of the project, was centered around making this message. I have often thought that, of all the possible forms of extraterrestrial creatures who might capture this record, Jon Lomberg's "twin" should be the lucky one. No one else would enjoy it, learn from it, or glory in it more.

Dan Mitler. An engineer with NAIC, he worked hand in hand with Valentin Boriakoff to convert the TV picture–quality signals into the lower frequency of recordable signals. Dan flew to Colorado, accompanied by a Honeywell recorder, and spent a few days of inconvenience shuttling between Ithaca, New York City and Boulder. Dan was like a pinch hitter—quiet, but there when he was needed.

Amahl Shakhashiri. As assistant to the director of NAIC (now also my wife), she was very close to the thinking underlying the making of the record. As a member of the team, she had something to do with almost every aspect of putting together the picture sequence. She was quick to spot concepts that were not included in our "draft" sets of pictures and was able to find in short order the appropriate photos to fill the voids. She gave up many nights as we toiled over the photos to make our final selections, and provided valuable suggestions for the content of the sequence as well as ideas for picture sources. Her voice extends the greeting in Arabic in the "greetings" part of the record.

Colorado-Video Inc. This is a small company located in Boulder, Colorado. As a public service, CVI contributed the use of its equipment and personnel. Its president, Glen Southworth, personally assisted, even in the wee hours of the morning, in the actual recording of the pictures. Technician Hannaway and Engineer McClelland spent many hours operating the equipment, and making adjustments that would assure that the quality of the recording was at its highest. CVI also played a key role in negotiating for the loan of a Honeywell 5600C recorder from Honeywell, Inc., in Denver. CVI's zeal and enthusiasm for this project was heartwarming. At the cost of disrupting their normal operations, they endorsed our wish to have a trial run prior to the final recording session; on short notice they accommodated our last-minute frantic efforts to include, in picture format, the message from President Carter and the names of both House and Senate members of space-related committees.

Finally, I would like to acknowledge the support of the National Astronomy and Ionosphere Center. Some members of our staff—even some of our graduate students—embraced the concept of the Voyager message and diverted considerable time and effort both from their primary duties at NAIC as well as from personal leisure to the completion of the project. Their biggest thrill came when they had a sneak preview of the entire "show," and their delight was beyond measure when they realized that their efforts might breach the long expanse of interstellar communication.

ACKNOWLEDGMENTS
Jon Lomberg

Elizabeth Lumley, Arthur Fuller, Michael Schulman, Pat Kellogg, Max Allen, Fred Durant, Shirley Arden, Toronto Library Picture Collection, Richard Lee, Stuart Edelstein, Steven Soter, Tom Prendergast, Hannah Bruce, Jon Schneeberger, Walter Shostal, Gary Davis, Joan Winterkorn, Lilly Lomberg

Acknowledgments
Ann Druyan

Joe Agresti	CBS
Hank Altman	CBS
Shirley Arden	Laboratory for Planetary Studies, Cornell University
Alan Botto	Vantage Sounds
Dr. Margaret Bullowa	Massachusetts Institute of Technology
Jonathan Cott	*Rolling Stone* Magazine
Marty Gindi	New York University Medical Center
Wendy Gradison	Laboratory for Planetary Studies, Cornell University
Bud Graham	CBS
Dr. Ronald Hoy	Department of Neurobiology and Behavior, Cornell University
Jimmy Iovine	
Mickey Kapp	Warner Special Productions
Dr. Julius Korein	New York University Medical Center
Phyllis Kronhaus	New York University Medical Center
Dr. Richard Lee	University of Toronto
Lucie Levidow	New York University Medical Center
Dr. Lise Menn	Massachusetts Institute of Technology
Dr. Roger Payne ⎫	Rockefeller University and
Katy Payne ⎭	The New York Zoological Society
Russ Payne	CBS
Dr. John Rogers	Yale University
Willie Ruff	Yale University
William R. Schoppe, Jr.	CBS
Dr. David Simpson	The Lamont-Doherty Geological Laboratories
Laurie Spiegel	Bell Laboratories

Acknowledgments
Timothy Ferris

Sandro Baratheli, William Boswell, Robert Brown, Chou Wen-chung, John Cohen, Sandra LeBrun Holmes, Bruce MacIntyre, Tim Oliver, Delfina Rattazzi, Colin Turnbull

Acknowledgments
Linda Salzman Sagan

Shirley Arden, Michael Bronfenbrenner, Department of Languages, Cornell University, Phillip Freedman, Suzanne Freedman, Cary Frumess, David Gluck, Wendy Gradison, Bishun Khare, Joe Leeming, Alexander Marshack, Clara T. Pierson, Susan A. Robinson, Debbie Sidlin, Murry Sidlin, Dr. Ralph Solecki, Dr. Steven Soter

APPENDICES

Appendix A

A Message to the Future

(Text of a NASA press release, April 15, 1976)
[Compare with the figure on page 10]

A message has been sealed inside Lageos in the event it should be retrieved from orbit or discovered after its return to Earth some 10 million years from now.

The message was prepared by Dr. Carl Sagan of the Laboratory for Planetary Studies at Cornell University, Ithaca, New York. Two copies of the message, which is etched on stainless steel sheets measuring 10 by 18 cm (4 by 7 inches), are installed in the satellite—one at each end of the bolt connecting the two hemispheres which make up Lageos.

In its upper center the message displays the simplest counting scheme, binary arithmetic, which uses only zeros and ones. The numbers 1 through 10 in binary notation are shown. At upper right is a schematic drawing of the Earth in orbit around the Sun, an arrow indicating the direction of motion. The arrowhead points to the right, the convention adopted for indicating the future. All arrows accompanying numbers are such "arrows of time." Under the Earth's orbit is the binary number one, denoting the period of time used on the plaque—one revolution of the Earth about the Sun, or one year.

The remainder of the Lageos plaque consists of three maps of the Earth's surface, all in a common projection that permits the entire surface of our planet to be viewed at once. Beneath the first map is an arrowhead pointing left, denoting the past, and connected to a large binary number. In decimal notation this number is equivalent to about 268 million years ago. The map shows the approximate configuration of the continents in the Permian period, about 225 million years ago. The binary number could have been made more accurate, but was "rounded off" to avoid giving the impression of spurious accuracy. Since detailed knowledge of continental drift is still very limited, all the continents are shown together in one mass, sometimes called "Pangaea."

The close fit of South America into West Africa was one of the first hints that continental drift actually occurs. Australia is shown as lying originally between Antarctica and West Africa; in other reconstructions, it is thought to have been in contact with Western Antarctica. These maps are not intended to be a precise representation of continental drift, but rather a means of portraying dramatically the existence and extent of continental drift.

The middle map displays the present configuration of the continents. Below it is a symbol indicating zero years, and arrows denoting simultaneously the past and the future; that is, the present. This map represents the zero point in time for the other two maps. Lageos is shown being launched into space from the Western Test Range at Vandenberg Air Force Base in California.

The final map is coded by an arrow pointing to the right and a binary number, again rounded off, denoting an epoch 8.4 million years from now—very roughly, the estimated lifetime of the Lageos spacecraft. The satellite is shown returning to the Earth. Many important changes in the Earth's surface are shown, including the drift of Vandenberg Air Force Base and the rest of southern California out into the Pacific Ocean. This separation, along the San Andreas Fault, is an expected consequence of the crustal motions which Lageos is designed to investigate. Many of the other changes in the map of the Earth shown are little more than guesses. Our knowledge of them should be significantly improved by Lageos.

Whoever comes upon the Lageos plaque need only compare a current map of the Earth's geography with that in the lower two maps to calculate roughly the time between his own epoch and ours. Drift rates of about an inch per year can, in fact, be estimated by comparing the bottom two maps. Thus, the prime objective of Lageos and the method of telling time of the spacecraft's plaque are identical.

Lageos will return to Earth at a time in the future more distant than the time in the past of the origin of the human species. The Earth will surely have changed profoundly by that future time, and not only with respect to the disposition of its continents. Whoever is inhabiting Earth in that distant epoch may appreciate a little greeting card from the remote past.

Appendix B

Messages of the UN Delegates Aboard the Voyager

Mohamed El-Zoeby of Egypt (Arabic):
"People and Djinn, if you could pierce the boundaries of Earth and Sky then do it, and you will do it only with authority."

Chaidir Anwar Sani of Indonesia (Indonesian):
"I want to give you a short message for this Voyager . . . "

Bernadette Lefort of France (French):
" 'Above the lakes, above the vales,
The mountains and the woods, the clouds, the seas,
Beyond the sun, beyond the ether,
Beyond the confines of the starry spheres,

'My soul, you move with ease,
And like a strong swimmer in rapture in the wave
You wing your way blithely through boundless space
With virile joy unspeakable.' "
(From Baudelaire's "Les Fleurs du Mal")

Syed Azmat Hassan of Pakistan (Punjabi):
". . . on behalf of my countrymen I am sending a message of friendship and greetings to our friends in space. It is our heartiest desire that there should be peace in the whole world and this peace is in all facets of life."

Peter Jankowitsch of Austria (German):
"As the chairman of the Outer Space Committee of the UN and the representative of Austria, I am pleased to extend to you our greetings in this way."

Robert B. Edmonds of Canada (English):
"I should like to extend the greetings of the government and people of Canada to the extraterrestrial inhabitants of outer space."

Wallace R. T. Macaulay of Nigeria (Efik):
"To extraterrestrial intelligent beings: We are supposed to inhabit this planet alone but we know this is not quite so. In Africa, we want to believe that we have you and you are all-knowing, and perhaps possess high intelligence and therefore can help us solve the many problems of our world here."

James F. Leonard of the United States of America (English):
"I wish to extend greetings and friendly wishes to all who may encounter this Voyager and receive this message."

Juan Carlos Valero of Chile (Spanish):
"[We] send to all beings in the universe an affectionate greeting of peace and happiness. May the future give us the opportunity [of getting together]."

Eric Duchêne of Belgium (Flemish):
"Belgium sends its greetings on board the Voyager and hopes that this message will reach the people of outer space."

Samuel Ramsay Nicol of Sierra Leone (English):
" . . . and good luck. Sierra Leone is a member of the Committee on Outer Space and we believe that this committee good for . . . "

Wallace R. T. Macaulay of Nigeria (English):
"My dear friends in outer space, as you probably know, my country is situated on the west coast of the continent of Africa, a land mass more or less in the shape of a question mark in the center of our planet."

Bahram Moghtaderi of Iran (Persian):
"[As a representative] of the Committee of the Peaceful Uses of Outer Space, I have the honor of sending the greeting of the people and government [of Iran.]"

Ralph Harry of Australia (Esperanto):
"We seek to live in peace with the peoples of the whole world, of the whole universe . . . "

Anders Thunboig of Sweden (Swedish):
"We saw a nebula in a telescope.
A golden mistcluster we thought we saw.
In larger telescopes it could seem as
the fathomless space of a thousand suns.

Our spinning thoughts made it appear
to rise, high above earth's wars,
away from time and space—our lives' naïveté—
to other dimensions' majesty.

No law rules there as in this life.
There reign the laws for the world of worlds.
There surge the suns away, mature,
and ring into the source of all the suns.

A multitude of suns are to be found.
Each sun there beats with cosmic law
in the unbearable light of greater suns.
And all is clearness there, the day of days."

(The poem "Visit to the Observatory" by the late Harry Martinson from *Passad.* Copyright 1945 by Harry Martinson. Published by permission of Albert Bonniers Förlag AB, Stockholm, Sweden. Unofficial translation by Marna Feldt, information officer, Swedish Information Service, with the help of Verne Moberg, translator.)

Appendix C

Robert Brown's Recommendations on Musical Repertoire

May 9, 1977

Dear Dr. Sagan:

I was glad to learn from you on Thursday that there might be a chance to extend the time allotted for human music on the Voyager recording.

My selection amounts to about thirty-eight minutes and is limited to pieces that are complete in themselves and are available on commercial recordings. I have tried, as far as possible, to make selections in a logical way from the whole range of human music, without the distinction of Western and non-Western or other ethnocentric viewpoints. Included are some different uses and timbres of the human voice; principal types of instruments, alone or in various densities of combination; a range of scales, modes and tuning systems to suggest the human variety thereof; different types of meter, rhythm, and tempo; examples of different kinds of harmony and counterpoint; and textures ranging from simple to complex. Without trying to reconstruct historical items from the Western past, I have at the same time attempted to glean living examples from different stages of human musical development.

Although all of these measurable elements are interesting and would, I hope, suggest some of the parameters of human music to an intelligence otherwise quite unfamiliar with it, they are obviously only secondary considerations for most listeners and performers here on earth. Music being primarily a means of communicating emotional, spiritual, and intellectual states, I have chosen only examples that have for me personally, a deep musical meaning. In the final analysis, then, the selection is subjective, and I believe that it has to be. I don't think that such comprehensive artistic choices are ever well decided by committees. The fact that no two ethnomusicologists would compile the same list is, after all, directly related to the characteristics of human nature responsible for the staggering number of items one has to choose from. The problem is rather like that which would confront a botanist asked to select a half-dozen varieties to represent the world's flowers. Let us hope that, among other things, he wouldn't have forgotten that most people think of them in terms of visual beauty and fragrance. If I could extend the list, it would include the following: a lively mridangam solo from India (in a tala of five beats, played by Palghat Mani Iyer, who may well be the world's best drummer); a representative piece of electronic music (hard to decide upon); a Balinese gamelan piece (my choice would be the ancient Gamelan Selundeng, recorded on Boîte à Musique LD 096M); a piece of Renaissance vocal polyphony by Des Pres, Dufay, or Ockeghem, bristling with contrapuntal devices; a Chinese ch'in solo; a West African dance piece with drum ensemble and voices; a Mozart aria; a Bulgarian folk song in diaphonic style; Melanesian panpipes, to relate to the Bach and shakuhachi; and a symphony of Beethoven's, probably the Eighth. This could conceivably produce more insight into human nature than an extraterrestrial intelligence might be prepared to handle!

A survey of the record shops in Portland, Oregon, has failed to produce your Chavez piece. Could it be the Hymn to the Sun? I was told that there are many releases subsidized by the Mexican government that are not available in the United States. Although I admire Chavez, and have performed his piano music, if the piece is an attempt to evoke the spirit of the Indian past, I would be more inclined to go directly to the source and select from one of the living traditions of Indian music in Central or South America (another excellent addition to the list, by the way). By the same token, I would avoid the presumptions inherent in trying to reconstruct ancient Greek, Egyptian, or Mesopotamian music, where the aural tradition is irrevocably lost. On the other hand, if you tell me, as you did, that the Chavez piece was deeply moving and represented special profundities of the human spirit to you, my position collapses. If we don't send things we passionately care for, why send them at all?

Finally, I have to thank you for providing a fine jolt of energy to my work at a time when it happened to be especially appreciated. In working toward the evolution of a new attitude toward human music commensurate with the present state of knowledge of its diverse manifestations and astonishing range, I sometimes feel as though I am pushing forward into new mental territory where it is difficult to communicate, even with colleagues in my field. A year ago, for instance, I read a paper concerned with the idea of entropy in world musical traditions before a small group of specialists in Quebec. (Among other things, I feel as concerned with the obliteration of musical species as I do in the case of the flora and fauna.) One of the points of that paper was a proposition that human education in the future might well center on the twin subjects of astronomy and music, representing that which is without (and beyond human), and that which is within (and intimately and exclusively human). I had the impression that no one there felt anything like a burning necessity to try to integrate these two areas of knowledge (the inside and outside? mind and spirit? science and art?), in a way that could make sense out of all the visible diversities of human knowledge and experience. But I sense that you do feel that need, and I have admired both the iconoclastic and benevolent nature of your activities. Having to deal with your request, whatever the results may be, has swept away a lot of mental debris, and helped me to concentrate again on some important realities of my own life's work. It also provided an immediate focus for an editorial in the Center for World Music Newsletter, with which I have been tussling for some time. I'm enclosing a copy of the whole Newsletter, for context. Perhaps it may amuse you as one of those uncontrollable spin-offs which any powerful idea is likely to generate. There was a lengthy release from UPI concerning the Voyager project and proposed recording in last night's local paper, so I feel mightily relieved not to have jumped the gun by more than a few days.

Robert E. Brown
Executive Director
Center for World Music and Related Arts
Berkeley, California

REB:py

World Music for Outer Space
proposed by Robert E. Brown

1. INDIAN VOCAL MUSIC. Surshri Kesar Bai Kerkar. HMV EALP 1278.

   Time: 3:25. Solo voice; seven-tone modal melody with auxiliary pitches; cyclic meter of fourteen beats; microtones; ornamentation; drone; drum accompaniment; improvisation. Words (probably less important than abstract melody and mood) mean: "Where are you going? Don't go alone—I haven't given you permission. Out in the street people are celebrating the Holi festival by throwing saffron color at each other. You are so young."

2. JAVANESE GAMELAN. Ketawang Puspawarna, with gamelan and singers of the Paku Alaman Palace in Jogyakarta, K.R.T. Wasitodipuro, director. Nonesuch H-72044.

   Time: 4:46. Orchestra of percussion instruments, solo and choral singing stratification of parts; pentatonic slendro tuning; colotomic structure of gong patterns. Words relatively unimportant (voices used instrumentally), refer symbolically to different kinds of flowers, related to the nine states (rasa) of Hindu philosophy.

3. BACH ORGAN CHORALE PRELUDE. Michel Chapuis, at the organ of the Erlöser-Kirche in Copenhagen. Das Alte Werk (Telefunken) 6-35083.

   Time: 3:55. Based on the chorale melody "Wenn wir in höchsten Nöten sind" (also used for the text "Vor deinen Thron tret ich hiermit"). This is said to Bach's last composition, dictated from his deathbed. Harmony; counterpoint; seven-tone modal melody with auxiliary pitches; organ as a complex wind instrument.

4. PYGMY HONEY-GATHERING SONG. Pygmies of the Ituri Forest, singing antiphonally. Ethnic Folkways FE 4457.

   Time: 2:45. Harmony; counterpoint; solo and choral singing; simple rhythmic accompaniment with clapper.

5. JOHN COLTRANE QUARTET. "Giant Steps," played by John Coltrane, tenor saxophone; Tommy Flanagan, piano; Paul Chambers, string bass; Art Taylor, drums. Atlantic 1311.

   Time: 4:43. Chamber music; wind, strings, drums; fast tempo; harmony; solo improvisations.

6. JAPANESE SHAKUHACHI. Shika no Tone, performed by Haruhiko Notomi and Tatsuya Araki. Bärenreiter BM 30 L 2014 (UNESCO Musical Anthology of the Orient, Japan, Volume III).

   Time: 7:45. Solo wind instrument; varieties of tone color; development of musical material; range; dynamic variation.

7. DEBUSSY: "Prélude à l'après-midi d'un faune." New York Philharmonic Orchestra, conducted by Leonard Bernstein. Columbia MS 6754.

   Time: 10:15. Varieties of instruments; contrast of dynamics; orchestration; tempo change; complex harmony; rhythmic variety; form and thematic development.

Appendix D

Jon Lomberg's Original Suggested Selections on Tape for One-Hour Voyager Record

1.	Sioux Medicine Chant	1:00	from *Music of the Sioux and Navaho* (Ethnic Folkways)
2.	"Seya wa mama ndalamba"	2:21	from *Missa Luba (and Congolese Folk Songs)* (Philips)
3.	Fugue No. 2 in C minor by Bach	1:33	from Glenn Gould, *The Well-Tempered Clavier,* Book 1 (Columbia)
4.	Gavotte en rondeaux by Bach	2:50	from *6 Sonatas and Partitas for Unaccompanied Violin,* Arthur Grumiaux, violin (Philips)
5.	"Alleluiah" from *Exsultate, Jubilate* by Mozart	2:40	from Elisabeth Schwarzkopf, *Mozart and Bach* (Seraphim)
6.	Beethoven's Fifth	6:53	from *Fifth Symphony,* Leonard Bernstein and the New York Philharmonic (Columbia)
7.	Fanfare for the Common Man by Aaron Copland	1:03	from *A Lincoln Portrait* (Columbia)
8.	First of *Six kleine Klavierstücke* by Arnold Schoenberg	:48	from *Schoenberg: The Complete Music for Solo Piano* by Glenn Gould (Columbia)
9.	"Summertime," by George Gershwin	2:30	from *Porgy and Bess,* with Ella Fitzgerald and Louis Armstrong (Verve)
10.	"Sgt. Pepper's Lonely Hearts Club Band" (reprise) by the Beatles	1:25	from *Sgt. Pepper's Lonely Hearts Club Band* (Capitol)

Appendix E

Voyager Science Teams

Imaging Science
    Bradford A. Smith, University of Arizona, team leader
    Geoffrey A. Briggs, Jet Propulsion Laboratory
    A. F. Cook, Smithsonian Institution
    G. E. Danielson, Jr., Jet Propulsion Laboratory
    Merton Davies, Rand Corp.
    G. E. Hunt, Meteorological Office, U.K.
    Tobias Owen, State University of New York
    Carl Sagan, Cornell University
    Lawrence Soderblom, U.S. Geological Survey
    V. E. Suomi, University of Wisconsin
    Harold Masursky, U.S. Geological Survey

Radio Science

    Von R. Eshelman, Stanford University, team leader
    J. D. Anderson, Jet Propulsion Laboratory
    T. A. Croft, Stanford Research Institute
    Gunnar Fjeldbo, Jet Propulsion Laboratory
    G. S. Levy, Jet Propulsion Laboratory
    G. L. Tyler, Stanford University
    G. E. Wood, Jet Propulsion Laboratory

Plasma Wave

    Frederick L. Scarf, TRW Systems, principal investigator
    D. A. Gurnett, University of Iowa

Infrared Spectroscopy and Radiometry

    Rudolf A. Hanel, Goddard Space Flight Center, principal investigator
    B. J. Conrath, Goddard Space Flight Center
    P. Gierasch, Cornell University
    V. Kunde, Goddard Space Flight Center

P. D. Lowman, Goddard Space Flight Center
W. Maguire, Goddard Space Flight Center
J. Pearl, Goddard Space Flight Center
J. Pirraglia, Goddard Space Flight Center
R. Samuelson, Goddard Space Flight Center
Cyril Ponnamperuma, University of Maryland
D. Gautier, Meudon, France

Ultraviolet Spectroscopy

A. Lyle Broadfoot, Kitt Peak National Observatory, principal investigator
J.B. Bertaux, Service d'Aéronomie du CNRS, France
J. Blamont, Service d'Aéronomie du CNRS, France
T. M. Donahue, University of Michigan
R. M. Goody, Harvard University
A. Dalgarno, Harvard College Observatory
Michael B. McElroy, Harvard University
J. C. McConnell, York University, Canada
H. W. Moos, Johns Hopkins University
M. J. S. Belton, Kitt Peak National Observatory
D. F. Strobel, Naval Research Laboratory

Photopolarimetry

Charles F. Lillie, University of Colorado, principal investigator
Charles W. Hord, University of Colorado
D. L. Coffeen, Goddard Institute for Space Studies
J. E. Hansen, Goddard Institute for Space Studies
K. Pang, Science Applications Inc.

Planetary Radio Astronomy

James W. Warwick, University of Colorado, principal investigator
J. K. Alexander, Goddard Space Flight Center
A. Boischot, Observatoire de Paris, France
W. E. Brown, Jet Propulsion Laboratory
T. D. Carr, University of Florida
Samuel Gulkis, Jet Propulsion Laboratory

F. T. Haddock, University of Michigan
C. C. Harvey, Observatoire de Paris, France
Y. LeBlanc, Observatoire de Paris, France
R. G. Peltzer, University of Colorado
R. J. Phillips, Jet Propulsion Laboratory
D. H. Staelin, Massachusetts Institute of Technology

Magnetic Fields

Norman F. Ness, Goddard Space Flight Center, principal investigator
Mario H. Acuna, Goddard Space Flight Center
K. W. Behannon, Goddard Space Flight Center
L. F. Burlaga, Goddard Space Flight Center
R. P. Lepping, Goddard Space Flight Center
F. M. Neubauer, Technische Universitat, F.R.G.

Plasma Science

Herbert S. Bridge, Massachusetts Institute of Technology, principal investigator
J. W. Belcher, Massachusetts Institute of Technology
J. H. Binsack, Massachusetts Institute of Technology
A. J. Lazarus, Massachusetts Institute of Technology
S. Olbert, Massachusetts Institute of Technology
V. M. Vasyliunas, Max Planck Institute, F.R.G.
L. F. Burlaga, Goddard Space Flight Center
R. E. Hartle, Goddard Space Flight Center
K. W. Ogilvie, Goddard Space Flight Center
G. L. Siscoe, University of California, Los Angeles
A. J. Hundhausen, High Altitude Observatory

Low-Energy Charged Particles

S. M. Krimigis, Johns Hopkins University, principal investigator
T. P. Armstrong, University of Kansas
W. I. Axford, Max Planck Institute, F.R.G.
C. O. Bostrom, Johns Hopkins University
C. Y. Fan, University of Arizona
G. Gloeckler, University of Maryland
L. J. Lanzerotti, Bell Telephone Laboratories

Cosmic Ray

R. E. Vogt, California Institute of Technology, principal investigator
J. R. Jokipii, University of Arizona
E. C. Stone, California Institute of Technology
F. B. McDonald, Goddard Space Flight Center
B. J. Teegarden, Goddard Space Flight Center
James H. Trainor, Goddard Space Flight Center
W. R. Webber, University of New Hampshire

Appendix F

Voyager Management Team

NASA Office of Space Science

Noel W. Hinners, Associate Administrator for Space Science
Anthony J. Calio, Deputy Associate Administrator
S. Ichtiaque Rasool, Deputy Associate Administrator—Science
A. Thomas Young, Director, Lunar and Planetary Programs
Rodney A. Mills, Program Manager
Arthur Reetz, Jr., Deputy Program Manager
Milton A. Mitz, Program Scientist
Earl W. Glahn, Flight Support Manager

NASA Office of Tracking and Data Acquisition

Gerald M. Truszynski, Associate Administrator for Tracking and
Data Acquisition
Charles A. Taylor, Director, Network Operations and Communica-
tion Programs
Arnold C. Belcher, Program Manager for DSN Operations
Frederick B. Bryant, Director, Network System Development Pro-
grams
Maurice E. Binkley, Director, DSN Systems

NASA Office of Space Flight

John F. Yardley, Associate Administrator for Space Flight
Joseph B. Mahon, Director, Expendable Launch Vehicles
Joseph E. McGolrick, Director, Small and Medium Launch Vehicles
B. C. Lam, Titan III Manager

Jet Propulsion Laboratory, Pasadena, California

Bruce C. Murray, Laboratory Director
Gen. Charles H. Terhune, Jr., Deputy Laboratory Director
Robert J. Parks, Assistant Laboratory Director for Flight Projects
John R. Casani, Project Manager

Raymond L. Heacock, Spacecraft System Manager
Charles E. Kohlhase, Jr., Mission Analysis and Engineering Manager
James E. Long, Science Manager
Richard P. Laeser, Mission Operations System Manager
Esker K. Davis, Tracking and Data Systems Manager
James F. Scott, Mission Computing System Manager
Michael J. Sander, Mission Control and Computing Center Manager
Ronald F. Draper, Spacecraft System Engineer
William S. Shipley, Spacecraft Development Manager
William G. Fawcett, Science Instruments Manager
Michael Devirian, Chief of Mission Operations

California Institute of Technology, Pasadena, California

Edward C. Stone, Project Scientist

Lewis Research Center, Cleveland, Ohio

Bruce T. Lundin, Center Director
Andrew J. Stofan, Director, Launch Vehicles
Carl B. Wentworth, Chief, Program Integration Division
Gary D. Sagerman, Voyager Mission Analyst
Richard P. Geye, Voyager Mission Project Engineer
Richard A. Flage, LV Test Integration Engineer
Richard E. Orzechowski, TDS Support Engineer
Larry J. Ross, Chief, Vehicles Engineering Division
James E. Patterson, Associate Chief, Engineering Division
Frank L. Manning, TC-6 and TC-7 Vehicle Engineer

Kennedy Space Center, Florida

Lee R. Scherer, Center Director
Walter J. Kapryan, Director of Space Vehicles Operations
George F. Page, Director, Expendable Vehicles
John D. Gossett, Chief, Centaur Operations Division
Creighton A. Terhune, Chief Engineer, Operations Division
Jack E. Baltar, Centaur Operations Branch
Donald C. Sheppard, Chief, Spacecraft and Support Operations Division
James E. Weir, Spacecraft Operations Branch

The Voyager Record label, Side One. Not apparent in this illustration is the background motif underneath the lettering—a photograph of the planet Earth from space.

INDEX

About the Authors

CARL SAGAN was chairman of the NASA Voyager Record Committee and executive producer of the record. He holds the David Duncan Chair as Professor of Astronomy and Space Sciences at Cornell University, where he is also director of the Laboratory for Planetary Studies. Sagan has played key roles in the Mariner, Viking, and Voyager missions to the planets; on Voyager he is a member of the Imaging Team. He is author of *The Cosmic Connection, The Dragons of Eden* (for which he received the Pulitzer Prize) and, with I. Shklovskii, *Intelligent Life in the Universe.*

F. D. DRAKE is director of the National Astronomy and Ionosphere Center (part of which is the Arecibo Observatory in Puerto Rico) and Goldwin Smith Professor of Astronomy at Cornell University. He is widely known for his belief that life exists elsewhere in the universe and is a leading authority on methods for the construction of messages and for the detection of extraterrestrial intelligent signals.

ANN DRUYAN was the creative director of the Voyager record and is the author of the recently published novel *A Famous Broken Heart.* Her articles have appeared in the *New York Times Magazine* and elsewhere.

JON LOMBERG is an artist and writer whose major interests are astronomy (particularly interstellar communication and the study of galaxies) and music. He won the Boston Visionary Cell Award for painting in 1971. He illustrated Carl Sagan's *The Cosmic Connection,* and his paintings appear at the Ontario Science Center and the Smithsonian Institution's Air and Space Museum.

TIMOTHY FERRIS, who served as producer of the Voyager record, is the author of a book on twentieth-century astronomy, *The Red Limit: The Search for the Edge of the Universe.* He is professor of English at Brooklyn College and contributing editor to *Rolling Stone* magazine.

LINDA SALZMAN SAGAN has worked as an artist, film-maker and picture researcher. She helped design the Pioneer 10 plaque, and was assistant director of the award-winning documentary *Two Ball Games.*